Enhancing Relationships
Between Children and Teachers

Enhancing Relationships
Between Children and Teachers

■ ▲ ●

Robert C. Pianta

American Psychological Association
Washington, DC

#39763464

Published by
American Psychological Association
750 First Street, NE
Washington, DC 20002

Copies may be ordered from
APA Order Department
P.O. Box 92984
Washington, DC 20090-2984

In the United Kingdom, Europe, Africa, and the Middle East, copies may be
ordered from
American Psychological Association
3 Henrietta Street
Covent Garden, London
WC2E 8LU England

Typeset in Century Schoolbook by EPS Group Inc., Easton, MD
Printer: Braun-Brumfield, Inc., Ann Arbor, MI
Cover Designer: Minker Design, Bethesda, MD
Technical/Production Editor: Anne Woodworth

Library of Congress Cataloging-in-Publication Data
Pianta, Robert C.
    Enhancing relationships between children and teachers / Robert C.
Pianta.—1st ed.
        p.   cm.
    Includes bibliographical references (p.   ) and index.
    ISBN 1-55798-542-1
    1. Teacher—student relationships.   2. Classroom environment.
3. School psychology.   I. Title.
LB1033.P563   1998
372.11023—dc21   98-42492
                                                            CIP

British Library Cataloguing-in-Publication Data
A CIP record is available from the British Library.

Printed in the United States of America
First edition

*To the sixth- and seventh-grade students
in my classes at Bloomfield Middle School.
They taught me the value of relationships
between teachers and children.*

Contents

Acknowledgments

This book is truly an integration of personal experiences, years of my own research and thinking, and ideas from a broad range of sources. I would like to acknowledge the colleagues and mentors who have influenced my thinking about relationships and their importance in development—Byron Egeland, Alan Sroufe, Arnold Sameroff, and Daniel Walsh. My undergraduate mentors, Jack Cawley and Miriam Cherkes, were instrumental in helping me keep one foot in the schools and one foot in developmental theory. I have received support for this work from the Center for Research on the Education of Teachers, directed by Bob McNergney here at Virginia and from the Curry School of Education in the form of various small grants and summer support. This work has also been supported, in part, by the Office of Educational Research and Improvement's National Center for Early Development and Learning.

But much of what's in this book is the result of experiences in the schools, and I am intellectually and personally indebted to the many children and professionals who have shared their experiences with me over the years. Nancy Gercke, Director of the Jefferson Preschool Center in Charlottesville, has been a valuable colleague and friend without whose support the ideas in this book would not have come to light. The staff of the Jefferson Preschool allowed me to meet with them for a year and shared many experiences that gave rise to ideas in the book. Over the years, many teachers have participated in interviews about relationships, and they gave generously of their time and personal life to help us understand relationships between children and teachers. My wife, Ann McAndrew, has worked for the past 10 years in schools in varying ways, and our discussions of her experiences have shaped an enormous amount of how I think about the importance of social processes in schools and have encouraged me to continue to conduct research to understand these processes. I am very grateful for her willingness to share these experiences with me and for the personal encouragement I received from her while writing this book. Finally, my children Meghan, Tony, and Timmy were all in elementary school while this book was being written, and watching them form connections with various teachers has been an important influence on my thinking.

Enhancing Relationships
Between Children and Teachers

Introduction

Ask any teachers why they teach. They will say "it's the kids" and will go on to describe effects that their students have had on them as people. These discussions invariably are about relationships between students and teachers, the experience of which constitutes a large proportion of what goes on in school. Unfortunately, researchers, teacher educators, and school administrators have been late in figuring this out and have not capitalized on what these experiences have to offer children (and teachers). The goal of this book is to place relationships between children and teachers squarely on the agenda of educators and applied child and adolescent psychologists, to frame a theory for understanding these relationships, and to present a set of tools for harnessing these relationships as resources for development.

My interest in relationships between children and teachers began when I was a teacher in Connecticut at Bloomfield Middle School in 1978. I had just finished training in special education at the University of Connecticut and was assigned to teach in a sixth-grade special education resource class. I was fortunate to be team-teaching with a colleague whose support, creativity, and dedication was invaluable to me as a beginning teacher. Most of my students were boys, and I quickly became aware that there was more to our interactions than instruction and learning academic skills. The social and emotional dimensions of our contacts fascinated me. I often thought about and talked about these children after I had gone home for the day; I noticed how as we came to know each others' patterns of behavior that we would anticipate each other and that interactions often were more smooth and effective, and I relied a lot on our knowledge of each other when I actually taught skills or had to manage behavior. At the time I did not know it, but these experiences demonstrated the value of building and enhancing relationships with these children.

Over the course of my 3 years teaching, I was fortunate enough to get to know my students well; in fact, the evolving organization of the school and the special education programs enabled me, serendipitously, to have some of the same children in my class for all 3 years that I taught. For these years, I noticed the effects on children (and myself) of a deepening of relationships that would otherwise not have occurred in the context of the usual grade-based transition in classroom membership. The added depth in the relationships I experienced with students had many effects.

3

I had little or no problems in classroom management, with children who oftentimes had great difficulty in self-regulation and who got in trouble with other teachers. And this was not because I ran a state-of-the-art classroom in terms of behavior management. Also, I watched my students' motivation for tough academic tasks increase far beyond expectations (most had dual diagnostic labels as "learning disabled" and "emotionally disturbed"), and their performance increased as well. And again, this was not because I was a great teacher or motivator. In retrospect, I believe my relationships with these students (most, but not all of them) "hooked" them in ways that enhanced their development in social areas and as learners. These relationships were resources.

Not all of these relationships worked in the way I have described. Some relationships caused more concern. I learned what happens when a child seems to dictate the terms of engagement—when interactions are consistently troubling or problematic—and I would get angry or feel helpless. Fortunately, in a team-teaching situation I had a place to go with these concerns, and my partner was readily available as a good listener who had constructive thoughts. Thus, I came to know the value of support and consultation for relationships that are not functioning well, and I experienced the results of such support.

My training as a school, child clinical, and developmental psychologist at the University of Minnesota could not have fit better with these experiences. It was there that I became acquainted with theory and research on parent–child relationships and often reflected on how they so easily and readily applied to my experiences as a teacher. The work described in the book flows from the integration of these experiences as a teacher and from the theory and research on relationships in which I was trained and have worked for the past 12 years.

Overview

This book aims to provide school psychologists, child clinical psychologists, and other mental health professionals working with children with the theoretical and technical basis for designing interventions that enhance relationships between children and teachers. In it, I draw on research in social development and relationship-systems theory to describe the role of child–adult relationships in the development of social and academic competencies and the potential of child–teacher relationships to promote healthy development. It is explicitly focused on the use of child–teacher relationships as a *preventive* intervention and the role of the psychologist as a consultant to the classroom teacher, the school, and the school district.

School and classroom contexts offer the child numerous relationship opportunities, and valuable relationships are formed between children and nonparental adults in these settings. These relationships provide children with emotional experiences and opportunities to learn social skills and self-regulatory capacities and to practice basic developmental functions, such as attachment, exploration, play, and mastery. In many ways, children's relationships with adults in school may mirror the relationships that they have with parents in the family context and may provide many of the same functions (i.e., play, mastery, affiliation–attachment). These relationships serve as a "natural context" for the infusion of intervention efforts that may serve large-scale prevention goals in relation to reducing risk. Thus, the book identifies aspects of the classroom and school contexts that have relationship-based components and similarities and differences across those contexts and applies relationship-based principles to designing interventions in the classroom. In this framework, the school is described as a context for development and relationships between children and teachers as resources for development that can be harnessed as a preventive intervention to enhance child competence and to reduce high levels of risk present in today's population of children. Throughout the book, examples of child–teacher relationships are used. Each chapter starts with one such example and includes more brief, specific examples in the text, and chapter 6 is entirely devoted to presenting three case studies. All of these examples are of actual children and teachers, although all names have been changed in the present text; none of these are composite descriptions, as they are actual experiences of individuals. The case studies are drawn from my own experience in the classroom as well as from extensive interviews with teachers and observations in their classrooms.

In the first four chapters, relevant theories of social development and interpersonal relationships, general systems theory, and ecological perspectives are used to provide the scientist-practitioner with a theoretical framework that can be applied to child–teacher relationships. Chapter 1 presents a conceptualization of the role that relationships can play for children, particularly for children who have the kinds of background experiences that tend to predict difficulty in school. The concept of risk as a social process and the way in which a focus on child–teacher relationships can be used to reduce risk are introduced, as is the notion that the practice of psychology with children is closely tied to the management of contexts that provide resources for development. Schools are viewed as a central context in this respect. Chapter 2 follows with a summary of concepts from general systems theory that can be used to understand the functioning of relationships between children and adults, particularly teachers. These concepts embrace the view that the child is an organized, active part of a relationship and that the asymmetric nature of child–adult relationships allows these relationships to function as a resource for development.

In chapter 3, there is a description of social and emotional development from a relational vantage point. This chapter outlines the role that social processes play in development and the way that developmental change can be understood as embedded in relationships. Chapter 4 extends this discussion to focus specifically on the role of child–adult relationships, with extended discussions of attachment and child–parent relationships as providing the infrastructure to development that is subsequently operated on by child–teacher relationships in the school context. Particular attention is paid to the role of adult–child relationships in forming a child's self-regulation capacities and for supporting the acquisition of knowledge and academic competencies.

Chapter 5 begins a more dedicated focus on child–teacher relationships and reviews the literature on a range of techniques that can be used to assess child–teacher relationships, including interviews, self-report measures, and observations. Attention is also devoted to consideration of research on key variables used for the description of child–teacher relationships. Chapter 6 follows this focus on assessment with a presentation of three case studies of child–teacher relationships. These case studies illuminate the theoretical framework outlined in chapters 1 through 4, highlight assessment issues raised in chapter 5, and provide the reader with a basis for considering the range of intervention issues and techniques discussed in chapters 7 through 9.

Chapters 7 through 9, present interventions of various types designed to enhance relationships between teachers and children. Chapter 7 presents a set of interventions that focus on individual teachers and their experiences with children in their classrooms. From this perspective, interventions discussed include dealing with teachers' perceptions of their relationships with children, assisting teachers in identifying children's cues for a variety of teacher-oriented behaviors, and addressing the teachers' emotional experiences in the classroom and the regulation of those experiences, vis-à-vis children's demands. Chapter 8 identifies classroom-level practices—such as behavior management, grouping, placement of children—that have implications for child–teacher relationships. A particular focus is on how operant behavior management techniques can function to enhance relationships, and vice versa. Chapter 9 looks more broadly at school-level policies and practices, such as child–teacher ratios and the use of resource pull-out programs, in relation to their implications for child–teacher relationships. Emphasis is placed on the intentional analysis and use of practices and policies that can strengthen, rather than inhibit, high-quality child–teacher relationships. Finally, chapter 10 summarizes the major issues raised in the previous chapters and looks ahead to their implications for the practice of psychology in relation to child–teacher relationships. This view includes a discussion of an agenda for research and practice and the important role of empirically based theory in the development of relationship-focused practices.

In sum, the book integrates developmental, clinical, and school psychology, links research on social development and applications in school and classroom contexts, and identifies a set of theoretically driven applications for intervention strategies. I believe it provides the reader with an important set of tools to address an almost completely neglected resource for children. By focusing on child–teacher relationships as a resource for development, and by harnessing the power of these relationships for the purpose of prevention of problems and enhancement of competencies, it is my hope that applied psychologists will be able to play key roles in the reform and enrichment of school contexts.

1

Why Supportive Relationships
Are Essential

Ms. Smith[1] describes her attitude toward teaching: "I like being a teacher . . . we live in a farming community and everyone knows one another . . . I'll see the kids at the ballpark, heck, I taught some of these kids' parents! One time I was at the park watching a softball game and Theresa came up and snuggled in my lap . . . watched the game with me. Then the next morning she came up and said, 'I saw you last night.' I will miss her when she goes to third grade. Theresa has struggled this year with some hard times at home and I know she has relied on me and on others in the school for some security. I hope she finds it next year."

A second teacher, Mr. Irvin, provides a different view: "Fred wouldn't do anything for me. At best he was content to sit in class and take up space. At his worst he'd dedicate himself to making my life miserable— nagging, getting other kids to misbehave. I felt like we were in a power struggle most of the year. It was exhausting. He will be a junior in high school this year. All in all he had a tremendous attitude problem and was extremely lazy, never worked up to his potential . . . he was actually pretty capable. Made me mad to see him waste it. I found it hard to like anything about him."

These two teachers are describing relationships with students. They differ in their characterizations of these relationships, but they do not differ in the intensity of their feelings. Both spoke in animated, lively terms, although whereas one was emotionally energized, the other appeared drained and tired. This book is about relationships like these—how to think about them and about their effects on development, how to assess them, and most important, how to harness the power of these important influences on all children's lives. This is particularly important for children living in high-risk circumstances for whom experiences in relationships may be compromised and preventive interventions are needed (Roberts, 1996).

---

[1]Although cases are based on actual classroom experiences, the names used throughout are not.

Stresses on Schools

By almost all estimates, levels of various forms of failure (e.g., social, behavioral, achievement) in the public schools are unacceptably high. Special education referrals and placements remain in 12% to 15% of the population (U.S. Department of Education, 1996), with the belief that if services were available to more children, more children would be identified. Rates of violent behavior in schools, once considered negligible, have become an index of a successful school, and rates of achievement, as measured by standardized tests or criteria such as "learning to read," have dropped steadily over the past decades. There is no question that schools and teachers are under tremendous pressure (Pianta & Walsh, 1996).

Furthermore, educating and ensuring the developmental competence of children exposed to the range of hazards and stressors found in many child-rearing contexts presents the single most difficult challenge to face the public schools and contemporary society. And the problem is growing. In fact, the downward trend in the quality of child-rearing contexts over the past 20 years reflects Senator Daniel Patrick Moynihan's contention that *deviance* (defined here as society's tolerance for poor living conditions for its children) has been "defined down." For example, it has been estimated that more than 25% of all children under 6 years and 60% of children under 6 years in single-mother families live in poverty, one of the most pernicious factors contributing to school failure (National Center for Children in Poverty, 1993). Rates of child maltreatment in the United States have skyrocketed in the last 20 years, with consequences of serious emotional and behavioral disturbance for its victims. Although the divorce rate has now stabilized at roughly 50% to 60% of all marriages, the literature on the effects of divorce and marital strife suggests a number of troublesome consequences for children's social and emotional development. Extrafamilial care for preschool and school-age children suffers from a lack of appropriate regulation and training that virtually ensures the low levels of quality found in most settings (e.g., Cost, Quality, and Child Outcomes Study Team, 1995). Many school-age children are unsupervised both before and after school, do not have a secure and safe adult to whom to turn, and live in dangerous and, at best, unpredictable and unstimulating environments.

The 1992 Fordham University Index of Social Health reported the lowest rating in 21 years for 1990. Nine of the 16 social problems rated (e.g., infant mortality, drug abuse, unemployment, homicide) grew worse, 3 improved, and 4 remained about the same. Of the 9 problems that worsened, 6 reached their worst recorded level, many of which involved children: abuse, homelessness, and family stress. By 1989, children living in doubled-up households increased 42%, to almost 5 million children (National Center for Children in Poverty, 1993). Homelessness threatened an increasing number of children. The U.S. Department of Education estimated that 220,000 school-age children are homeless and that 65,000 of them do not attend school (Reed & Sautter, 1990). On any given night, 186,000 children who are not actually homeless are "precariously housed," living on the verge of homelessness. An estimated ½ million children, up by more than half from 1986, depend on an overwhelmed and inadequate foster care system.

The demographic realities described above are not all new to the United States, although the level of need and the rate of exposure in the population are unprecedented. The increased numbers of children coming to school exposed to these dire circumstances, and the difficulty in educating them, are, in part, two of the conditions that gave rise to a number of reports, calling the nation's attention to the realities facing schools and the high failure rates associated with these realities.

The Carnegie Commission report (see Young, 1994) on the development of young children in relation to schooling and other outcomes concluded that an increasing number of children were growing up in seriously compromised circumstances that affected brain development, cognition, learning, and socialization. This report and others (see Duncan & Brooks-Gunn, 1997) have codified the associations between the demographic indexes described above and child failure—low achievement, inattentiveness, psychiatric symptoms and behavior problems, grade retention, and other forms.

These reports do not tell the whole story because they fail to identify the often subtle processes that account for the links between these child outcomes and hazards, such as maltreatment, poor child care, divorce, and so on. It is important that each day, children bring to school the consequences of the experiences and conditions described above, most of which have to do with problems in emotional and social behavior related to family and adult–child interactions that are undermined in these living circumstances (Erickson & Pianta, 1989). There is widespread consensus that the quality of *social experiences* for very large numbers of children (both poverty and higher income) accounts for the links between these life hazards and poor outcomes for children (see Duncan & Brooks-Gunn, 1997). In particular, the relationships between adults (usually parents) and children have been implicated as key factors in linking social stressors with poor outcomes for children. Because adult–child relationships are so important to healthy development, and underlie much of what a child is called to do in school, the erosion of, or strains placed on, these relationships contribute heavily to the rates of school-related difficulties reported in the press. Thus, risk for poor school outcomes is at least somewhat social in nature and involves relationships with adults. It is the contention of this book that relationships between teachers and children are a resource for development that can counteract relationship-related risk.

Theory, Empirical Tests, and Practice

The efforts of a very large number of people and large amounts of money are expended in the endeavor of educating children raised under the conditions noted above. Yet recent reviews of the literature on educating high-risk children underscore the high levels of disagreement about what approaches work best (Alexander, Entwisle, & Dauber, 1995; Wang & Kovach, 1995). Although programs proliferate at the local level, only a few are theory based or subjected to systematic evaluation (e.g., Henggeler, 1994; Roberts, 1996). For this reason, many local efforts and dollars expended to help children in need, although well-intended, may not be well-informed.

Theory is important when designing solutions for the concerns noted above. Theory provides a reason to choose certain alternatives for an intervention and, even more important, guides decisions about whether something works or not and where to go next. Theory provides a map with which to direct efforts and resources. For example, E. D. Hirsch (1997) has argued that "progressive" theories of education, which emphasize the acquisition of problem-solving skills, reasoning, and higher order processes, neglect the importance of acquiring knowledge about the world. Hirsch's argument is compelling, in part, because he links theories of how children acquire knowledge and the role that knowledge plays in later achievement to instructional practices that attempt to increase knowledge. Not surprising, this debate has led to scrutinizing and improving some of the theories and practices that Hirsch labeled "progressive," such as developmentally appropriate practice for young children (Bredekamp, 1987).

It has been argued that one difficulty in educating "at-risk" students is the absence of theory. It is understandable that at the local level, where pressure is high to solve the problems of children, educators have focused on practice (Pianta & Walsh, 1996). Such pressure creates a debate about practices (which is most effective, etc.) without an accompanying focus on theories about the development of those children in the very areas in which practice is focused. As just one example, Diaz and Berk (1995) have argued that the widespread use of "cognitive-behavioral interventions" for children with problems with impulsivity neglects the literature on how links among cognition, emotion, and behavior develop into a system for self-regulation. In the view of Diaz and Berk, the jump to use what appears to be an effective practice, without an accompanying understanding of developmental processes underlying that problem, accounts for the fact that the practice designed as a solution for the problem is not effective across a wide range of conditions (i.e., lacks generalizability). Doll (1996) provided a clear example of linking developmental theory to the practice of psychology in the schools with her analysis of the literature on peer relations—an analysis that resulted in recommendations that psychologists participate in the peer relations of children on the playground and in the lunchroom!

In the ideal world, theory provides the rationale for designing solutions (interventions) for problems in development and behavior. These solutions are subjected to scrutiny through well-controlled tests of their effectiveness, and ultimately, the solutions that pass scrutiny of this form are introduced as practices in schools and clinics. Although to a certain degree this theory–empirical test–practice sequence functions as described, the intense pressure—at the local level—to address the pressing concerns of children creates a vacuum that is filled by practices that are less and less linked to theory. Furthermore, there is a distinction between empirically validated practices and empirically validated theories that is not often observed when discussions emphasize the need for psychologists to implement practices that have demonstrated effectiveness. As in the case of the cognitive behavior modification example above, it is possible for a set of practices to have been shown to be effective in fairly rigorous tests but to lack a connection to a validated theory of how the practice works or how the problem (which the practice is designed to address) develops. Thus, in both cases—the absence of a link between practice and theory and a focus on empirical tests of practices as opposed to an empirically validated theory of a problem—there is a lack of attention to how understanding basic processes related to particular problems, and theories regarding those processes, can directly contribute to designing useful practice.

In this book, theories of social development are used to understand how social processes in classrooms—relationships between teachers and children—can be enhanced. More specifically, theories on the social impoverishment of high risk children are described and linked with practices designed to reduce risk by addressing relationships between teachers and children. The book presents ideas related to relationships between children and adults—at home and in school—and ways to improve relationships with teachers. It is designed to help psychologists, counselors, teachers, and others make decisions about how best to use the resources available to children in the form of child–adult relationships and to help improve the educational outcomes of high risk children. In this case, theoretical perspectives that emphasize development and systems theory guide the discussion of child–adult relationships. It will be apparent to the reader that the discussion is not saturated with empirically validated interventions or practices. This is for two reasons. First, consideration of child–teacher relationships in the context of specific interventions is only emerging (see Pianta, 1997a). This book represents one of the first attempts to consider these relationships in an intervention context. Second, and perhaps more important, the emphasis is on empirically validated theories that describe how social processes are related to risk and problem outcomes and why child–teacher relationships might be used preventively to ameliorate these concerns. For reasons described above, it is argued that knowledgeable psychologists, armed with a solid informational and theoretical base, can design (and evaluate) local solutions to local problems for individual and groups of children.

Before delving into a discussion of developmental systems theory as it applies to relationships between teachers and children, it is important to further discuss risk, helpful ways to think about risk, and the way that risk and relationships are linked within the kinds of social impoverishment that was mentioned earlier.

Risk

In technical terms, *risk* refers to a probability linking a predictor, such as poor academic skills, with an outcome, such as dropping out of school. For example, in a certain school district, 85% of third graders with standardized test scores falling below the 25th percentile drop out of school before 12th grade. Thus, the 25th percentile could be used as a cut point distinguishing a group of third graders with a high probability (high risk) of dropping out. Risk does not refer to a cause or an etiological relation, although a risk factor may be part of etiological processes (Eaton, 1981). Instead, risk status is a way of describing the likelihood that a given individual will attain a specific outcome, given certain conditions. The concept of risk emphasizes the probabilistic relations between a certain set of conditions and outcomes; it is not a diagnosis. For the example above, the 85% likelihood of failure signals only a need for intervention; it does not suggest why that link exists for a given individual (e.g., whether a particular child scoring at the 19th percentile has an auditory processing disorder). Eaton defined a *risk factor* as any event, condition, or characteristic that increases the probability of the occurrence of a target outcome (e.g., mental disorder, heart attacks, school failure, school age pregnancy).

When one is using the term *risk* it is important (as in the example above) to specify both the outcome and the level of risk. To the extent possible, these statements should be data based (as above). Specifying educational outcomes has been difficult. Educators have only started to grapple with defining the outcomes in which they are most interested (both positive and negative). Witness the debate on Goals 2000. Establishing standards for performance—the things we want children to know and do in school and as a function of schooling—is mired in disagreement and is under attack. Also, because education is heavily invested in improving outcomes regardless of the level of risk, even if standards were written and agreed on, because education is primarily an effort to induce change, it is even more critical to know the processes by which risk can be reduced.

The "At-Risk" Label

Despite these conventions, most often the term *at-risk* is used as a labeling device to describe individual children. In this way, risk is just another way of labeling a problem. But the wider context in which risk is used—the context of prevention—is a more helpful way for educators to think about risk and has implications for focusing on child–teacher relationships as a preventive intervention. Thus, it is argued that child–teacher relationships can counteract the social consequences, or dimension, of the risk conditions described earlier. Furthermore, because adult–child relationships are a resource for development, strengthening these relationships in nonrisk populations can have added benefits to development. In both risk and nonrisk samples, then, a focus on enhancing child–teacher relationships can be expected to elevate competence levels and to help attenuate the rates of failure currently present in public schools.

It is critical to understand that risk is relative. It changes across individuals who have the same risk status (not all children with test scores below the 25th percentile are equally likely to drop out), and it changes for a given individual, depending on time and situation (our hypothetical at-risk child might be exposed to experiences that lead to improved test scores). One's risk of not learning to read varies greatly depending on the extent to which one is read to at home, is familiar with the alphabet, has a caring and knowledgeable teacher, is learning to read a language that one speaks fluently, or has a meaningful reading experience. Understanding that risk is dynamic is essential to developing preventive-oriented programs that unlink risk from problem outcomes.

Risk and its links to prevention have been emphasized. Probabilities of different forms of failure are associated with certain risk factors. These probabilities can be used to deploy resources aimed at unlinking risk factors and outcomes to lower the probabilities. In a preventive-oriented system, resources are deployed at various stages prior to the time at which problem outcomes are expected to appear (Consortium on the School-Based Promotion of Social Competence, CSBPSC, 1994; Henngeler, 1994; Roberts, 1996). Drawing on the example used above, implementing a package of interventions (lower class size, intensive instruction in reading, mathematics, and content knowledge) in the primary grades, for children whose Grade 1 standardized test scores fell below the 25th percentile, might lead to only 15% of children scoring below the 25th percentile eventually dropping out. Research on protective factors—naturally occurring experiences and conditions that are related to success among high risk individuals and groups—and educational programs that emulate these protective mechanisms, can inform a prevention-oriented service delivery system (Pianta, 1990). By and large, this research base suggests that adult–child relationships are some of the most frequently reported protective factors in relation to associations with competence in school-age risk samples (Garmezy, 1994).

Prevention: Vulnerability and Protective Mechanisms

Rutter (1987) has discussed how risk status translates into outcomes—in terms of vulnerability and protective mechanisms that influence the response to risk. For Rutter, protective mechanisms operate to reduce the effects of risk factors that in ordinary circumstances lead to a negative outcome—they interrupt the chain that links, for example, child maltreatment and social problems. In other words, they create a branch on an expected developmental pathway. In this scenario, a protective mechanism could be something as simple as a teacher's spending extra time with a young child who she knows is experiencing conflict at home. In contrast, vulnerability mechanisms intensify the reaction to risk factors and lead to poor outcomes—they actually increase the likelihood that risk status will lead to problems. In the example above, vulnerability mechanisms operate when a maltreated child with social problems is subsequently rejected by peers and teachers. Doll (1996) provided an example of the schools' role as vulnerability mechanisms when she described how children with peer problems are often cut off (usually as a result of disciplinary actions) from contact with peers (as at recess or lunch).

Vulnerability and protective mechanisms operate within a window of opportunity; a period of relative plasticity when responses to risk are being formulated. Little is known about these windows, despite the fact that nearly all professionals concerned with children exposed to risk pose the question "can this be overcome with [intervention]?" What is known is that typically, the earlier in the risk response period that one is provided protective resources, the better.

Unfortunately, schools most often provide services for children after they have failed in some way. Typically, students' needs are responded to after they start having problems (Gartner & Lipsky, 1987). Yet, by understanding links between risk status and prevention, efforts in schools can be directed toward reducing failure before it emerges (at least for some high risk children) and reducing the level of need for children who continue to experience problems.

Pianta (1990) and others (CSBPSC, 1994; Johnson, Malone, & Hightower, 1997; Knoff, 1996) have summarized the three forms of intervention actions in relation to risk status and school outcomes. The three forms of intervention differ with respect to scope and timing. Primary prevention actions are those that are aimed at the entire population, without respect to risk status, and are delivered before the causal process underlying the problem outcome begins—for example, inoculating all children for certain diseases. The aim of such interventions is to eliminate the problem outcome in the population. Secondary prevention actions are those interventions that are delivered to a particular group—a high-risk group—whose probability of attaining the problem outcome is elevated. The link between high risk status and secondary prevention enables the intervention to be targeted more narrowly than for primary prevention efforts. Prekindergarten programs for poor 4-year-olds are examples of secondary prevention. Secondary prevention actions are delivered before the problem outcome is attained by the group members and are evaluated in terms of how they lower the risk coefficient for the target group. Finally, tertiary prevention actions are those interventions delivered after a problem outcome has been attained. These actions basically involve prevention of additional negative effects of a problem outcome and are offered to only those individuals who have attained problem outcome status. Special education or programs for children with certain disorders or disabilities are tertiary prevention efforts. These forms of preventive intervention will return in subsequent discussions of actions to enhance relationships between teachers and children.

In an example central to the thesis of this book, Pianta, Steinberg, and Rollins (1995) discovered that within a group of children at-risk for retention in kindergarten, first grade, or second grade, those children with whom teachers could openly communicate about personal matters, and with whom a teacher shared a warm relationship, were not retained. Thus, these components of the relationship between a child and a teacher were related to a reduced risk coefficient for individuals within a high risk category. These "protective factors" could form the basis of theoretically informed prevention efforts, including efforts to stabilize and extend contact between children and a given teacher. This finding corroborated findings from a number of other investigations indicating that a positive relationship with a teacher is associated with better than expected or improved outcomes for both risk and nonrisk samples (e.g., Garmezy, 1994; Pederson, Faucher, & Eaton, 1978; Werner & Smith, 1980). Thus, a major goal of this book is to integrate theory on risk and its effect on developmental pathways through school, with the use of child–teacher relationships in the school context to intervene early in the risk response period and improve outcomes for children.

What is critical then to risk-reducing efforts in schools is understanding how individuals' responses to risk factors vary and how school contexts shape those responses either by supporting the individual or acting directly on the risk factor or factors that affect the individual. In this way, school contexts can play a key role in shaping the pathways of development. The term "pathways" is a means of understanding the links between early and later developmental status (Sroufe, 1989a). Educators have interests in understanding these relations, such as whether the aggressive first grader becomes the violent sixth grader or whether the disinterested elementary school student will drop out of school. These examples involve a relation between prior and future status that can be understood in terms of pathways.

Risk and Pathways

One lesson learned from many years of developmental research is that there is no single, linear, one-to-one mapping of early risk (or nonrisk) status onto problem (or competent) outcomes. Thus, although many maltreated children have learning and behavior problems in school, a minority become successful students (Erickson, Egeland, & Pianta, 1989). Impulsive first graders may have a higher likelihood of becoming aggressive sixth graders, but not all of them do. Instead, the relation between risk and outcome depends on many things that happen in the intervening period. Thus a risk coefficient, no matter how high, does not really describe a process. What is needed is attention to the processes by which a certain risk factor (maltreatment or impulsivity) translates into failure (learning–behavior problems or aggression). Targeting these processes for intervention could be a key to interrupting the risk–problem relation (Loeber, 1990). Thus, the path the child follows from first grade to adolescence may take many turns, depending on intervening experiences and how those experiences shape development.

Development, as noted by Sroufe (1989a), can be thought of as a branching tree. Developmental paths of individuals can overlap at the start (looking like a trunk) but, over time, will branch and deviate from one another. Individuals with common histories may look quite different later in life. How do schools play a role in creating and sustaining these branching pathways? How might relationships between teachers and children move high risk children from one path to another?

Interest in the pathways of school-age children must be approached from long and short views—birth to adulthood, preschool through high school graduation, and the small windows in between. These windows offer opportunities to shape pathways connecting the long-view endpoints. They include the possibilities offered by learning to develop friendships, to read, to adjust to new schools, and to form a relationship with a teacher. All too often, educators are forced, in one way or another, to take a short view of children's school careers. Teachers most often have a 9-month window of opportunity with which to work with a child. Psychologists, counselors, and other service personnel can have an even shorter window if they only see a child on a time-limited basis. Yet from the perspective advocated here, it is important for educators to have a sense of the developmental pathway along which the child is proceeding and to act in relation to that pathway. Knowledge of risk status and risk factors is important in understanding and making judgments about a child's developmental pathway. Critical to this perspective is the role of relationships in risk itself and in the process of forming and shaping these pathways of development over the course of children's school careers.

In this context, two issues are of importance: First, the early school years exert a disproportionate influence on the trajectories of children's later adjustment in school, and second, social processes—in particular relationships with adults (and also with peers)—play a critical role in shaping pathways and in altering their trajectories and direction. Relationships are central at almost every juncture.

Windows of Opportunity

With respect to the timing of interventions, Doris Entwisle, Karl Alexander, and colleagues (Alexander & Entwisle, 1988; Alexander et al., 1995) have conducted an important longitudinal study of a cohort of children enrolled in the Baltimore City schools, following them from kindergarten throughout their school careers. One of the conclusions that can be drawn from this research is that by the end of third grade, children's pathways through school are fairly set. By the end of third grade, one can predict with a fairly high degree of accuracy how well a child will do in their later years. It appears that relatively little significant "branching" occurs after third grade. In other terms, development in school becomes less plastic or malleable with respect to broad outcomes, such as failure and success. This suggests that the early school years are what can be termed a sensitive period (Pianta & Walsh, 1996). This is a period in which the window of opportunity for influencing later outcomes is open and in which experiences will have disproportionate influence. In one sense, this may be a period in which significant branching of developmental pathways (either toward positive or negative outcomes) may occur. Thus, there is a need to know what factors produce branching and if such factors can be used to produce branching toward positive outcomes.

All too often, little branching occurs in this elementary school period;

in fact, one could argue that in many cases, the early school years are not a period in which developmental trajectories change (Entwisle & Alexander, 1993). Recent studies suggest that data from preschool periods predict elementary outcomes fairly well—risk status at school entry predicts problem outcomes with about 75% accuracy (Pianta & McCoy, 1997). This is one of the central problems of early schooling: how to disrupt these well-entrenched relations between early risk and elementary school problems—between poverty and the acquisition of basic academic competencies, for example. In other words, this is an issue of how to enable school contexts to create pathways branching toward competent outcomes.

Relationships and Pathways

In this book, I focus on the role of schools and relationships, particularly child–teacher relationships, in forming and shaping pathways in school. Subsequent chapters discuss literature that supports the view that child competence, especially in the birth to late elementary school period, is not a property of the child per se but is distributed across the child and the context or contexts that support competence. More specifically, child competence is often embedded in and a property of relationships with adults. In other words, adult–child relationships are critical regulators of development; they form and shape it. In the early years, relationships with adults, primarily parents (usually mothers) but often child-care providers or other family members, form the infrastructure of development that supports nearly all of what a child is asked to do in school—relate to other people, be persistent and focused, stay motivated to perform, be compliant–assertive, communicate, and explore the world. In the school years, this infrastructure is carried forward, hopefully sustained by ongoing support from parents (Bradley, Caldwell, & Rock, 1988) but possibly undermined by changes in relationships (e.g., death of a parent, divorce, parental depression or illness, etc.).

This relationship-based infrastructure is transferred to the classroom—in relationships with teachers and in the challenges of classroom adjustment. It is here that a window of opportunity exists for teachers—the opportunity afforded by the relationship they will form with a child. Evidence supports the view that, indeed, this relationship can shape the course of development—can create a branch in a developmental pathway (Pederson et al, 1978; Pianta et al., 1995, Werner & Smith, 1980). It is important to understand how relationships with teachers can intersect children's developmental pathways and can influence the creation of branches toward health. For these reasons, it is very important to understand the role of relationships in the early school years—this book devotes many pages to promoting a fuller understanding of this.

Psychology in Schools

Applied child and adolescent psychologists face the needs of the very large and growing population of children called "at risk" in the public schools nearly every day. Most frequently, psychologists are called in after a problem has developed to a fairly serious level, and their time and efforts are used to document the severity of the problem. On other occasions, a psychologist might be called in to consult with school personnel regarding a child demonstrating serious difficulties. This could involve coordinating meetings with parents and teachers, linking mental health with school-based services, or developing specific intervention plans for a teacher to implement. Problems or failure can be described in many terms and can include academic, social, mental health, and family concerns. But rarely are psychologists involved early enough to prevent the kind of problems they see most often.

Application in Context

Earlier, the links among theory, empirical validation, and practice were discussed. In that context, it was argued that too much reliance on empirical validation (e.g., a statistically significant difference between an intervention and a control group) as the sole criterion or standard for applications of interventions in professional practice may be mistaken. Local factors (e.g., a teacher's willingness to change, a parent's involvement, a child's attendance) always constrain the applicability of any intervention or practice (Molnar & Lindquist, 1990). Thus, there is substantial need for theory—knowledge about the processes that produce the problem under consideration and knowledge about what factors alter the problem. This knowledge should be well validated and can serve as a means for practitioners to make the many important local decisions they face.

As experts in development and behavior, psychologists can formulate theory-driven responses to the challenges posed by children struggling to succeed. Psychologists must take seriously the need for their knowledge and understanding of development and behavior, not just their technical expertise in assessment or application of intervention protocols. The field of school psychology, in particular, has a large stake in this task. Failure to ground practice in developmental theory and to develop theory-driven techniques will inevitably result in the practice of psychology in the schools being increasingly marginalized. Services considered "psychological," such as counseling, behavioral consultation, and assessment, will become usurped by personnel who are often less well trained and who use techniques that are less well grounded in psychological and developmental principles (Adelman, 1996; Dwyer & Gorin, 1996).

It is increasingly recognized that interventions applied in the context or contexts in which a problem occurs are more effective agents of change than are efforts at change that take place in an office or a context remote to the problem at hand. Although somewhat effective at producing desired changes, typical office-situated psychological intervention services are inefficient agents of change for many problems in childhood. Rarely is it the case that children referred for mental health services display problems only at home or only in contexts other than school. In fact, it can be argued that the school context is the place in which children most frequently demonstrate social, behavioral, and emotional problems and that school may in fact contribute to these problems. Thus, the design of many clinical intervention treatment plans must recognize the school context, and work within it, to produce change (Adelman, 1996; Roberts, 1996). For this reason, it has been argued that applied child and adolescent psychologists adopt the role of "context manager": designing interventions to be carried out by others in natural contexts (parents, teachers, peers), training the intervenors, and monitoring progress. With increasing pressure to deliver effective services, and many psychological services being contracted to paraprofessionals and frontline workers, applied child and adolescent psychologists have a stake in working in schools in a preventive intervention framework. One of the key resources psychologists bring to this set of tasks is their knowledge and understanding of development and their capacity to translate that knowledge into informing local decisions about children.

Relationships in Prevention and Remediation Services

Relationships between adults and children—in particular, teachers and children—can be a legitimate target of the efforts of psychologists in relation to two modes of service delivery: (a) developing prevention-oriented services and (b) enhancing existing, remediation-oriented services. Subsequent chapters build the theoretical basis from which to conduct such work, linking the role of adult–child relationships in development to the classroom context.

The need for a focus on preventive mental health services, using schools as contexts in which to deliver such services, has been articulated by many professionals (Adelman, 1996; Johnson et al., 1996; Roberts, 1996; Weissberg, Caplan, & Harwood, 1991). For children exposed to risk factors that undermine their capacity to adapt competently, interventions triggered early in the window of opportunity have a greater chance of altering the response to risk and of shaping the pathway of development. This requires a prevention mind-set on the part of the professional. Often, by the time a child is put through various forms of eligibility mechanisms, opportunities for change may be lost. Pianta (1990) has delineated the distinction between the prevailing service delivery mind-set (remedial) versus a preventive orientation and the reasons why a preventive orientation is preferable.

However, such an orientation requires that professionals recognize the role of schools as a context for development, that they understand the mechanisms of change and development present within the school context, and that they mobilize resources in such a way to maximize the benefit of those mechanisms. Relationships between children and teachers are one such mechanism of development, and these resources present in the school context can be used more systematically. The importance of relationships between children and adults is hardly of debate—what is new is the recognition that schools play a major role in providing and regulating this form of relationship.

Every child in every elementary school (and middle and high school) has the opportunity to develop a relationship with an adult that can serve as a buffer to risk—a resource for development. In many schools and for many children, there are several adults available for this role (ratios of adults to children in elementary schools are typically 1:12 or 1:15). Thus from a service delivery view, the resources for intervention are already in place, making it possible to affect all children and certainly possible to affect children at greater need. Yet teachers, psychologists, and other school professionals are often in the dark as to how to harness, direct, and refine these resources to benefit children. Thus, the purpose of this book is to use teacher–child relationships as resources for preventing the translating of risk into pathology. These relationships can interrupt pathways to problems and direct them toward competent outcomes. Examples of this approach include policies and practices that affect teacher–child ratios, enhance teachers' understanding of development and the life circumstances of children, facilitate communication between children and teachers, and enhance stability of teacher–child contacts.

With respect to a remedial framework, applied child and adolescent psychologists spend a lot of time (and educators are very concerned) with children already identified as having learning, behavioral, or emotional difficulties and for whom some level of individualized help is required. For these children, child–adult relationships also play a role in competent development. Children with identified problems in learning or behavior often experience conflict in relationships with teachers (Pianta et al., 1995). Thus, the teacher's (or the child's) feelings and beliefs about their experiences with one another can be a correlate of more serious problems. More importantly, it is through these relationships that the social behavior, self-control, and achievement motivation of children with serious problems can be improved and that any other intervention (e.g., a behavior modification plan, consultation services) must be delivered (Meyers, Parsons, & Martin, 1979).

Thus, regardless of a child's classroom problems or needs and the intervention applied to meet those needs, relationships between teachers and children play a role in the identification of those problems and in the intervention delivered. Parallel (or integrated) efforts to improve the relationship between teacher and child will almost always have the added benefit of improving the response to the intervention. Therefore, even with children who already have considerable problems in school—the children with whom psychologists most frequently come in contact—there is a role for working in and through their relationships with adults. A discussion of how one meets these children's needs using the child–teacher relationships involves the assessment of teacher–child relationships (observation, interview, questionnaires) and specific techniques for improving child–teacher relationships and linking child–teacher relationship interventions with other classroom interventions.

The perspective advocated here is that psychologists working with children and adolescents are well situated (and hopefully well suited) to apply developmental and educational theory in an educational context. The role of the psychologist as program developer, consultant, and context manager will allow for the fuller use of the resources present to children in the form of relationships with teachers. However, before leaping into a discussion of assessment or intervention practices, the next chapters provide the theoretical background necessary for a full understanding of techniques.

Summary

Relationships between children and adults are a critical resource for development. For many children, relationships with adults are impoverished or conflictual and, in these cases, are a source of risk. Relationships with teachers are an essential part of classroom experience for all children and a potential resource for improving developmental outcomes. Psychologists working in school settings can play a major role in harnessing this potential resource for development.

2

How the Parts Affect the Whole: Systems Theory in Classroom Relationships

One first-year teacher of second graders describes her life in a school. "It was very hard working with the other second-grade teachers. I never understood it, but I guess they were told that the new hires (me) were going to improve things around here. What a set-up! They hated us before we even got there . . . they even made wisecracks about what I knew! I found others to go to and learn from so it was a workable year, but I'm leaving. My parents are getting older and I want to live near family again. I'll really miss the kids though, one came up to me at the beginning of the year and said, 'I really like you Ms. Gilbert, I'm so glad, I love school.' I'll really miss her."

This teacher's story suggests the complexity of life in a school and life as an educator. Ms. Gilbert is caught in the middle of a struggle between administrators and veteran teachers. She enjoys working with children and has energy and enthusiasm for her work. At the same time, she misses her parents, who are important figures for her. In another set of reflections, Ms. Gilbert notes that she feels her relationship with her grandmother echoes in her relationships with children. She is thoughtful and responsive to her students. But Ms. Gilbert is miserable. She is caught in a set of social circumstances that are confusing. Her story is all about systems and the need for a broad perspective.

Intervention practices must be grounded in a theory of change. General systems theory, especially as applied to developmental psychology (Ford & Lerner, 1992; Sameroff, 1989), has certain advantages for understanding risk and schooling as well as ways to use interactions between students and teachers to change student pathways. Systems theory principles frame the analysis used in this book; therefore, I will discuss them in considerable detail in this chapter. Pianta and Walsh (1996) have written on the application of general systems theory to schooling and have found that it is a useful alternative, both conceptually and practically, to current "best practices" models that disregard theory as a means to generate practical solutions. Pianta (1997a) has applied these concepts to relationships between children and teachers in discussing how these relationships function as a system.

The previous chapter described a number of problems in the application of a risk and prevention framework for addressing problems of school failure. These included the multiple ways in which risk factors and outcomes are linked with one another; the way in which links between risk factors and outcomes change with time and situations; and the social, relational nature of many forms of risk. Designing solutions for high-risk children in schools is complex. In this chapter, general systems theory is used as a tool for addressing this complexity in a way that real-world solutions can be generated. The chapter presents an overview of general systems theory and its underlying principles; examples from classrooms and adult-child relationships are used throughout to illustrate important concepts. Rather than addressing complexity by oversimplification, or neglecting it altogether, general systems theory provides a set of principles that can help educators wade through and make sense of the complex nature of developmental pathways under conditions of risk. Thus, one of the problems facing educators is the sheer complexity of the task of understanding the links between risk, outcome, and education. Systems theory helps order inquiry and analysis. This ordering of inquiry, in the context of fresh perspectives (in this case, knowledge about child–teacher relationships), can be an asset to local decision making that governs practices with children (Molnar & Lindquist, 1990).

In abbreviated terms, *systems* are units composed of sets of interrelated parts that act in organized, interdependent ways to promote the adaptation or the survival of the whole unit. Classrooms, schools, reading groups, disciplinary practices, child–teacher relationships, literacy behaviors, and families each are, or can be, systems of one form or another. In some, the systemic nature of the unit is easy to see (e.g., classrooms); in others, it is not as readily apparent (e.g., literacy behaviors). Nonetheless, the definition holds in each of these cases, with the focus of the ensuing discussion being child–teacher relationships as systems.

General systems theory (GST) has a long history in the understanding of biological, ecological, and other complex living systems (Ford & Ford, 1987). The concepts and principles of GST allow for the description and the analysis of the kinds of systems described above. Most familiar to educators is the application of systems theory to the organization of schools. The principles of GST emphasize understanding the behavior of the system's parts in relation to the unit as a whole and understanding the dynamic properties of the whole in relation to its context. In other words, understanding the social behavior of a child is improved by knowing about how that child relates to his or her teacher in the context of what the teacher (and the school) is trying to accomplish in that classroom. Thus, there are lots of reasons why a child may be distracted in the context of a reading group and not attend to a teacher's request. General systems theory concepts have been applied to child development by Ford and Lerner (1992) in what they called developmental systems theory, some of which bears important similarities to Vygotsky's ideas. These perspectives attempt to capture the dynamic, multicomponent, interactive nature of children's development.

For example, Vygotsky's concept of the "zone of proximal development" (ZPD) embodies systemic principles. The ZPD refers to the difference between the levels of competence a child displays when performing a task alone or when in the context of interacting with an experienced teacher. Children typically display considerably higher levels of competence and more sophistication when interacting with a teacher. Thus, child competence or performance is not a characteristic of the child per se but a dynamic attribute of a system (child–context). Also important in determining performance levels is the quality of child–context interactions, particularly the levels of support and challenge provided by the teacher. Thus, the balance among all these elements determines where, within the ZPD, a child's performance will be displayed.

General systems theory can be applied to a broad array of systems involved in the education of children (Pianta & Walsh, 1996). The principles of GST help integrate analysis of the multiple factors that influence young children, such as families, communities, social processes, cognitive development, schools, teachers, peers, and poverty. In this discussion of GST, the reader should apply these concepts to systems present in the school contexts with which they are familiar. By doing so, it should become very clear that terms such as *readiness to learn*, *skill acquisition*, *direct instruction*, *effective schools*, and even *at-risk children* are not consistent with this framework because they tend to oversimplify phenomena to the point that an appreciation of the dynamic connection between child and context is lost.

This discussion of systems theory focuses on types and levels of systems in child development and principles of systems that are manifest in classrooms and schools. Examples are drawn from schools, classrooms, and teacher–child relationships to illustrate these principles, with a specific focus on how child–teacher relationships function as developmental systems. Unfortunately, when analyzed from a developmental systems perspective, many current educational practices (e.g., services delivered by specialists in different locations in a building) can be viewed as actually increasing risk.

Types and Levels of Systems

First, a map of the playing field introduces the types and levels of systems. Any comprehensive discussion of the influences on children's learning and development has to describe those influences and their relations with one another, such as Bronfenbrenner (1979) has discussed. Such a description can be depicted topographically, as a kind of map, that includes the various contexts, or systems, that affect development. These systems have influences ranging from distal (governments) to proximal (families) and include the culture, the small social group, the dyad, the child, the behavioral system, and the genetic–biological system (see Figure 2.1). These systems, as emphasized by Bronfenbrenner (1979) and Sameroff (1989) constantly interact with one another, across and within levels of the model depicted.

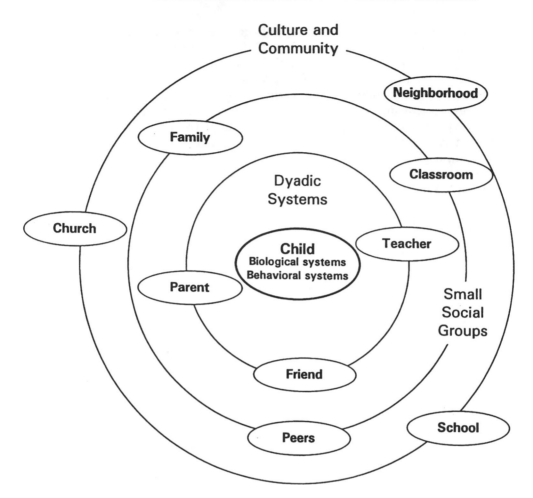

Figure 2.1. Contexts for development. Adapted from Pianta and Walsh (1996) and Sameroff (1989).

Each of these systems is a context for development, carrying with it a particular mechanism for influencing child outcomes. Sameroff (1989) used the concept of the environtype to describe the influence of contexts–systems. The environment is conceptualized to have as powerful an influence on development (the child) as do genetics. In this context, Sameroff was interested in discussing the *regulation* of developmental change—how development is orderly, organized, and planful as opposed to random, chaotic, or unpredictable. This concept of regulation can be thought of in simplest terms, such as what happens when a thermostat is used to control (or to regulate) temperature in a room. The thermostat functions as a mechanism to maintain a certain state, and in doing so monitors that state and responds to changes in state or demand, accordingly. Systems theorists have argued that development also contains regulatory mechanisms that, like thermostats, maintain organization and calibration of certain functions or states. In the discussion of Vygotsky's ZPD above, the child–context (or child–teacher) relationship regulates performance of certain skills within the ZPD.

As discussed later, child–teacher relationships (can) regulate a child's experience in classroom settings. Child–teacher relationships stabilize a child's emotional experience in classrooms (Lynch & Cicchetti, 1992), provide structure and guides for his or her interactions with peers (Howes, Hamilton, & Matheson, 1994), serve as a source of security that supports his or her exploration and mastery (Birch & Ladd, 1997; Pianta, 1997a), and provide interactions that help shape the child's self-regulation (Pianta, 1997a).

But concerning influences other than child–teacher relationships, it is important that Sameroff (1983) differentiated systems within the environment that regulate development in specific ways. These systems (or contexts) contain codes that prescribe regulatory actions of the system vis-à-vis the child. These regulatory actions shape the proximal context in which the child must adapt. For example, schools (as systems) have rules that govern the behavior of teachers and children. These rules constrain the kinds of interactions that take place in classrooms (e.g., teachers cannot hit students, students cannot hit teachers).

Cultures and Large Communities

At a quite distal level, cultures and large communities have considerable impact on the education of children. Systems typically known as cultures, subcultures, states, and communities are included within this broad category. Cultures and communities regulate the behavior of individuals and smaller social groups through creating, organizing, and maintaining roles within the larger group (Boulding, 1985). Thus, one way in which a community influences schools is through creating, sustaining, and filling the role of the "school board member."

The set of culture-level codes that affects development can be called a *developmental agenda* (Sameroff, 1989). One way of thinking about a culture's developmental agenda is as the shared timetable for developmental milestones or generally held beliefs and expectations for child development. The developmental agenda is a series of culturally defined points in the child's life when the child-rearing context is restructured to provide different experiences to the child. These restructurings include toilet training, attending preschool, entering school, being taught to read, having increased academic expectations, or participating in testing programs linked to age or grade that sort children into different education tracks. These restructurings are large-scale, long-term actions called *macroregulations* in Sameroff's model.

Many, if not all, enactments of cultural codes tend to be keyed to the chronological age of children in that culture, not the developmental level of an individual child. Thus, all children who are 5 years old by September 1 go to school in a given state, all first graders are taught to read, and all sixth graders go to middle school. Teacher–child ratios are another such macroregulation, as they are often dictated by administrative policies that are invariant across individual differences in children.

Macroregulations may produce opportunity or trigger failure of one sort or another. Powerful challenges (relating to four teachers instead of one, maintaining peer relations, doing seat work) are enacted on the basis of chronological age (or some proxy like grade in school) and may exceed either the child's or family's capacity to adapt or the teacher's capacity to teach. Macroregulations may require certain skills or capacities or assume previous developmental successes that are not part of the child's life history or present status. Thus, such macroregulations may stress the functioning of the ZPD by introducing too much challenge and too little support for performance.

For example, school policies often prescribe that children change teachers annually, and specific schools often require that young elementary students be taught by more than one teacher (i.e., teaming). But when a socially impoverished child—one who is being raised by a single parent who is often depressed and harsh, with little in the way of predictable routines and regular relationships with adults—is placed in this classroom, these policies can produce risk. Absent the opportunity to develop a close, long-term relationship with a sensitive adult that can enhance social and emotional development, this child may maintain a distanced, avoidant stance, and hence be unable to use an adult to help negotiate peer relations and other developmental skills. When challenged in these areas, the child will often fail. Macroregulations of this sort increase the child's risk when they are beyond the ZPD. Often, they are too great a challenge for the developmental level of the child, or too little support is provided to meet that challenge. The result is some form of "child failure" or "school failure," but it is more accurately characterized as a failure of the system (Pianta & Walsh, 1996).

Families and Small Social Groups

At the next level, moving from distal to more proximal, are systems of families and small social groups (peer groups, gangs, church groups, schools, classrooms). These groups are concerned with the regulation of the individual child's behavior, and a large part of their activity toward the child is oriented toward the goal of producing individuals who adequately fulfill roles in the larger social structure (culture). For example, classroom teachers have the intentional goal of regulating children's behavior within the school and of helping the child become a functional member of society.

Codes within these small social groups regulate the behavior of individuals with respect to the goals of the group, which may or may not be consonant with the larger culture's developmental agenda. Such is the case when teens belong to gangs, in which individual behavior is tightly constrained by gang rules, but the function of gang membership is often at odds with the goals of the larger community.

Small-group codes trigger behaviors of the group that operate within a shorter time span than cultural-level codes. Small-group regulations often reflect the colliding demands of living together in small social groups and of meeting the larger developmental agenda. Sameroff (1989) called these *mini-regulations*. Caregiving practices, such as feeding and discipline, expectations for performance, and patterns of emotional expression allowed within the group, are all coded at this level and are enacted through regulations that involve rules for the behavior of adults. These regulatory influences allow the group to function as a cohesive social unit to accomplish its purpose in a social structure. Family- and classroom-code influences are apparent, for example, in family expectations for performance and discipline practices in school.

Closer to the focus of this book, classroom codes and regulations constrain how teachers and children relate to one another in many ways. In an example that later in the book serves as a focus of intervention, teachers often adopt discipline practices that provide for one-to-one contact with students on only a *conditional* basis. That is, individual time is seen as reinforcing to children and therefore is allotted only when a child meets certain behavioral expectations. Such an approach can make it difficult to establish the kind of child–teacher interactions that are conducive to enhancing child–teacher relationships. Or teachers may use a system for behavior management that provides for systematic feedback and consequences for behavior (both positive and negative). This system, which calls for predictable and contingent responding on the part of an adult, provides a structure that supports the development of relationships between teachers and children.

Interpersonal Relationships

Interpersonal relationships (child–parent, peer–peer, parent–parent, teacher–child) are dyadic systems that play key roles in the regulation of child behavior within small social groups. Interactions between two people, over time and across many situations, come to be patterned; when they do, these patterns reflect a relationship shared by the two individuals (Hinde, 1987). This relationship, and its qualities, can play a role in shaping the behaviors of the individuals involved—the relationship, through countless interactions, will regulate or constrain the development of the two individuals. It takes time for teachers and children to come to know one another in a way that has this type of influence, but with time and repeated encounters, they come to know what to expect from one another, the cues that each other gives for certain responses, and the limits that will be enforced within this relationship. The fact that relationships (as dyadic systems) take time to develop, and that time is needed for the regulatory influence of these relationships to take shape, supports school and classroom policies or practices that maximize and lengthen contact between children and their teacher.

Regulation at the relationship level is enacted through *individual codes,* according to Sameroff (1989). With respect to relationships between adults and children, these codes involve the adult's (caretaker, teacher) accumulated feelings and beliefs about their behaviors with children— what works and does not work—their motivation styles, and their goals of interaction with children in general and specific children in particular (Pianta, 1997a). These feelings and beliefs are enacted in very brief, often subtle aspects of moment-to-moment interaction with children (micro-regulations). The qualities of this interaction are described not by what is being done by the adult or child (i.e., feeding, punishing, attending) but more by how it is being done in relation to the other. Thus, constructs such as reciprocity, sensitivity, coordination, and synchrony are considered important and can be used to describe relationships and interactions between teachers and children (Howes & Hamilton, 1992a, 1992b; Pianta, Nimetz, & Bennett, 1997; Sameroff, 1989). A teacher and a child who share a laugh (mutuality or synchrony) or a teacher who reads a child's subtle frustration cues and slides a puzzle piece closer to the child's hand (sensitivity) are examples of the qualitative aspects of interaction that stand for individual-level codes. Teachers' preferred styles of emotional expression (calm and easy or tense and stressed), their tending to and responding to children's emotional needs (personalized or autonomous), and their perceptions or beliefs regarding children's social behavior and emotions (emotions are important or not) are all other examples of variables that can be considered when discussing how teacher-level codes affect regulation of the teacher–child relationship.

Considerable evidence shows that adult–child relationships play important roles in the adaptation of the child within a specific situation— home or classroom (e.g., Birch & Ladd, 1996; Howes & Hamilton, 1992a; Pianta, 1997a). Adult–child relationships are asymmetrical (the adult is more mature and has greater weight in determining the quality of the relationship), therefore, these relationships, and individual codes within them, can have great influence. Many child problems can be linked to Sameroff's notion of individual codes, as these erode a context's function as a ZPD. For example, a teachers' style of relating to children may assume certain prior experiences in a relationship on the part of the child—a style that is aloof and businesslike and that tends to remain emotionally distant from children may trigger a negative emotional and behavioral response from a child who seeks emotional contact with such a teacher and is rebuffed (Lynch & Cicchetti, 1992). Furthermore, children bring with them certain individual codes that can be enacted in relationships with teachers and that can affect the quality of these relationships. Variables such as child temperament or a child's beliefs about adults based on his or her past experiences (such as with parents) are also crucial codes enacted within the adult–child dyadic system.

In sum, considering child–teacher relationships as systems emphasizes their dynamic, multicomponent, interactive qualities. An expanded discussion of these qualities appears in chapters 4 and 5.

The Child as a System

The developing child is also a system. One way to view the child as a system is to recognize that behavior is organized across many developmental domains (motor, cognitive, emotional) to produce an integrated whole (the "whole child"). From this point of view, motor, cognitive, social, and emotional development are not independent entities on parallel paths but are integrated within an organized, dynamic process.

Educational practices that focus solely on one of these domains (e.g., assessment of cognitive development or reading achievement) often reinforce the fiction that children's behaviors can be isolated from one another and from the context or function in which they are embedded. Testing and evaluation of children often falls into the trap of drawing somewhat artificial boundaries between these domains. However, the whole child, as a system, cannot be explained in terms of its parts, much less in terms of one part. Thus, research on interpersonal relationships suggests that *emotional* and *social* qualities of parent–child or teacher–child interaction predict *cognitive* competencies in that and in other situations (Pianta & Harbers, 1996; Pianta et al., 1997; Rogoff, 1990). Taking a developmental systems perspective, many psychologists have argued that child assessment should focus on broad indexes reflecting integrated functions across a number of behavioral domains (e.g., Greenspan & Greenspan, 1991). Terms such as *adaptation* have been used to capture these broad qualities of behavioral organization, and although fairly abstract, they call attention to a focus on how children use the range of resources available to them (including their own skills and the resources of peers, adults, and materials) to respond to internal and external demands.

When considering the child as a developing system, one focuses not only on one domain of functioning or an isolated behavior, such as aggression, but also on the organization of behavior from multiple domains with respect to particular situational or developmental demands. In these respects, a child's particular behavior such as aggression cannot be understood on its own but in the context of related factors, such as the level of language skills used, the use of self-regulation processes, and the role that aggression, as a social behavior, plays in the situations in which it is displayed. This conceptualization of the child and the child's functioning has many implications for schooling. Assumptions about performance, indicators of progress, and targets of instruction are all affected by viewing the child as a developing system in the context of social relationships.

Teachers are systems, too, as the example given at the beginning of the chapter indicates. Understanding the relationship-oriented behavior of a teacher with a given student requires consideration of many elements—training and knowledge, experience, current concerns or experiences (e.g., financial, family, marital), hobbies or interests, and so forth. Thus, it is critical not to approach teachers as if the only dimension of their experience or the only resource (liability) they bring to a relationship is what is seen in the classroom (Goodlad, 1991; Molnar & Lindquist, 1990).

Biological Systems

Finally, increasing attention is being paid to biological systems (e.g., genetics, neuroanatomy, neurophysiology) as explanations for risk and school failure. Biological "causes" have been offered for such functional problems as reading failure, overactivity and attention problems, and conduct problems (Pennington & Ozonoff, 1991; Riccio, Hynd, Cohen, & Gonzalez, 1993). Unfortunately, this is a problem with interpretation of research relating biological processes and problem outcomes. Research pointing to biological or genetic reasons for school failure is too often misinterpreted to suggest a "causal" role for biology and ignores the reality that biological systems are embedded in and interact with other systems (Gottlieb, 1991; Greenough & Black, 1991). At best, studies must be viewed in light of evidence that biochemical and genetic activity are affected by experience and environmental parameters (Gottlieb, 1991; Greenough & Black, 1991) and that biological influences on behavior operate within the larger systems influences described above. Recent evidence has, in fact, made it very clear that neurophysiology and neuroanatomy are strongly affected by environmental input, including the qualities of interaction between young children and parents, the predictability of routines, and the emotional climate of the home (see Young, 1994).

The fact that neurological processes respond to environmental input should be obvious. The ease with which biological interpretations are made for children's school-related problems (e.g., reading failure, behavioral maladaptation) reflects an unfortunate inclination to attribute the cause of problem outcomes in schools to forces that schools cannot influence or control (a macroregulation in present-day American culture). These interpretations place responsibility for school progress on some unknown, unseen force within children, blaming not so much the children as their gene pools or their brains. The role of context—in particular, the regulatory role of relationships—is ignored in these interpretations.

Interaction of Systems

The previous discussion has outlined some of the key systems involved in child development, creating a topography of units. These units are themselves interconnected and constantly interact with one another. Peer relations are affected by the quality of child–parent relationships (Sroufe, 1989b) and by the quality of child–teacher relationships (Howes, Matheson, & Hamilton, 1994). Policies made at school board levels (community systems) affect the interactions of children and teachers with one another (dyadic systems). Systems within this topography are interdependent and act in concert (for better or worse) with one another (Gottlieb, 1991).

The activity of a given system—for example, the brain or the classroom—is not independent; it relies on activity elsewhere, and itself affects the activity of other systems. This web of systems acts together, and this activity is patterned and predictable (to some degree, although never completely). As has been argued previously, *social processes,* or interactions, are the strands that hold together this web. Garbarino (1982) has likened this web to a fabric that supports the development of the child—the more connections, and the more these connections have a positive, supportive tone to them, the better they are able to sustain developmental progress.

This web, or fabric of connections, is a package that has been referred to as a "developmental niche" (Super & Harkness, 1986). This niche reflects the organized patterning of these codes, itself an influence on children. In a stark example of a developmental niche, or web, Garbarino and colleagues (Garbarino, Dubrow, Kostelny, & Pardo, 1992) have described life for children in what they call "urban war zones." Life in these areas is harsh, accompanied by stresses that produce psychiatric symptoms in children that are consistent with those suffered by combat soldiers. These children fail miserably in school—they cannot attend to information, they suffer serious emotional difficulties, and they are socially unregulated. These behavioral profiles are the output from a set of interlocking systems that reflect the niche of poverty—poor housing, widespread unemployment, no health care, decrepit schools and stressed teachers, and dangerously violent and unsafe neighborhoods.

Thus, educators need to attend not only to the ways a given system (e.g., families, schools, parents, or teachers) regulates development but also to the interactions among systems. This requires attending to the regulatory codes present in many systems. For example, certain codes for discipline govern the regulation of child misbehavior in some contexts (a home in which physical punishment is acceptable) but not in others (a classroom in which physical punishment is not acceptable). When codes conflict like this, these systems fail to contribute to a niche, or fabric, that will support development. Cultural-level codes, like educational standards or testing programs that are used to determine whether a child can be promoted to the next grade are often inconsistent with the support provided to the child or the schools to meet these demands (Kozol, 1991). A developmental systems perspective requires this type of analysis of the developmental niche to more fully understand processes related to risk or failure.

Within the developmental niche of a given child, relationships with adults are midlevel systems—strongly affected by forces from all directions while influencing the child's development. These relationships are like the keystone or the linchpin of development—they are in large part responsible for developmental success under conditions of risk and, more often than not, transmit those risk conditions to the child. These relationships and their role within a developmental niche are the focus of chapters 3 and 4.

Implications of GST Principles for Schooling

Having described the topography of systems involved in development, the following is a brief discussion of principles related to the functioning of systems, and to the analysis of systems, that aids in later discussions of child–teacher relationships as systems that regulate children's development.

Units of Analysis

In GST, the unit of analysis is at a macrolevel. In terms of parts and wholes, interest is in the whole. Thus, the behavior of "larger" systems (such as child–teacher relationships) is used to explain the behavior of "smaller" systems (such as children). Attention and analysis are often focused at a level that is higher than the one in which the initial question is framed. To understand the discipline-related behavior of a teacher in his or her classroom, one must know something about the school, the school system, and the community in which they are embedded as well as the teacher's history of experience in relation to behavioral expectations in the classroom. It is not possible to understand why a teacher has difficulty maintaining behavioral expectations (the part) without knowing how that activity relates to the purpose of these other concerns (the whole). One cannot understand or explain a teacher's interactions with students without understanding how those interactions fit within and are shaped by goals (implicit or explicit) of the school, the school system, or the community. The whole gives meaning to the activity of the parts. Similarly, behaviors (e.g., attention, motivation) of a child in a classroom may be best understood in relation to the relationship the child shares with a teacher and the way that relationship functions (or not) to support the child in those behaviors.

Most educators raised on behaviorism have learned to take a complex behavior such as reading or social competence and break it down into parts through task analysis. In theory, these parts account for the complex tasks they reflect and can be reassembled by teaching them in a prescribed sequence through direct instruction (or cognitive behavior modification, social skills curricula, etc.). Presumably, when the component parts have been learned in proper order, the *ability* to read or to be socially competent has been acquired and will be displayed spontaneously and on demand in various situations. But for children whose experiences have undermined the *development* of these competencies, task analysis and instruction (intervention at the level of parts), often leads to the acquisition of the parts, not the whole. Thus, *developmental change is not reflected by progressive acquisition of isolated skills*. Clearly skills help, but they are not the whole story.

Earlier it was noted that one explanation given for the failure of cognitive behavior modification techniques to produce generalizable changes in self-control or impulsivity was that these techniques tend to be isolated skills extracted from developmental processes that are more holistic and systemic in nature (Diaz & Berk, 1995). In this criticism, Diaz and Berk suggested that self-regulation is a function of a system of cognitive, emotional, linguistic, behavioral, and interactive processes that develop over time and as a function of experiences in many contexts. They suggested that isolating skills that appear to distinguish regulated and impulsive children and then teaching those skills to impulsive children cannot replicate the development of self-regulation and thus is likely to have serious limitations as an intervention, if the intervention is expected to produce behavioral gains in contexts other than the therapist's office.

Developmental, and by implication educational, processes are both whole- and part-oriented. From the perspective of the whole, many things change as a child learns to read or to be socially competent. Complex behavioral *systems* come into play. Reading involves hundreds of isolated behaviors (decoding, encoding, memory, comprehension). Self-regulation involves similarly numerous and complex behaviors. These behaviors must become organized in a whole unit—a system—that itself functions smoothly on demand. This system also functions in a social context—such as reading to your teacher, being read to by your parents, or complying with a parent's or a teacher's directions. This system cannot be broken down in component parts and learned.

Functional Relations Between Parts and Wholes

Systems are embedded within other systems. What is a unit in one system—for example, the child in the classroom—is also a system itself. Systems theorists discuss relations between systems and their component units in terms of *differentiation* and *integration*.

Differentiation refers to the fact that over time, in response to internal and external pressures, one of the ways in which systems adapt is by the emergence of subunits. These subunits take on different roles for the system as a whole to function. Conversely, integration refers to the fact that for the system as a whole to maintain its integrity and identity, differentiated subunits must also be integrated, or connected, with one another to accomplish the primary function of the system.

In education, for example, special education is a subunit of a school that responds to needs of children that cannot be addressed by general educational procedures. But for the school system to function, special education and general education must be integrated within a given school instead of operating as two separate entities within one building. Reading skills, as they progress with increasing organization, often differentiate into skills used in reading different forms of text—poetry, algebra books, and novels.

Relationships between teachers and children develop different forms (differentiate) as well, as one teacher recalled in the following:

> I've known her since the third grade, she was a wonderful student in my class, and I enjoyed teaching her. Then I coached her in soccer for another 3 years in fourth, fifth, and sixth grades. I saw her grow up from a young girl to a teenager, and our relationship changed as we both saw sides of each other that most students and teachers do not see.

In a developing system, there is always a tension between differentiation and integration. This tension is a consequence of relations between units that are active and connected with one another.

It is important that differentiation and integration allow systems to behave efficiently. In a system in which units are both differentiated (serving different functions) and integrated (the right hand knows what the left is doing), there is a much wider variety of ways that the system can adapt to pressure than if units were redundant and not connected. Thus, in the context of a teacher–child relationship, teachers can instruct, discipline, and comfort a particular student. It is not necessary for a different adult to take on each of these functions.

Early in the development of a system, each unit within it has the potential to develop the properties of other units within the system. In the beginning of the school year, before roles are created for students, there are many possible ways in which different students will sort themselves out. Who will become a teacher's favorite? Who will have trouble adjusting? This property is called *equipotentiality* and refers to the equal potential of different units to perform each other's function. It refers to something like *replaceability* and can make a system very flexible. In the example of regular and special education, it is conceivable that under some conditions, each classroom in a school has the potential of serving many children with different needs. Classrooms may not have to be sorted to perform this function.

With respect to relationships within the classroom, teachers and aides are two adults that often replace one another in multiple ways—assisting and comforting children. Yet at the same time, these two adults perform different roles and functions—they are hierarchically related to one another—one is charged with responsibility for instruction and the other is charged with assisting. Two interesting questions to ask of classrooms with a teacher and an aide concern the differential responsiveness of these adults to children in the class: Does this enable these two to meet the wide range of needs in the class better than if there were one adult? Does this enable each to develop a special relationship with different children or do the same children develop special relationships with both?

On the one hand, equipotentiality allows a system to recover the function it would lose if a part was lost. If one thinks of occasions when a highly skilled and valued staff member leaves a school, there is frequently a period of reorganization, which often entails a search for another staff member, or members, who can perform the lost function or functions. To the extent that someone else in the building knows how to do what the person could do, then the "recovery" period is quick. When a teacher is absent, the aide usually performs the "in charge" functions, children seek the aide out, and the aide assumes the function of the teacher for more children in the class. On the other hand, equipotentiality also carries redundancy and, at times, inefficiency. It might not be useful for everyone in a school or a classroom to be able to perform all functions.

Solutions for many of the challenges of educating children (and often for high-risk children) have involved the creation of new units—a strategy of differentiation. New programs, new classes, new types of professionals, and new services are all part of this response in most schools. This response has led to overdifferentiation and lack of integration in current practices related to special education and, more generally, in solutions for high-risk students. Typically, when a child demonstrates difficulty learning or has problems in behavior, the "solution" to this pressure involves a referral to an "expert" based outside the classroom. Intervention services are then offered that involve contact between another expert and the child, most frequently in the form of "resource" or "pull out" help in which the child's normal classroom activity is disrupted. From a systems theory perspective, this is a high degree of differentiation and specialization, the consequences of which will require even more resources to harmonize the functions and the roles within this system (Pianta & Walsh, 1996).

This highly differentiated approach to special services for high-risk children reflects a disintegration of the child and of child–teacher relationships, which itself can be a negative force. The child, the skills the child brings to the classroom, the staffing of a school, and the services within the school are all carved up under the assumption that when they are put back together, the resulting educational program reflects some functional improvement for the child. This may not be the case. Eligibility procedures (referral, assessment, labeling) are costly to schools; assessment procedures and services often have little connection to the skills the child needs to perform competently in the "regular" classroom (Wang & Kovach, 1995).

From a different perspective, resources can be focused within a given classroom to provide for preventive effects of classroom experiences (Pianta, 1990). To the extent possible, a child can be maintained within the classroom with a focus on using interactions between the child and the teacher to buffer the likelihood of failure. These interventions are the focus of later chapters, but the point is that children need smaller or more integrated systems within which to thrive in school. This is especially true of children whose social experiences have been fragmented, unpredictable, and unsupportive. When a school's response to these children is overdifferentiated, the school experience can promote risk.

As noted above, how schools integrate their responses to risk is a critical component of building a preventive context. How schools schedule time is one aspect of this response. In one kindergarten classroom, about half of the 18 children were high risk. This classroom had a skilled teacher and an aide. The daily schedule was pinned next to the door and reflected the comings and goings of children in the room. The children having the most difficulty adapting to the classroom routine also spent the most time coming and going to services. These children and this teacher had to manage an average of seven transitions each morning. The teacher had more uninterrupted time with the well-adjusted children. One boy identified as one of the most "at-risk" children in the classroom came and went more than three times a day just to "services" that were in addition to the other extra services offered to all the children, such as music, art, and gym. This child probably spent more time in the hallway than in the classroom.

Thus, the differentiated approach to services created transitions that interacted with the child's own risk status to increase risk.

Motivation

Systems theory offers alternative views of the locus of motivation and change. Within behavioral perspectives, change and motivation to change are often viewed as derived extrinsically—from being acted on by positive (or negative) reinforcement or reinforcement history. Maturationist views of change posit that the locus of change is the unfolding of genetic programs, or chronological age. From both perspectives, the child is a somewhat passive participant in change—change is something that happens to the child whether from within or without.

General systems theory holds that the motivation to change is an intrinsic property of any system and an inherent aspect in the fact that systems are active. Developmental change follows naturally as a consequence of the activity and the evolution of interacting systems. The child is inherently active: constructing meaning, adapting to changes, seeking challenges, and practicing emergent capacities. This is a different view of the child than that of the passive child who is acted on by contingencies or that of the equally passive child whose behaviors are preprogrammed. Furthermore, the child acts within contexts that are dynamic and fluid. Motivation, or the "desire" to change, is derived from the *co-action of systems*: both of child and of context.

One can think of the kind of activity in any classroom: Children interact with other children, with teachers, and with materials. There are standards for performance, thousands of opportunities for feedback and correction, and numerous chances to alter one's behavior. One can argue about the appropriateness of any of these activities, but it is hard to argue that classrooms lack activity.

Developmental change occurs regardless of the nature of the "input" variables in this process. In most classrooms, children learn regardless of whether they are reinforced or whether they are "old enough." Children acquire skills that facilitate their adaptation in a given context. In some cases, these may be skills, such as drug dealing or theft, that enable them to be thrown out of school so that they can engage in the street economy. In other cases, these skills can enable them to disengage from an overwhelming classroom with excessive demands for coping (e.g., the boy with three transitions in and out of the classroom each morning). Children learn not to approach the teacher who is emotionally withholding and hostile; they engage and deepen connections with teachers who comfort and challenge them.

An active organism interacting with a context will learn, adapt, and change over time. Some extrinsic contingencies may guide the performance of behavior and may influence the acquisition of certain behaviors, and some behavioral systems (such as written language or formal mathematics) depend on external input. Nonetheless, a system's basic propensity to change (motivation) is not inside or outside the system but is integrated in its basic properties. For example, the evidence for children's intuitive use of higher order mathematics skills and concepts in the absence of formal instruction (Resnick, 1994; Rogoff, 1990) clearly demonstrates that motivation, even for academic skills, does not depend on formal schooling. It is ironic that children are often better intuitive mathematicians before formal instruction than after.

Assumptions about the locus of change and motivation have fundamental consequences for the organization of schools and for the delivery of instruction. Views of motivation as existing in an external form and of change as resulting from input to the child will inevitably result in instruction that is driven by curricular scope and sequence charts, behavioral objectives, and drill and practice—which are the dominant modes of instruction in the United States (Stigler & Fernandez, 1995). Biological views of motivation result in schools using "transitional" grades that delay entry in formal schooling in the hope that a year of maturation will help the child catch up to his or her chronologically aged peers or, worse yet, doctors prescribing medication as a means to address a lack of fit between child and classroom (e.g., Shepard & Smith, 1986).

These views of motivation are inadequate because they fail to acknowledge that instruction is a social process—a process that occurs in the context of a relationship between teacher and student, as described earlier in terms of Vygotsky's ZPD. The child is an active participant in this. Teachers pose challenges and guide activity toward adapting to those challenges. This relationship is a system that regulates the child's development of competencies and skills in the context of the classroom. This relationship creates a "holding environment" for the interactions between the child (as a system), the teacher (as a system) and the curriculum—from which will emerge new skills and competencies. In later chapters, I describe the elements of this system in more detail.

Change

In most educators' views, change is a function of acquiring or adding new skills—progressing from two-word sentences to three-word sentences or learning more letters in the alphabet. In GST, change is often viewed as discontinuous and qualitative. It occurs when systems reorganize and transform under pressure to adapt. In this context, change is not the acquisition of skills or the addition of new units to an existing repertoire but a reorganization of relations among units (old and new) within the system. The following illustrates how a teacher describes change in relating to a student in his second-grade class:

> Mark was socially backwards—he had not had many opportunities to spend time with children his own age and had few friends—so he spent a lot of time with me. He seemed afraid of forming attachments, he'd shy away from the other kids and cling to me—almost to the point where I felt burdened by his neediness. One day Mark had an emo-

tional outburst in response to some frustration he was feeling, and he bit me. I did not get mad and lose my temper (although I did feel pretty angry); I tried to respond differently than what I think he was expecting from adults. I held him until he stopped crying and quieted down. I tried to reassure him. After this incident, he seemed more trusting. At the end of the year I asked to have Mark retained in my class for another year; I felt it would enable him to build upon our connection and not start over. During the summer I invited him to visit the classroom, and I took him home after the visit. The year went smoothly, he became increasingly independent and less needy—he seemed more oriented to persist when challenged and seemed a bit more robust socially—there were fewer emotional outbursts. He seemed more secure in himself and with me.

Many things changed in this teacher's relationship with Mark, and Mark changed as well. What properties of systems may account for these changes? Are these properties evident in this teacher's relationship with Mark?

Self-stabilization and adaptive self-reorganization refer to GST principles describing both stability and adaptive change of a complex system. *Self-stabilization* refers to the gyroscopic property of complex systems in which the system can respond to perturbations or demands while not reorganizing in response to this demand. The system responds by rearranging internal dynamics or relations and adapts to pressure without altering its basic structure or identity. Self-stabilization is a very important property of systems; it preserves their identity in the face of contextual pressures or demands and ensures that major change, or reorganization, occurs at a slow, regulated pace. If it were not for self-stabilization, the behavior of systems and individuals would be wildly unpredictable and unstable.

In the example above, this teacher remains stable in his interactions with Mark. He concentrates on being consistent and on responding to Mark's outbursts with stability and calm—he consciously "reins in" his own emotions in the service of maintaining this sense of stability. This provides a consistency and a constancy to their interactions—no matter how far Mark may stray or his behavior may vary from the norm, there is a consistent response. This is self-stabilization; it is the essence of security and enables Mark to grow more independent.

Adaptive self-reorganization refers to the response of a complex system to more constant or intense environmental (or internal) pressure or demand. In this process, the self-stabilizing properties of the system are inadequate to meet the demands placed on them, and the system must reorganize to respond adaptively. As noted above, in his second year with this teacher, Mark eventually became a more "robust" student, able to deal with some of his own frustrations and social experiences without the outbursts that accompanied these experiences. He also became more persistent as well. In short, he grew—a more confident and flexible stance allows Mark to cope with a wider range of emotions, social interactions, and classroom experiences. Are these changes a function of maturation or were they related to his experiences in relationship with his teacher?

This kind of reorganization takes place as a system (Mark) accumulates a pattern of self-stabilizing responses to internal (maturational) pressures, external (relationship) pressures, or both. Also, reorganization can take place in response to external pressures of sufficient intensity or duration—in this case, Mark's relationship with his teacher may have been of sufficient intensity and duration to enable change of this magnitude. Change of complex systems takes time and does not usually come about by large, one-time reorganizations but by incremental changes that are constant adaptions to the demands of contact with other systems. Mark had hundreds of opportunities for contact with his teacher, opportunities that allowed him to respond in ways that restructured Mark's social and emotional experiences in the classroom and in relation to adults. This teacher became a salient figure in Mark's development as a function of these interactions. Over time, these individual interactions— such as eye contact, tone of voice, touches on the head, hugs, soothing talk, small helps in the context of building tension and frustration—all added up to large-scale change.

Time

Action and change take place in time. Time will influence the extent or the degree of change, even with all else equal. This is all the more important for relationships between teachers and children. Would Mark have grown as much if not placed with this teacher for a second year? Almost all models of schooling or education have no code for time as an input variable. In fact, the way schools organize time usually acts against the formation of relationships between teachers and children; certainly, it acts against the formation of relationships with the kind of intensity and stability that marked Mark's relationship with his teacher. For example, most school systems organize the several-year school career of children into 9-month grades, and within a grade, children often attend different classes or programs at different times of the year. It is important that time be accorded importance in any consideration of systems' activity and change.

Prediction and Assessment

Educators spend a lot of time and energy wrestling with the problem of predictability, usually in the context of assessing children's skills or progress. It is fundamental to education in the United States that judgments are made about the likelihood of success or failure. Within a GST perspective, perfect predictability is recognized as impossible; all prediction is highly probabilistic and fraught with uncertainty.

Recalling that living systems are active and that the behavior one tries to predict is part of this activity, one can use GST to recognize that attempts to measure activity are largely artificial; relations between assessments (correlations and validity coefficients) are of necessity bounded. Estimates of abilities, skills, or future performance will never approach 1.0 not because measures are unreliable but because the complex, dynamic systems are active; hence, actual description of them in static terms can never be more than an estimate. General systems theory also posits that the interrelated and complex behaviors of systems transform the system over time, such that new and different organizations govern the system's activity, making prediction over time even more difficult. In terms of relationships between teachers and children, not all outcomes are predictable. Instead, a focus on general principles, and understanding specific circumstances in terms of those principles, will be helpful in trying to understand whether child X will benefit from teacher Y.

"Fit" Systems

Finally, GST suggests a set of principles for the assessment of systems that can be used to guide observations of relationships between teachers and children or other systems in relation to this relationship. These are a set of variables on which systems differ that index the degree of fitness of a given system to respond to challenge or to regulate the behavior of individuals (subsystems) organized within the system.

Flexibility is a hallmark of systemic fitness or capacity to adapt. A *flexible system* is able to respond to a wide range of contextual conditions and internal pressures. Flexible relationships between teachers and children accommodate a range of children's needs; they function across many contexts (e.g., home, classroom, playground), and they support the child in a number of ways (e.g., emotionally, with respect to instruction and learning, in relation to peers). Flexible relationships with teachers allow the child to benefit from the resources in this relationship in many ways.

Another aspect of systems that can be evaluated is the extent of differentiation present. Under most circumstances, less differentiation is better for building relationships between teachers and children that will buffer the effects of risk. For relationships to function as regulatory mechanisms in development (like for Mark above), there must be sufficient intensity of interaction and frequency of interaction. Too many adults dilute these interactions and distribute them too widely for the desired buffering effect to occur.

Relationship systems can also be evaluated with respect to feedback functions. Again, the interrelated nature of systems requires a large number of feedback loops through which information is transmitted. Rich, varied, contingent, multimodal feedback loops that are reciprocal and mutual make for the kind of relationship system that can regulate development. These topics are the focus of extended discussion in chapter 4.

Summary

General systems theory offers a set of tools for examining behavioral development that acknowledge the complexity of the processes involved.

Such tools provide psychologists with alternative ways to view the behaviors of children and teachers, particularly complex social behaviors. Systems theory encourages a holistic level of analysis that embraces the dynamic properties of behaviors as they are displayed in context.

Critical to this perspective is an understanding of how behavior cannot be easily isolated from its context, how change takes place as a function of processes of self-stabilization and self-reorganization, how differentiation and integration describe relations between parts and wholes in a system, and how activity is a hallmark of developing systems. A perspective informed by systems theory embraces the uncertainty of predicting behavior and recognizes that behavior is always determined by multiple influences. Relationships between children and adults (teachers) are systems and are, in turn, part of larger systems (e.g., classrooms). This perspective is helpful in understanding how relationships between children and teachers form, how they are maintained, and how they are important for development.

3

The Child as a Developing System

They are so wonderful to watch, even the children who struggle. They are always moving, always trying to figure something out (even when this is troublesome for me), and they always seem to be watching what I'm doing. I am amazed at how they pay attention—to something—maybe not to what I want them to attend to, but they are always watching . . . I also wonder about them a lot . . . what their lives are like at home, especially the ones that have trouble at school. What puzzles me sometimes is how different they can be one minute to the next—one time almost nonverbal and acting like a preschooler, other times so sophisticated. Lots of times you can just see how they hurt, or see how much they need . . . sometimes I can give it and other times I can't or just don't know how. I'm only their teacher.

This example highlights one fifth-grade teacher's thoughts about the children with whom she works. She wonders about children's development as well as doubts her own influence. This chapter attends to the connection between development and the kinds of contexts discussed in the last chapter—families, schools, and classrooms. It also provides a window on some of this teacher's questions about development—what develops and how—focusing on socioemotional processes.

Applications of systems theory principles in schools were introduced in the previous chapter. The present chapter focuses in more detail on the child as a developing system and the implications of this perspective for understanding relationships that children form with their teachers. Within this chapter, there is a specific focus on understanding the origins and course of problem behaviors from the developmental psychopathology perspective (Sroufe & Rutter, 1984). Developmental psychopathology is of importance to school and clinical child psychologists because it focuses on processes related to how problem outcomes develop and how risk is translated into problem behaviors or school failure, with an emphasis on how contexts (school, home, and community) interact with one another and with child characteristics to produce competence or maladaptation.

Thus, the focus is not on the issues that tend to dominate professional practice with children—eligibility for services or distinctions between diagnostic groups—but on the processes that describe a particular developmental pathway. For applied child and adolescent psychologists and other professionals working in schools, this perspective offers a way for viewing schools as contexts for development, assessing the resources for development that are available in schools, and identifying ways to deliver those resources to children. Because this perspective is explicitly developmental and is focused on how certain outcomes are shaped over time, it lends itself well, as a theory, to practices that are preventive. That is, developmental psychopathology is concerned with the early detection of pathways to problem outcomes and the role of contexts in altering those pathways.

Developmental psychopathology embraces systems theory and its implications for understanding human behavior and development. It recognizes the multifactorial, dynamic nature of behavioral development as well as the ways in which systems at multiple levels interact with one another. One focus of developmental psychopathology has been on the role of social processes in the development of problem outcomes in children. Social processes, and the relationships (parent–child, child–peer) that reflect these processes, are fundamental to understanding the origins and the course of child adaptation and maladaptation. These social relationships regulate much of what children learn—cognition, language, self-regulation, knowledge of emotions, self-esteem, and work habits (see Sroufe, 1989a, 1989b). Furthermore, developmental psychopathology recognizes that how children perform across different domains is connected—for example, language skills facilitate self-regulation. Thus, the focus of analysis is not the individual or the behaviors in a given domain but the pattern of behaviors across multiple domains shown in response to key developmental challenges. These patterns are best viewed in the context of relationships between the individual and the context or contexts. Thus, the developmental psychopathology perspective forces psychologists to take a holistic perspective when addressing questions regarding understanding or treating a problem behavior.

This holistic perspective is often embodied in the approach to inquiry taken in a psychologist assessment. A whole set of approaches to assessment pursue a line of inquiry that leads to progressively narrower and narrower slices of human behavior. Thus, something like a learning problem is approached in terms of a global achievement–intelligence discrepancy that is further narrowed to specific domains of achievement (reading, mathematics) or cognitive abilities (verbal, nonverbal), then further narrowed to more specific abilities, skills, or processes (auditory sequential processing, phonemic awareness, freedom from distractibility), and maybe even further refined to neurological processes and brain physiology. Not all cases are treated this way, but the general tendency is toward this reductionist stance or trend—to seek explanations for complex behaviors by breaking those behaviors into smaller and smaller units of behavior. And although the better psychological assessments incorporate observation and interview data in an attempt to focus attention more broadly and more functionally, the typical response to inconclusive assessment information is to focus more narrowly—to seek answers in tests of more discrete abilities.

The developmental psychopathology perspective supports a focus at broader levels—not at smaller units of behavior but at larger units of interactions. Thus, a problem in classroom functioning is not initially framed as a "learning problem" per se but is approached as a problem in adaptation in the classroom that likely involves multiple interacting components (within the child and between the child and the classroom context). Like many "best practice" approaches in consultation and assessment (Shriner, Ysseldyke, & Christenson, 1989), data are gathered about the functional meaning of the problem in light of an array of information—the teacher's and the child's perceptions and beliefs, and also important, the child's performance in similar and different situations and in response to different inputs—interactions. Thus, there is a strong effort to prevent the premature narrowing of focus. Unfortunately, many best practice models provide only guidelines on "how" to approach cases from this functional standpoint but lack information on "what" to look for. Thus, the contents of development—the processes and behaviors that can be the focus of this holistic approach—are missing from most descriptions of functional assessment or consultation (Meyers et al., 1979; Shriner et al., 1989). The bulk of this chapter provides this kind of description.

A Developmental Psychopathology Framework

Applied child and adolescent psychologists working in school settings, or with school-related problems, spend a great deal of time addressing the concern of whether a problem is "severe" enough to warrant intervention. At times, this takes the form of whether the problem fits with established diagnostic criteria for problem behaviors (such as are found in the system of the *Diagnostic and Statistical Manual of Mental Disorders*, 4th ed.; American Psychiatric Association, 1994) or whether the behavior can be attributed to some "cause," which can include physiological, psychological, sociological, or educational factors. Many times the "cause" is sought in another disorder. There is little argument, however, that these issues occupy the majority of psychologists' time and that increasingly, physiological or biological factors are viewed as causal to the problem behaviors shown by children in classrooms. These efforts aimed at knowing diagnosis and cause are largely inferential. They rely on interpretation of data in the context of a theoretical framework for understanding those data; in these instances, a developmental psychopathology perspective is helpful.

For no other problem behavior is the need for a developmental perspective more evident than for attention deficit hyperactivity disorder (ADHD) in children. Attention deficit hyperactivity disorder is considered to be a frequent and problematic condition for children and families and is often coincident with school-related concerns (e.g., Campbell, 1990; Kazdin, 1992; McBurnett, Lahey, & Pfiffner, 1993). Not surprising, inattention, overactivity, and disruptive behavior comprise a constellation of symptoms that is the single most frequent cause for referral for behavioral and mental health services in childhood (Greenberg, Kusche, & Speltz,

1991; Richman, Stevenson, & Graham 1982). Teachers are particularly bothered by these behaviors.

Reflecting the general tendency to narrow the frame of reference, researchers often cite neurochemical or neuroanatomical factors as *causes* of these behavioral symptoms (e.g., Riccio et al., 1993) and use these factors to support the use of stimulant medication for treatment (Swanson et al., 1993). Currently, stimulant medication is the treatment of choice for such problems, with the incidence of medication use rising dramatically in the last 10 years, to the extent that a significant proportion (up to 5% in some estimates) of the population of children in the United States receives prescription medication for these problem behaviors daily (Jacobvitz & Sroufe, 1987; Reid, Maag, & Vasa, 1993). The use of pharmacological products prescribed for adult mood and behavior symptoms (e.g., Prozac) has also risen dramatically.

However, the vast majority of studies conducted on the identification and treatment of problems with attention and impulsivity are plagued by two flaws: They are correlational in design and lack adequate controls. For example, studies demonstrating links between attentional deficits and neurological measures by and large do not reveal *predictive relations* between these neurological factors and behavior over time but report relations derived from research designs that compare already diagnosed or identified children with nondiagnosed or unidentified children. Results that demonstrate neurological differences between these groups are often used to infer neurological causes—a mistaken inference. Furthermore, the contention that children benefit from prescription drugs aimed at these neurological or physiological "causes" frequently results from research that examines symptom changes in a diagnostic group as a function of medication, without comparison data on the extent to which the behavior of "normal" children changes as a function of the same medication.

Results of research on the development of attention, or the developmental processes regulating motor and attention behaviors, have not been well-integrated with the literature on ADHD (Riccio et al., 1993). How biological, psychological, and social mechanisms interact to produce the attentional and self-regulating behaviors of children in classrooms is not typically a focus of research on ADHD, although there is ample support for the contention that attention and activity are related to social interactions with adults, predictability of environments, and even cultural norms and expectations (Jacobvitz & Sroufe, 1987; Reid et al., 1993). In one prospective study of children from economically disadvantaged households studied from birth through the early grades of school, Jacobvitz and Sroufe demonstrated that the diagnosis of ADHD was predicted by disregulated parent–child interaction in the early years of life and was unrelated to a variety of child characteristics, such as temperament, IQ, or neurobehavioral state.

Thus, developmentally informed research designs and theory are not often used in generating the information base from which practicing psychologists draw in making decisions and inferences about practice with specific children. Consequently, treatment approaches (e.g., stimulant medication for ADHD) are not informed by theory of how developmental mechanisms regulate change in target behaviors (e.g., attention). There is little discussion of how any of the variety of systems discussed in chapter 2 (behavioral, cultural, or relationship) contribute to a theory of the problem on which there is so much focus. Instead, as has been discussed, much effort has been directed toward generating empirically validated treatments.

Yet, without a discussion of theory informed by longitudinal research on how self-regulating behaviors develop, it is impossible to design interventions that interrupt developmental pathways that lead to inattention, overactivity, and impulsivity in the classroom, and practice will default to what appears to be the valid, but more narrow, approach. Thus, for the practicing psychologist, although a developmental psychopathology perspective complicates matters a bit by introducing multiple factors and processes into discussions of children's problems and by emphasizing the uncertainty of prediction, this perspective nonetheless frames a view of school-related problems in a way that focuses attention and energy on how contexts influence development, which is consistent with what schools are designed to do.

The developmental psychopathology perspective embraces the idea that *the child is a system developing in a context* and that behavior in one domain (such as attention) cannot be understood without reference to other domains and to contexts in which that behavior is demanded, supported, or both. In the discussion of Vygotsky's ZPD from chapter 2, children, as systems, are in dynamic interchange with contexts—exchanging information, material, energy, and activity (Ford & Ford, 1987). The child has quite permeable boundaries, and properties that appear to "reside" in the child are actually distributed across the child and these contexts (Hofer, 1994; Resnick, 1994). For example, Campbell and colleagues' (e.g., Campbell, 1994; Campbell, March, Pierce, Ewing, & Szumowski, 1991) work on hard-to-manage children demonstrates that externalizing behaviors are embedded within (or a precipitate of) a system of family factors, parenting behaviors, life stresses, and child characteristics. No single element is sufficient to explain the externalizing symptoms.

Because context cannot be separated from child adaptation, adaptation is distributed (Resnick, 1994). Attention, problem solving, literacy, emotion, social behavior, social cognition, peer relations, and self-control are distributed across the child, the situation or situations in which the challenge occurs, and the relation of the child to the challenge and the situation or situations. All aspects of this distributed network need to be considered before adaptation can be understood and described. This view suggests that child competence is located in this network.

Thus, any discussion of the child's competencies is qualified by knowledge of the contextual supports for those competencies—inferences about diagnostic status, or etiology, are fundamentally inaccurate and premature, without a full understanding of the contribution of context both currently and over time. In this view, context is not equivalent to reinforcement contingencies but encompasses a wider point of view. Central among considerations is the nature of the child's relationships with socialization agents and caregivers—parents, teachers, and others.

Children and the contexts in which they develop are complex systems, the interactions of which can be thought of in terms of *co-action* (Gottlieb, 1991). Co-action refers to the premise that activity of a given system (e.g., the brain or the classroom) relies on and affects the activity of other systems. The networked nature of systems allows for activity to be regulated by relations within the system or systems in which that unit is embedded (such as relationships with teachers or parents). Developmental change follows as a consequence of regulated activity (Ford & Ford, 1987; Sameroff, 1983).

In this view, the child is inherently active: constructing meaning, adapting, seeking challenges, practicing emergent capacities, and creating endless opportunities for transformation and change. This notion of change and activity suggests developmental views of treatment in which intervention involves one's intentional structuring or harnessing of developmental activity or one's using context in a skillful way to developmental advantage (Lieberman, 1992). This approach to intervention frames the discussions of the importance of child–teacher relationships in development and the interventions designed to improve them. It is inherently a prevention-oriented view (CSBPSC, 1994).

It is from this point of view that this chapter now turns to a more extended discussion of developmental themes in childhood and the role of relationships in the development of children's competencies. This discussion forms the cornerstone of efforts to understand and improve these relationships (with teachers) through a variety of interventions. This discussion is focused on processes that are common to normal and abnormal development in childhood. As noted above, a central question in the practice of psychology is the differentiation between normal and abnormal. Most forms of "abnormal" development seen in clinical and school settings have their roots in these normative developmental processes.

Key Developmental Themes in Early Childhood

Sroufe (1989a, 1989b) and Greenspan (1989) approached development as a series of themes around which child behavior and interactions with context are organized. These themes emerge at different ages and become organized within later patterns of adaptation. For each theme, there is a specific role for context in facilitating adaptation to this (and hence later) themes. In particular, adult–child relationships play a key role in the regulation of a child's adaptation with respect to each of these themes. Understanding these themes, their organization, and the role for context is critical to understanding the role of relationships with adults in development for all children. This also contributes to understanding the role that relationships with teachers can play in relation to high-risk children in schools. As noted earlier, this discussion of developmental themes or challenges also describes the content of development that can inform current functional approaches to behavioral intervention and consultation.

These key themes involve the following aspects of early childhood: (a) the regulation and modulation of physiological arousal, (b) the formation of an effective attachment relationship, (c) the development of self-reliance or autonomy, (d) the formation of an expanded ability to organize and coordinate environmental and personal resources, (e) the establishment of effective peer relations, and (f) the formation of a sense of self, an effective use of self-control, and the use of abstract symbols.

This section describes the course of development in childhood, emphasizing child–context relationships (Greenspan & Greenspan, 1991; Sroufe, 1989a, 1989b; Sroufe & Rutter, 1984). Central to this perspective is that as development proceeds, the child *as a developing system* is faced with adaptational challenges of increasing complexity that are both a product of his or her own behavior and the response of his or her context to the perceived level of adaptation (Ford & Lerner, 1992; Greenspan, 1989; Sroufe, 1989a, 1989b). In Greenspan and Greenspan's view, child–context systems increase in level of organization over time. Interactions between child and context move from primarily reflexive and simple engagement to intentional, reciprocal, and symbolic relations. These interactions, increasingly complex over time, are embodied in these themes of adaptation at a given developmental phase (Greenspan, 1989; Sroufe & Rutter, 1984).

Developmental history is also important in two related ways. First, early adaptation lays the foundation for subsequent competence. Thus, whether children effectively explore the world in an independent or autonomous fashion, using their own internal resources, depends on how well they had learned earlier to use their primary caregiver as a source of support for exploration (Sroufe, 1989a). Thus, development builds on itself. However, "old" patterns of adaptation do not disappear. Patterns of adaptation to earlier developmental challenges are organized within responses to subsequent challenges and are mobilized in response to these later challenges. For example, the competent, autonomous fifth grader who is overwhelmed by the social, academic, and peer challenges of a new middle school might respond in what appears to be the "immature" manner of seeking lots of help at home, staying close to the teacher, and not wanting to extend himself or herself in the peer group. This is merely an activation of an adaptive strategy that was effective in relation to attachment challenges. Thus, this situation for this fifth grader was responded to as an attachment challenge, with strategies that were effective for seeking comfort and assistance from a caregiver earlier in development, instead of as a challenge in the arena of identity and peer relations. Earlier strategies were mobilized in response to a current challenge.

Most important, adaptation occurs in a relational context: It is embedded in relationships—with parents, peers, and teachers (and the wider social context). Context plays a central role in affording the conditions for adaptation at a given period or in a particular situation (Ford & Lerner, 1992). This concept of *affordance* embodies the idea that contexts contain resources for the child that can be activated to sustain the child's adaptation to the demands of that setting. Similar to the concept of ZPD, contexts can be evaluated on the extent to which they are high affordance or low affordance by examining them in relation to how they help children adapt to these development challenges. It is important that the affordance of a context has to be accessed by interactions between the child and those affordances. Everyone has noticed the difference in functional capacity of a fourth grader under circumstances of differing structure and support (affordance). When faced with a particular academic or behavioral challenge, the child's response might vary as a function of the context. One can recognize the differences in these scenarios:

> *Scenario A*: Harold was sitting at his desk, struggling to read the book he had chosen from the library, during "free read" time. Ms. Jones had just asked the children to put away their books and to get ready for the weekly spelling test. Harold's response to this request was "oh no"; he tossed his book aside and hurriedly grabbed for a clean sheet of paper and a pencil. Finding neither, and with Ms. Jones occupied with other children, Harold focused on the child sitting next to him, starting to engage in conversation. Ms. Jones, noticing Harold's behavior and interpreting it as noncompliance, scolded him mildly and encouraged him to get ready. By this time, most of the class's attention was on Harold and Ms. Jones, and he started to show off, anxious about performing poorly on a test for which he knew he was ill-prepared. Things got worse from there.
> *Scenario B*: Harold was sitting at his desk, struggling to read the book he had chosen from the library, during "free read" time. Ms. Jones had just asked the children to put away their books and to get ready for the weekly spelling test. Ms. Jones approached Harold and put her hand on his shoulder as a reminder to stay focused on her request. She stood there with her hand on him as she spoke to the other children; meanwhile Harold rummaged through his desk for the necessary materials, at times glancing sideways at his neighbor. At one point, Ms. Jones guided his hand to his pencil and pushed his chair in a bit. She leaned down and told him that she would be standing here during the test, noticing the words he spelled correctly and incorrectly so that they could work together on them later. Harold managed a response to each of the words.

Clearly, context plays a role in adaptation. In this example, Ms. Jones's response to Harold in the second scenario can be characterized as good teaching but can also be discussed in terms of how these behaviors are embedded in, and characteristic of, her relationship with Harold and how this relationship affords Harold a higher level of competence in the second scenario than in the first. The discussion now turns to the themes of development in childhood. For each theme, it is important to note the ways in which contexts, specifically relationships with adults, support (or inhibit) competence.

Regulation and Modulation of Physiological Arousal and Joint Attention

The first theme involves the regulation and modulation of physiological arousal and joint attention. The infant (and caregiver) must tolerate increasingly complex physical and social stimulation and must maintain an organized state in the face of this increasing arousal. This organized state leads to periods of joint attention and mutuality—the basis of exploration of the object and the interpersonal world. Cycles of sleep and alertness, feeding, interest, and arousal all begin to become organized very early on within this period. The immature status of the newborn predisposes the child to require caregiver interactions to help maintain organization in the face of cyclic variations (Hofer, 1994; Sander, 1975) to the extent that many infant researchers argue that the infant is really only as competent as the environment affords competence.

In competent forms of adaptation, the infant responds to routines set by caregivers and, with caregivers, establishes regular rhythms of feeding, activity–alertness, and sleep. High affordance contexts ensure the maintenance of smooth, regular, predictable routines and practices that are contingent on infant cues. In the context of interaction, the infant and caregiver mesh behaviors to establish these routines that form the basis of self and relationships (Sroufe, 1989b). These patterns broaden to include interactive play and form a relational matrix that organizes the infant in the face of increasingly complex stimulation.

In less competent forms of adaptation at this stage, the infant may show a tendency toward over- and underarousal, little or no predictability in terms of routines, little interest in interactions, or difficulty being settled and soothed so that caregivers become increasingly stressed and unpredictable. These maladaptive patterns of behavior are linked with patterns of incompetent adaptation later in development: insecure attachment, poor exploration, and inadequate self-regulation (Greenspan, 1989; Sroufe, 1996). From an affordance point of view, these patterns of infant maladaptation are also linked to highly stressful environments in terms of financial or psychosocial stress, intrusive caregiving interactions, over- and understimulating households, maternal depression, and child maltreatment. These factors contribute to infant and relational maladaptation through disordered child–caregiver interactions (e.g., Cohn, Campbell, Matias, & Hopkins, 1990; Egeland, Pianta, & O'Brien, 1993).

This early phase of development has marked consequences for problems in school. Children's difficulties in establishing shared attention and engagement predict problems in behavioral and emotional regulation in kindergarten to Grade 2 (Egeland et al., 1993), and early experiences of maltreatment are so strongly related to social and academic problems in school that they have been labeled as an insult to children's "secure readiness to learn" (Aber & Allen, 1987; Cummings, Hennessy, Rabideau, & Cicchetti, 1994; Dodge, Pettit, & Bates, 1994). In this way, problems in the caregiving regulatory system (Hofer, 1994) early in infancy strongly influence the emergent self-regulatory capacities of the preschool- and elementary school-age child.

Formation and Maintenance of an Effective Attachment Relationship

A major theme for the second 6 months of life and throughout childhood is the formation and maintenance of an effective attachment relationship. In nearly every theoretical consideration of child development, an effective attachment develops as a consequence of early patterns of interaction, affords the child a sense of security in the context of a relationship, and provides a basis for exploration of the object and the interpersonal world. Adult responsiveness, emotional availability, and use of an effective signaling system all play important roles in regulating experience in relation to this theme (Ainsworth, Blehar, Waters, & Wall, 1978), as does the caregiver's previous attachment experiences and self-regulation of attention and emotion (Fonagy, Steele, & Steele, 1991; Main & Hesse, 1990; Zeanah et al., 1993).

Ineffective attachment relationships reflect one of three ways of regulating emotional arousal through contact with the caregiver (Cassidy, 1994):

1. Avoidant—the child avoids the caregiver in situations of distress because he or she has learned that the caregiver is unlikely to be available and will reject the child's bids for comfort.
2. Ambivalent—the child amplifies distress in an attempt to always keep the caregiver close. This strategy of attachment regulation is consistent with a caregiving pattern of inconsistency—at times available and at times hostile and punitive—leaving the child in uncertainty regarding the caregiver's availability, hence encouraging his or her "need" to always stay close.
3. Disorganized—a mixture of approach and avoidance behaviors in situations in which the child needs comfort or support. In this pattern, the child simultaneously emits both approach and avoidance behaviors, behaving in a style that appears confused and disorganized. The disorganized pattern of behavior is consistent with caregiving styles that are frightening to the child, as in cases in which the child has been maltreated (Carlson, Cicchetti, Barnett, & Braunwald, 1989) and in which the caregiver is made anxious by the child's expressed desire for closeness (Main & Hesse, 1990).

It is interesting that these patterns have been observed in children's interactions with other caregiving adults, such as child-care providers and teachers. This observation suggests that these strategies for emotional and behavioral regulation, learned in the context of child–parent relationships, may color relationships with nonparental figures on whom the child relies for assistance and, at times, protection and comfort (Howes, Hamilton, & Matheson, 1994; Pianta et al., 1997). Thus nonparental adults, such as teachers, can be the targets of attachment-related strategies that have developed in other relational contexts and, more important, these adults may provide the child with new relationship experiences of sufficient strength, intensity, and consistency that can enable the child to use adults more competently.

In many theories of development, attachment is accorded special significance. It is the first emotional, intimate relationship in which the child is involved, and patterns of emotion regulation, attention to emotion, and strategies for behavioral regulation are developed in this context (Cassidy, 1994). To the extent that attachment behaviors (proximity seeking under threat) and secure base behaviors (exploration in the presence of the caregiver) have a strong evolutionary function, development has a bias toward attachment, affiliation, and social–emotional engagement with a caregiver (Breger, 1974).

The child develops an internal "model" of his or her attachment relationship with a caregiver or caregivers that contains beliefs about the self as worthy of care (the roots of self-esteem) and about the providers of care that are the roots of security and exploration (Blatt, 1995; Bowlby, 1969). Children classified as insecurely attached to their primary caregivers perform more poorly than those classified as severely attached on measures of language development, emergent literacy and reading, cognitive development and play, and social interaction with peers and other adults (Bus & van IJzendoorn, 1988; Erickson, Sroufe, & Egeland, 1985; Sroufe, 1983; 1989a, 1989b). Internal models of self and other are carried forward and predict behavior in several relationship contexts (Elicker, Egeland, & Sroufe, 1992).

Attachment strategies involve functions such as selective attention and working memory concerning attachment-related needs and interactions that shape how the child processes emotions and social behaviors (Main & Hesse, 1990). These processes account for some of the relational difficulties that teachers have to overcome when interacting with students who see them as "punitive," "withholding," or "hostile" on the basis of their experiences with parents or other attachment figures.

The early child–caregiver relationship provides a context for the development of a close, intimate, emotion-laden relationship that helps shape later development in many domains. This emotional investment by a child (and a parent) is a developmental consequence of predictable, responsive care earlier in infancy. Thus, emotional attachment (from the child's point of view) depends on the history of caregiving interactions and particularly their regularity, timing, predictability, and coordination with the infant's signals.

However, attachment relationships do not exist between only mothers and children nor are children limited to only one such relationship (Pianta, 1992). Instead, the centrality of attachment is, in part, a consequence of the developing child's being an *open system*. Thus, attachment behaviors, beliefs, and emotions can be organized around several individuals, including teachers. Evolution, for a variety of selective purposes, requires considerable input to the child from relationships with caregiving adults (Hofer, 1994). Therefore, teachers are very salient figures for parents for the development of close, intimate relationships that can serve the kind of regulatory role described in this section.

Effective Self-Reliance or Autonomy

During the second year of life and continuing throughout childhood, effective self-reliance or autonomy (persistence, mastery, active problem solving, motivation), the third theme, becomes increasingly important. The concept of self-reliance recognizes the relational base of the child's efforts to meet social and task-related demands and focuses on the child's use of his or her own and others' resources. Effective self-reliance is observed when the child enthusiastically engages in problems in the world, persists in using his or her own efforts to address the problem, and before giving up or frustrating, signals for and uses resources from others to solve the problem. Confidence in self and other are hallmarks of competent adaptation. Thus, what appears to be a child-based skill or capacity (e.g., self-reliance or independence) is truly relational—this capacity for exploring the world is built on the relationship foundations of attachment and is supported in context by the relationships currently available to the child and the way that those relationships tolerate and support the child's emerging autonomy.

Part of competent exploration and mastery of the world is knowledge that there is a secure base from which to explore. Building on the effective attachment relationship developed within infancy, the caregiver–child dyad organizes the child's advancing motor, cognitive, and communicative skills to support exploratory forays, with the caregiver providing regulation (comfort, information) at a distance while the child practices autonomy and emerging skills (Breger, 1974; Crittenden, 1992). This practice creates new challenges and rewards to the child–caregiver interaction— on the one hand, it affords some relief from some physical aspects of caregiving, whereas on the other hand, it elicits new feelings in the parent (e.g., anxiety over control, pride) and child limit testing as a challenge to the relationship. Thus, the child–caregiver relationship reorganizes in this period—it must tolerate the child's autonomy strivings while at the same time must provide substantial support. The relationship is more complex, especially as experienced by the caregiver, than it was in infancy, during which predictable routines were by and large the primary challenge.

Educators should recognize the connections between self-reliance, as defined here, and competence in the classroom. Clearly, the roots of classroom behavior—support and limit setting by the adult, an orientation to problem solving, exploration, and mastery by the child—are inherent in this phase of development that emerges in the second year of life and continues for many years. This background helps frame an understanding of the role that child–teacher relationships play in supporting competence in the classroom. In fact, self-reliance in the classroom, as has been argued, is based both on the child's previous relationship history related to exploration and on the extent to which the classroom teacher provides a secure base for exploration. For example, in a recent study, Pianta et al. (1997) demonstrated that the social and task-related competencies of children in kindergarten were related to secure base features of their relationships with their mother and with their teachers.

Greenspan and Greenspan (1991) and Kopp and Wyer (1994) suggested that nonverbal communication involving gestures and social–emotional behaviors (body posture, intentional movements, facial expressions) is a core process in the regulation of self-reliance. Thus, in the context of adult–child interactions, gestural communication is more salient to the regulation of self-reliance than are words. In the second scenario of the example given earlier in this chapter, Ms. Jones physically approached Harold, touched her hand to his shoulder, and remained standing next to him. She bent closer to him when she spoke. Would her words of encouragement and verbal cues to focus attention and effort been as effective had they been delivered without those gestures or from a greater distance? Which would be the more potent intervention—use words only or gestures only? This example goes to the heart of the role of relationships in regulating developmental functions and the notion of the ZPD. In the situation embodied in these scenarios, Harold is faced with a challenge. The level of support offered to him in the context of his relationship with Ms. Jones differs in these examples. In one, support (gestural) is commensurate with Harold's capacity to adapt to the challenge; in the other, it is not. The example also illustrates the general principle that often the best support (higher affordance value) for a child in a situation is not input that corresponds in form to the task at hand (e.g., verbal or symbolic) but input that is somewhat less complex or abstract in form (gestural).

Nonetheless, maintaining balanced interest and arousal while exploring the world requires a more advanced level of communication and organization than do the simpler forms of action and reaction of infancy and early toddlerhood. In the view of Greenspan and Greenspan (1991), gestural, preverbal communication with a supportive caregiver provides this balance, out of which emerges the child's sense of self as being effective (Kopp & Wyer, 1994).

Self-reliance in the early childhood period is not equivalent to popular notions of independence. Instead, self-reliance refers to the child's motivation to explore, persistence in the face of frustration, and effective use of adults as resources. Self-reliance, like most other personality and behavioral constructs in childhood, is distributed across child and context. As conceptualized in terms of relationships and the emergence of self-esteem, self-reliance will play a prominent role in the child's capacity to adapt to the challenges of school settings, including aspects of social interaction with peers, response to instruction, and motivation to perform academic tasks.

Expanded Ability to Organize and Coordinate Environmental and Personal Resources

An expanded ability to organize and coordinate environmental and personal resources, the fourth theme, builds on attachment and early self-reliance as demands on the child become more complex and abstract. This is the challenge of elementary school and is embodied in the challenge of self-regulation. In Greenspan's model (Greenspan & Greenspan, 1991), creating internal images and sharing them with others through symbols (words) and ideas is a core process involved in the challenge of self-regulation. The organized and intentional use of words, thoughts, ideas, concepts, and interactions for the purposes of self-regulation is the hallmark of development in childhood (Crittenden, 1992; Greenspan, 1989; Kopp & Wyer, 1994; Thompson, 1994), a key factor in internalizing and externalizing symptoms (e.g., Greenberg et al., 1991; Stewart & Rubin, 1995), and a predictor of academic performance in the classroom. These skills mark the competent elementary school-age child.

Unlike the toddler and preschooler whose systems of self and social engagement were organized preverbally, words and symbolic actions (e.g., play) are used intentionally and functionally to communicate goals, desires, expectations, and meanings. In the elementary school years, these symbolic processes are used in the service of behavioral and emotional self-regulation. Children's behavioral and emotional flexibility and their capacity to modulate arousal using available resources are signs of competent adaptation in this and in future periods. Thus, words and symbols can be used effectively in the context of child–context interactions to influence a child's performance within the ZPD. As we saw in the case of Harold, if there is too much stress or challenge, though, even words may not function, and gestural communication may be necessary to establish a functional connection between the child and the context.

A key feature of competent adaptation in childhood is the development of "representational capacity" (Greenspan, 1989) to mediate child–context interactions. In this capacity, children connect symbols and words to experience and use them to regulate it. Words and sentences ("I don't like it when you bother me that way") are substituted for behavior (e.g., a hit on the arm or a push) in the expression of one's emotion, intent, need, comfort, or goal. Bowlby (1969) discussed this as a phase of "goal connected partnership," when child and parent negotiate mutual goals and plans using symbols that mesh (Crittenden, 1992). This notion of having symbols that mesh captures the fact that for the child to access the resources available to them in a context, interactions between the child and the context, usually in the form of interactions with teachers or parents, must be mutual and must share similar meanings or perceptions of the situation. At this phase of development, words, drawings, and symbolic play begin to serve this function, whereas prior to this, physical gestures and behavior were more functional.

Again, one can see the connections to relationships with teachers in which the child voices needs and goals for interactions with the teacher, and these can be discussed verbally in a way that addresses the concerns of the child.

> Tommy, a sensitive 6-year-old boy, had all the attributes to mark him as cute. His teacher and aide loved him and were quite affectionate toward him. He found the affection and attention at times overwhelming. Sometimes he backed away from this contact, and at other times, he just tolerated it. One day, when asked by his parents how school went, he said, "I hate Ms. Freeman, I hate it when she picks me up and kisses me in front of the other kids." His parents mentioned that his teacher probably meant no harm and really liked him, but if he did not want this contact, he should tell her. A couple of days later, he came home saying, "I told Ms. Freeman that I did not like to be hugged in front of the other kids, and she said she wouldn't do that anymore."

One can think of the differences between this child's handling of this situation and what would have occurred had words (symbols) not been used to mediate his experience and to create shared meanings and perceptions. Parents would not have been told, he would likely never have told his teacher directly, and would not have had the experience of sharing his concern with his teacher and of having her respond to it. Instead, there would probably have been increasing tension and many indirect, unclear signals to the teacher, who may or may not have picked up on them. The emergence of a representational capacity is a fundamental shift through which experience is no longer coded only in behavior but in symbols that can be used.

The emergence of representation introduces new capacities into many behavioral domains, provides the foundation for sophisticated self-control mechanisms (such as the self-management skills taught in cognitive behavioral modification techniques, e.g., telling oneself to relax or to think ahead) and for many aspects of friendships (in the form of perspective taking and social cognition). Representational capacity defines popular notions of maturity. This capacity to symbolically represent experience dramatically alters the way in which the child's relationship with the world is organized.

Context plays an important role in the emergence of representational skills, and problems in development can be traced to how contexts support representation. Greenberg et al. (1991) related problems in impulse control to the regulation of the child–caregiver system in interactions around attachment and in representations of emotional experience. In their studies of children with disruptive behavior disorders, caregivers were more coercive, were less able to follow their child's lead in play, gave more commands, were less responsive to the child's cues, and showed fewer expressions of positive affect. These controlling, coercive, negative, power-oriented behaviors indicate contexts that fail to support a child's representational capacity (Campbell, 1990; Campbell, March, Pierce, Ewing, & Szumowski, 1991).

However, interactions that recognize and label the child's experience, respond to the child's signals for help or assistance, and allow the child "room" to explore and to try alternatives are all styles that encourage a shift to representational processing. These interactions give the child symbols that connect to his or her emotional experience; they regulate, through symbols and interactions, the child's experience and they follow the child's lead. It should come as no surprise that these aspects of interaction would be readily recognized in interactions between a child and a "good" teacher. Strategies for enhancing individual child–teacher relationships that involve working with child–teacher interactions (chap. 7) reflect these elements of how a relationship supports the development of self-regulation.

Effective Peer Relationships

The fifth theme concerns effective peer relations, which are a central issue of concern from the preschool years onward. Peers are sources of challenges and resources, and the child must learn to integrate the affiliative nature of peer systems with other aspects, such as competition and mastery. Like child–parent relationships, peer relationships become characterized over time by increasingly abstract and representational forms of exchange (Dodge et al., 1994). Doll (1996) has outlined connections between peer relationships and the practice of school psychology in terms of the ways in which school psychologists can use naturally occurring interactions with peers in contexts, such as recess and the lunchroom, to facilitate developmental growth and, in turn, to reduce risk. Doll's emphasis on the use of developmental theory to provide a rationale for preventive interventions "in context" is entirely consistent with the views advocated in this book. Such work harnesses the relationship resources available to the child in the school context.

Peer relations are linked with the child's early relationship history with parents, caregivers, and other family members. Sroufe (1983) provided a clear example of how early forms of adaptation become layered within peer relations in the preschool and early school context. In a sample of high-risk children studied from birth through the preschool years, children with histories of secure attachment tended to become friends with one another. They related better to teachers, were rated by teachers as the most competent, and were considered well suited to activities that went on in a school setting (i.e., attentive, flexible, sociable, compliant, self-reliant, and persistent). By contrast, children with histories of insecure attachment were more poorly adapted. Children classified as showing avoidant attachment in infancy were rated by teachers as aggressive, noncompliant, and inattentive and tended toward a bullying style of peer relations, especially if paired with another child with a history of insecurity. Children with histories of anxious-ambivalent attachment were whiny, petulant, dependent, and generally lacked resilience or persistence. In peer relations, they were typically victimized, especially if paired with a child with a history of avoidance. Past research (Berlin, Cassidy, & Belsky, in press) has indicated that children with anxious-ambivalent attachment histories also report considerably more loneliness than their avoidant or securely attached counterparts. They process social information consistent with views of themselves as victims and of peers as victimizers (Dodge, 1991). They alienate both peers and teachers.

Birch and Ladd (1996) identified three relational styles that characterize relationships with teachers, parents, and peers: moving toward, moving against, and moving away. These three styles have been shown as common to childrens' interactions with teacher and peers and account for many relational similarities. In turn, they are similar to the three groups used to classify attachment with parents. Birch and Ladd suggested that these similarities reflect an integration of experience across relationships and a common set of strategies for organizing interpersonal behavior.

In sum, peer relations are a core component of adaptation in childhood. Children are expected to have stable, fairly close friendships or "chums," and peer relations become the focus for self-regulatory skills that are mastered (or not) in the context of family and child–caregiver relationships (Elicker et al., 1992). Failure in peer relations frequently indicates referral for mental health problems because it is both a salient feature of adaptation at that time and it is a strong predictor of later disorder (Kazdin, 1992; Loeber, 1990).

This area of development has many implications for teachers, as oftentimes they are called on to regulate children's interactions with peers. It is interesting that Howes et al. (1994) have shown that the quality of relationships between children and teachers is, in part, related to how well the child does with peers in a school-like setting. Thus, many of the principles of child–teacher interaction that have been mentioned in this chapter and have been reflected in the examples (especially that of Harold and Ms. Jones), can be directly applied to how teacher–child relationships afford the child resources for use in adapting to the challenge of peer relations.

Stable Sense of Self

The sixth theme involves the formation of a stable sense of self, an effective use of self-control, and the use of symbolic representation; these developmental processes expand rapidly in childhood and affect, and are products of, interactions between the child and many systems. They emerge from and influence relationships with parents, teachers, and peers and are key elements of cognitive–academic achievement, cooperation in social groups, and identity. Self-regulation is the hallmark of competence at this phase of late childhood and is a nearly universal expectation of schools and other settings.

Greenspan (1989) suggested that by the late elementary school ages, adaptation is a function of fairly sophisticated representational processes. Children intentionally manipulate language, symbols, and internal representations (images, etc.) in the service of self-control, peer interaction, conflict resolution, goal attainment, problem solving, and mastery of information. These complex internal representations are mirrored by more complex relationships with the external world.

The use of symbols to self-regulate can be traced to early and concurrent experiences in relationships. Representational capacity, language, metacognition, and problem solving are all linked to relationships (Greenberg et al., 1991). Crittenden (1992) suggested that being in the presence of safe, supportive adults (i.e., having a secure attachment) enables children to regulate anxiety, allowing for creativity and problem solving. Greenberg et al. (1991) suggested that secure relationships with adults allow children to freely communicate (gesturally, verbally, etc.) and to share meanings. In this context, the adult can accurately interpret the child's signals and meanings and can provide labels for experience and support for meeting situational challenges. Thus the child, in this situation, experiences emotional regulation in the context of a relationship with an adult, observes regulated behavior of the adult, and acquires the labels and descriptions of experience that will support the development of true self-regulation.

However, children with avoidant attachments, who experience the caregiver as rejecting or hostile, must develop emotion regulation strategies that are prematurely autonomous. They use internal resources to minimize anxiety, reducing attention to negative social or emotional experiences. These children learn to shut out negative emotion from awareness; thus the skills that enable a child to regulate these emotions and experiences are not acquired because such emotions and experiences are rarely expressed, especially in the context of interactions with an adult who can provide labels and support.

Likewise, children with resistant or ambivalent attachment relations rarely acquire the skills necessary to assume responsibility for regulating their emotional and social experiences because their stance toward interactions with adults is to have caregivers perform these regulations (Sroufe, 1986). Consequently, their adaptation in peer contexts, often requiring fairly advanced skills, is poor.

Like previous phases of adaptation, context plays a considerable role in the extent to which representational capacity is extended and organized within middle-late childhood and is used in the service of competent adaptation to issues of self-control and identity. Availability of appropriate role models is one important feature of context—adult and older peer models play an increasingly important role in the regulation of children's behavior through middle childhood. Thus, relationships affect children also in terms of what they see—models for regulated behavior. Furthermore, academic tasks must also be linked to the ways in which the child has come to make meaning of the world—again, in connection with role models and in connection to real-world problem solving (Resnick, 1994).

> Mr. Patten, a soft-spoken, yet forceful fifth-grade teacher, emphasized community building in his classroom. Children were encouraged to have a voice in how the classroom was run; they formed a government that was charged with roles that included behavior management and

maintenance of the class environment. Students rotated roles. Conflicts were discussed in classroom meetings in which Mr. Patten was present and facilitated. Even academic assignments were used for community building. Daily written language assignments (journals) were shared by all class members with one another, an activity used to encourage "voice." There were few, if any, management problems in Mr. Patten's classroom; the children spoke of him with reverence and respect, and as they approached adolescence, they sought him out as individuals to help manage concerns with peers and with the demands of other teachers. Mr. Patten was never threatened by the autonomy of his students; he modeled self-control and created a context of respect.

This classroom was filled with opportunities for the children who were involved to extend and consolidate self-regulation at the individual level and at the group level. Mr. Patten offered himself as a role model for regulation that children observed over and over. In addition, he created predictable routines and interactions (like debates) that served as opportunities for the children to practice using representational modes of regulation. Finally, his warmth and involvement with each child created a relationship context that children invariably experienced as supportive, and he was frequently sought out by students for advice and problem solving. In this way, Mr. Patten's room was a high-affordance context for representational functioning, and he supported the children with opportunities to master or to adapt to the challenges of the peer environment and identity formation.

Summary: The Role of Relationships in Child Adaptation

It is important to reiterate the distributed nature of development during childhood. Adaptation with respect to the themes described above is a function of many contexts' support with respect to that theme—in particular, relationships with prominent adults (parents, teachers). In fact, for many so-called at-risk children, the very nature or risk is bound up in the inability of social contexts (mostly relationships with parents and in the family) to appropriately regulate the child's emotional and social development vis-à-vis the key themes described above. It is in these social processes, mostly involving relationships between children and adults, that risk can be recognized and so easily transmitted to children (and later carried to school by children). It is for this reason that relationships were described as the cornerstone of development—they are in large part the infrastructure of school success not only for high-risk children but also for all children.

Thus, we find that children who lack supportive social relationships prior to school do not do well in school. In turn, it is unlikely for a third grader to function effectively in a classroom when the teacher, for one reason or another, requires children's attention to his or her own emotional needs. Much of the second half of this book is devoted to strategies that can help relationships between teachers and children in situations such as this.

For all school-age children, and especially those whose caregiving relationships have not afforded them opportunities to master many of the challenges of development just described, one cannot underestimate the extent to which relationships with people and environments support or inhibit developmental progress and functioning in school. Children are only as competent as their context affords them the opportunity to be. In short, their competence is a property of these systems, and some of these systems are relationships—with parents and with teachers. Perhaps the single biggest error that educators make when working with children is to assume that competence is a property of the child and to fail to make the necessary observations of the child in context. This focus on relationships with adults and their importance in relation to child functioning is extended in subsequent chapters.

4

The Emotional Bond Between Children and Adults

A young teacher, Ms. Brown, was describing her relationship with an 8-year-old boy, Gary, from an upper-middle-class home. She went to great lengths to talk about how tenuous his hold was on competence. "He would come into the room in the morning, and we would wonder what level of support he would need to make it through the day. I remember one day when he seemed fine—getting along with the rest of the kids—until I asked him to put away this book he was looking at and to come to the table for a group lesson I was doing. He just went off—tossing the book aside, withdrawing in a sullen, angry sort of way yet, at the same time, letting me know how explosive he felt at the time. I managed to approach him, gently and slowly, offering just to leave the room with him, which we did. Once we got into the hall, he was a combination of angry and sad—and he broke down crying. He was so confused—hurt about his dad being unavailable and out of the house, about his mom not being around much either—he worried about both of them. He sounded so tired and weary—just a little 8-year-old boy with such big troubles on his shoulders."

Teachers and other educators are constantly trying to make sense of the connection between children's family lives and what transpires between adults and children in the school building. Does Gary's reaction to his teacher reflect, in a direct way, his relationships at home? What processes carry over from home to school in terms of his response to adults? What impact do these relationships have on his competence? And the big question—can relationships with adults in school overcome whatever vulnerabilities this child has that are based on his experience at home?

Mr. Underwood, a fourth-grade teacher, describes his relationship with Delia: "She's distant, very cautious toward me and other adults. So I became the 'teacher' and she was the 'student'; she really didn't interact much with me. I wondered about this, although I did not think about her at home as much as I think about other kids in the class. I wonder why she is so nervous, and intimidated, and concerned about being wrong or doing the wrong thing. What caused that? How can I do anything about it? I had her brother a couple years ago and he was really difficult—bright but terrible social skills. She's better socially. What caused these two kids to have these problems relating? I work hard to get her to believe in herself, that she can do things. I give her praise and words of encouragement, but I also try to show her through my tone of voice, my actions—that seems to be helping. Lately she seems to hang around my desk more."

This is a thoughtful and perceptive teacher talking about how he experiences his relationship with a girl in his class. He raises many of the same issues as were raised in the previous anecdote. What are the connections between relationships in school and at home? How can relationships with students be used to help them overcome some of their vulnerabilities?

These are the central issues of this book. These anecdotes frame competence and risk in social terms—the strengths or the vulnerabilities are acquired through relationships and how these strengths and vulnerabilities are played out in school. The type of relationship-based risk that has been discussed in this context is a core of many forms of school failure (social and academic) in the preschool/elementary/middle-school years (Aber & Allen, 1987). Similarly, relationships with adults during these years (particularly in school) offer resources for combating the effects of this form of risk on children's competencies. For example, a teacher's style of relating to children—a style that is aloof, businesslike and emotionally distant—may trigger a different response in each child, depending on the child's history of relationships with parents (Lynch & Cicchetti, 1992; Pianta, 1994; Toth & Cicchetti, 1996). Recently, a national survey of adolescents revealed that the single most common factor associated with healthy outcomes across all domains assessed was that youth reported having a relationship with an adult that they experienced as supportive to them (Resnick et al., 1997). In particular, these relationships were described as being emotionally supportive—with someone the youth could count on to understand their problems and to offer advice. Teachers and other school personnel were among those adults mentioned most frequently as the source of this support. It is important that relationships with adults functioned in this way for all adolescents sampled in this large survey of a normative population.

This chapter describes processes involved in dyadic relationships, drawing heavily from work in the area of parent–child attachment and adult attachment and following from discussions of systems theory and its implications for understanding child development. This chapter first describes findings relating qualities of child–adult relationships to school-related outcomes and then describes processes in relationships between children and teachers, drawing parallels when necessary between children and parents. The model of child–adult relationships presented in this chapter provides much of the basis for many of the applications that follow in later chapters.

Adult–Child Relationship Processes and Schooling

Relationships between children and adults play a prominent role in the development of competencies in the preschool, elementary, and middle-school years (Birch & Ladd, 1996; Pianta & Walsh, 1996; Wentzel, 1996). They form the "developmental infrastructure" on which school experiences build. Considerable evidence shows that child–adult relationships play an important role in the adaptation of the child within a given context—home or classroom (e.g., Howes, Hamilton, & Matheson, 1994; Howes, Matheson, & Hamilton, 1994). The key qualities of these relationships appear to be related to the ability or skill of the adult to read the child's signals accurately, to respond contingently on the basis of these signals (e.g., to "follow the child's lead"), to convey acceptance and emotional warmth, to offer assistance as necessary, to model regulated behavior, and to enact appropriate structures and limits for the child's behavior. These qualities determine, in part, that context's affordance value for a particular child and are discussed in greater detail later in this chapter.

Child–parent and child–teacher relationships play important roles in developing skills in the areas of peer relations (e.g., Elicker et al., 1992; Howes et al., 1994), emotional development, and self-regulation (Denham & Burton, 1996) and in school competencies, such as attention, motivation, problem solving, and self-esteem (Birch & Ladd, 1996; Pianta & Harbers, 1996). Relationships with adults also figure prominently in developmental pathways toward behavior problems and psychopathology (Campbell, 1994; Greenberg, Speltz, & DeKlyen, 1993; Toth & Cicchetti, 1996).

Child–Parent Relationships

Relationships with parents influence a range of competencies in classroom contexts (Belsky & MacKinnon, 1994; Elicker et al., 1992; Sroufe, 1983; LaFreniere & Sroufe, 1985; Pianta & Harbers, 1996). Research has established the importance of child–parent (often mother) relationships in the prediction and the development of behavior problems (Campbell, 1990; Egeland et al., 1993), peer competencies (Elicker et al., 1992; Howes, Hamilton, & Matheson, 1994), academic achievement, and classroom adjustment (Pianta & Harbers, 1996; Pianta, Smith, & Reeve, 1991). Consistent with the developmental systems model proposed in chapters 2 and 3, various forms of adaptation in childhood are, in part, a function of the quality of child–parent relationships.

For example, a large number of studies have demonstrated the importance of various parameters of child–parent interaction in the prediction of a range of academic competencies in the early school years (e.g., de Ruiter & van IJzendoorn, 1993; Pianta & Harbers, 1996; Pianta et al., 1991; Rogoff, 1990). These relations between mother–child interaction and children's competence in mastering classroom academic tasks reflect the extent to which basic task-related skills, such as attention, conceptual development, communication skills, and reasoning, emerge from and remain embedded within a matrix of interactions with caregivers and other adults. Furthermore, in the context of these interactions, children acquire the capacity to approach tasks in an organized and confident manner, to seek help when needed, and to use help appropriately. This perspective is consistent with Vygotsky's theories regarding the social nature of learning and instruction.

School adjustment has also been traced to qualities of the child–mother relationship in a series of prospective studies on the Minnesota high-risk sample (e.g., Elicker et al., 1992; Sroufe, 1983, 1989b; Troy & Sroufe, 1987). These outcomes included teachers' ratings of self-esteem (Sroufe, 1983), peer competencies and friendships (LaFreniere & Sroufe, 1985), and popularity (Pancake, 1985) as well as peer competence in kindergarten (Bergmann, Egeland, & Sroufe, 1986).

Furthermore, there is evidence to suggest that a disturbed parent–child relationship places a child at risk for developing conduct problems in the early school years (Campbell, 1990; Campbell, March, Pierce, Ewing, & Szumowski, 1991; Greenberg et al., 1993). The work of Campbell and colleagues (Campbell, 1990, 1994; Campbell et al., 1991) has clearly established a link between controlling, hostile behavior by parents and disruptive behavior problems in early childhood. Reviews of this literature have indicated that child–mother interaction patterns account for between 10% and 15% of the variance in behavior problems in childhood (Pianta & Ferguson, 1997). Few contexts (or systems) have been as widely linked to child psychopathology, especially in childhood, as the child–caregiver relationship.

Qualities of the mother–child relationship also affect the quality of the relationship that a child forms with a teacher. In one study, teachers characterized children with ambivalent attachments as needy and displayed toward them high levels of nurturance and tolerance for immaturity, whereas their anger was directed almost exclusively at children with histories of avoidant attachment (Motti, 1986). These findings are consistent with results in which maltreated and nonmaltreated children's perceptions of their relationships with mothers were related to their needs for closeness with their teachers (Lynch & Cicchetti, 1992) and to the teachers' ratings of children's adjustment (Toth & Cicchetti, 1996). Cohn (1990) found that boys classified as insecurely attached to their mothers were rated by teachers to be less competent and to have more behavior problems than boys classified as securely attached. In addition, teachers reported that they liked these boys less. This link between the quality of the child–parent relationship and the nature of the relationship a child forms with a teacher confirms Bowlby's (1969) contention that the mother–child relationship establishes for the child a set of internal guides for interacting with adults that are carried forward into subsequent relationships and affect behavior in those relationships (Sroufe, 1983). These representations can affect the child's perceptions of the teacher (Lynch & Cicchetti, 1992), the child's behavior toward the teacher and the teacher's behavior toward the child (Motti, 1986), and the teacher's perceptions of the child (Pianta, 1992; Toth & Cicchetti, 1996). In sum, there is evidence for continuity across these child–adult relationships (Howes & Matheson, 1992).

Child–Teacher Relationships

Relationships with teachers also influence many school-related outcomes (Birch & Ladd, 1996; Howes, Matheson, & Hamilton, 1994; Pianta, 1992; Wentzel, 1996). Teacher–child relationships influence children's competencies with peers in the classroom (e.g., Howes et al., 1994) and their trajectories toward academic success or failure (Birch & Ladd, 1996; Pianta et al., 1995; van IJzendoorn, Sagi, & Lambermon, 1992). There is a growing body of evidence suggesting that teacher–child relationships influence child adjustment in preschool, the early grades, and beyond (Pianta, 1992; Lynch & Cicchetti, 1992).

During the early school years, teachers may assume a parent-surrogate role with the children they teach and may develop a relationship with the child that has considerable salience (Hamilton & Howes, 1992). The teacher not only controls rewards and punishments in the classroom, evaluates student performance, and maintains control over the classroom but she also "wipes runny noses and consoles hurt feelings, joining formal and nurturant responsibilities in a role peculiar to the elementary teacher" (Alexander, Entwistle, & Thompson, 1987). Like the parent–child relationship, the teacher–child relationship may vary in nature and quality. Some teacher–child relationships can be characterized as close and affectionate, others as distant and formal, and still others as conflictual (Howes & Matheson, 1992; Pianta et al., 1995).

Pianta (1994) reported on 26 teachers' perceptions of their relationships with more than 400 students. Six groups emerged from this analysis that characterized the types of child–teacher relationships: dependent (excessive reliance), positively involved (warmth, communication), dysfunctional (low involvement, anger, annoyance), average–functional, angry (high conflict), and uninvolved (low warmth, low communication, low anger). These patterns were related to children's behavior in the classroom, and there was a range of how these relationship types were distributed across classrooms. In one classroom, the teacher reported that more than 50% of her relationships with children were in the negative groups (angry or dysfunctional). Of the 8 teachers with more than 30% of the class identified in one of the negative relationship groups, 3 were in their last year of teaching (for various reasons) and were ranked by their supervisor at the bottom of the group of 26 in terms of their competence as teachers. Broad child risk indicators (e.g., socioeconomic status, school readiness) were distributed fairly evenly across the classrooms; however, there remained differences between the modal forms of teacher–child relationships, despite any differences across classrooms in child risk. Thus, like for parent–child relationships (e.g., attachment), teacher–child relationships can be characterized and profiled in groups that have meaningful relations to important teacher and child outcomes.

Howes and colleagues (Hamilton & Howes, 1992; Howes, Hamilton, & Matheson, 1994; Howes, Matheson, & Hamilton, 1994) have conducted a series of studies relating child–parent and child–teacher relationships to each other and to early childhood outcomes. They have established that there is a low-to-moderate degree of continuity in the quality of relationships children have with mothers and form with teachers (Howes & Matheson, 1992) and that both of these relationships play a role in children's peer competencies, albeit relationships with teachers are stronger predictors of behavior with peers in the classroom than are relationships with parents (Howes, Matheson, & Hamilton, 1994). However, Howes's work suggests that child–mother relationships influence relationships with teachers that, in turn, facilitate adjustment in the classroom.

Pianta and colleagues have reported links between teachers' reports of relationships with children and a range of school outcomes in the early grades. In one such study (Pianta et al., 1997) kindergarten teachers' reports of the degree to which children displayed security toward them was related to first-grade teachers' reports of the children's competence. In a series of descriptive studies, Pianta and Steinberg (1992) and Pianta (1994) showed that teacher–child relationships, as reported from the teachers' perspectives, can be characterized by dimensions of conflict, closeness, and overdependency. These dimensions consistently appear in samples that vary by age, ethnicity, and economic status (e.g., Saft, 1994; Taylor & Machida, 1996). They are also fairly stable across the kindergarten-to-Grade-2 period and correlate with concurrent and future teacher-reported measures of adjustment, grade retention, and special education referrals (Birch & Ladd, 1997; Pianta et al., 1995). Furthermore, changes in student adjustment from year to year are correlated in expected directions with these dimensions (Pianta et al., 1995): Downward deflections are correlated with child–teacher conflict, whereas upward deflections are related to child–teacher closeness. (Chapter 5 describes these dimensions in more detail and discusses issues related to the assessment of relationships.) Finally, there is evidence that child–teacher relationships operate as a protective factor against risk—children at high risk for retention or referral for special education who are not referred or retained are reported to be in closer relationships with their teachers, whereas their retained–referred counterparts are in greater conflict with teachers (Pianta et al., 1995).

It is important that the work described above assesses teacher–child relationships from the teacher's perspective. Thus, associations between these perceptions of relationships and the child's behavior in the classroom and in other contexts could, in fact, be partly due to characteristics of the child (e.g., temperament, problem behavior, etc.) that relate to both the teacher's perceptions and the other variables, including observed child–teacher interactions. Nonetheless, despite these limitations, it is clear that teachers' perceptions and experiences of relationships with students provide a window on classroom processes that do, in fact, correlate with important indicators of child success or failure.

The work of several other investigators also supports the child–teacher relationship as a key context in which early school outcomes are developed. For example, van IJzendoorn et al. (1992) demonstrated that child–caregiver security added unique variance over and above that contributed by the child–mother relationship in the prediction of a range of developmental status and school readiness variables. Studies have also used children's reports of their relationships with teachers, with findings similar to those with teachers' perceptions. Wentzel (1996) reported that middle school students benefited from relationships with teachers characterized by open communication and a sense of closeness, suggesting that this is a relational context with salience for children beyond the early grades and the preschool years. Similarly, Lynch and Cicchetti (1992) have established that maltreated children, as a result of experiences with parents, are sensitized to seek certain relational experiences with teachers—they are less likely to form optimal relational patterns, and they seek psychological proximity and support from teachers.

Birch and Ladd (1996) have studied teacher–child relationships extensively in early elementary classrooms and have suggested that children have a generalized interpersonal style (moving toward, moving against, moving away) that characterizes their interactions with peers and with teachers. Presumably, this style is a product of interactions with parents. This style is correlated with children's behavior with peers (moving against predicts conflict, moving away predicts isolation), teachers' reports of externalizing behavior (for the moving-against style), and some academic competencies. The work of Birch and Ladd confirms Howes's and Pianta's work in suggesting the importance of social, particularly relationship, processes in many aspects of classroom performance.

Now, after having discussed findings relating adult–child relationships to child school-related outcomes, the next step in understanding relationships and their effects is to identify and describe the processes by which adult–child relationships affect early school outcomes. With respect to the examples of Gary and Delia, what aspects of their relationships with parents (felt security, discipline–management, sensitive teaching) affected children's behavior in school? How did these processes affect relationships with their teachers? What level or form of intervention, in the context of relationships with teachers, could support these children?

Despite widespread and well-accepted knowledge about the importance of adult–child relationships on school-age child outcomes, very little is known about the kind of issues raised by these questions, especially with respect to the role of child–teacher relationships. For example, although there are studies linking insecure attachment to poor outcomes in early childhood (Elicker et al., 1992; Greenberg et al., 1993), not all children with insecure attachments are maladjusted in the early grades, and less is known about how (and whether) children form compensatory attachments with teachers. More specifically, studies have regularly linked factors such as maternal intrusiveness to child behavior problems (Egeland et al., 1993); however, it is not clear what particular levels of intrusiveness provide for a deleterious developmental effect. That is, although intrusiveness is not helpful to development, little is known about what differentiates a harmful level of intrusiveness from what might be normative structuring. Thus, there is a need for attention to the specific processes of adult–child relationships that can be observed in child–teacher and child–parent relationships and how these processes affect the child.

A Model of Adult–Child Relationship Processes

The model depicted in Figure 4.1 is an attempt to depict some of the processes involved in a relationship between a child and an adult. This model, like relationships, contains many facets, or components. These components are organized in a system that involves two persons—this dyadic system is a relationship. In Figure 4.1, the relationship between the adult and the child is represented by the oval that encircles the two individuals.

Hinde (1987) and others (Sameroff & Emde, 1989) described relationships as dyadic systems. As such, a relationship is subject to the principles of systems' behavior described earlier in chapter 2. A relationship between a parent (or a teacher) and a child is not equivalent to only their interactions with one another or to their characteristics as individuals. A relationship between a teacher and a child is not wholly determined by that child's temperament, intelligence, or communication skills. Nor can their relationship be reduced to the pattern of reinforcement between them. Thus, relationships have their own identity apart from the features of interactions or individuals (Sroufe, 1989b).

Child–adult relationships are asymmetrical. In the context of this dyadic relationship system, the child is the less mature system or organism.

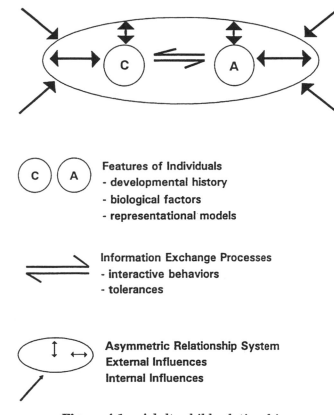

Figure 4.1.   Adult–child relationships.

For reasons that probably have to do with evolutionary processes (Bowlby, 1969; Breger, 1974), but at the minimum have to do with ensuring some degree of developmental competence, this less mature organism is tethered to a more mature organism (usually a parent) that is responsible for its development and survival. In this way, how this relationship develops and influences the child is biased toward input from the adult. The asymmetry inherent in child–adult relationship systems places a disproportionate responsibility on the adult for the quality of this relationship. Subsequent chapters address ways in which the adult's (teacher's) contribution to such a relationship can be enhanced.

Relationships, as dyadic systems, have several components, each of which can be the focus of assessment and intervention. First, relationships embody features of the individuals involved. These features include biologically predisposed characteristics (e.g. temperament), personality factors, and developmental history as well as features closely connected to the quality of the relationship itself—what Bowlby (1969) called the members' "representation" of the relationship. Next, relationships include feedback processes, the purpose of which is to exchange information between the two individuals. These processes include behavioral interactions, language and communication, and perceptions of self and other—which serve as feedback mechanisms in the context of this dyadic system. These feedback, or information exchange, processes are critical to the smooth functioning of the relationship. Finally, adult–child relationships embody certain asymmetries. That is, there are differential levels of responsibility for interaction and quality that are a function of the discrepancy in roles and maturity of the adult and the child. Each of these components is discussed below.

Features of Individuals in Relationships

At the most basic level, relationships incorporate features of individuals. These include biological facts (such as gender) or biological processes (such as temperament, genetics, responsivity to stressors) as well as developed features (such as personality, self-esteem, or intelligence). In this way, developmental history affects the interactions with others and, in turn, influences relationships (Fonagy et al., 1991; Zeanah et al., 1993). For example, a teacher's history of being cared for can relate to the way he or she understands the goals of teaching and, in turn, interprets and attends to a child's emotional behavior and cues (Zeanah et al., 1993). In the example used above for Gary, one can think about the different ways this teacher might have interpreted Gary's behavior, and responded to his behavior, had she been raised to believe that children should keep their feelings to themselves or be strong in the face of emotional stress. The fact that children bring certain features to a relationship with an adult is also evident in the case of Gary. What difference would it make if Gary was a girl? What if he was 4 instead of 8 years old, or if he was 12 instead of 8 years old? What if he was a high achieving student?

One feature that individuals bring to relationships is what is termed an "internal working model" or "representational model" of relationships (Bowlby, 1969; Stern 1989). In layman's terms, this model is like a map, a guide, or a template that the individual carries with him or her that contains a set of rules or guides for behavior in relationships, on the basis of previous and current experience in relationships. It can be fairly specific, like a model for relationships with children (in your own family or in your own classroom), or general, like a model for all relationships. From an adult's perspective, these models encompass adults' (parents' or teachers') accumulated feelings and beliefs about their behaviors with children (what works and does not work in getting children to comply), their motivation styles, their goals for interaction with children (how they relate to 5-year-olds), and their goals for interacting with a specific child in a specific situation (such as described above for Gary).

There are several key points about representational models. First, they are systems; that is, they are feelings, beliefs, memories, and experiences that have been encoded and stored in some abstracted but organized form. This organization is a system—feelings that have been stored about one relationship have the potential to affect feelings about another relationship or the interpretation of new experiences with that, or a different, person. Second, these models are open systems; that is, the content of representational models (e.g., the information stored in them), although fairly stable, is open to being changed on the basis of new experience. This is the potential of psychotherapy—for example, when a relationship with a therapist can provide experiences that alter people's perceptions of themselves and others. This is a critical feature of representational models with respect to intervention. Third, representational models reflect two sides of a relationship (Sroufe & Fleeson, 1988). In Gary's teacher's representational model of how children relate to teachers are both her experience of being taught (and parented) and her own experience as a teacher. She clearly believes that adults should support children and should encourage children to express feelings and that they should respond sensitively to those feelings. It is important that this belief holds for both positive and negative feelings. One can contrast this belief with what another teacher reports: "I don't see children as misbehaving. I never get frustrated . . . they are always so wonderful. I almost never have to worry about them being too demanding or needing me." In this example, the teacher expresses that positive feelings are allowable but that negative experiences are not part of adult–child relationships. Presumably, he may find it difficult to recognize the needs of children as well as his own needs. Both sides of a relationship or both roles (adult and child) are reflected in the representations each person holds about that relationship.

Representational models encode the history of a relationship; they function as a relationship's memory. This memory takes form in the expectations that each person holds for the other's behavior. In the case of Gary above, his teacher had certain expectations for his handling of the situation described that were based on previous experiences in similar situations. These expectations affected how she handled the situation described (e.g., responded very slowly and gently). In fact, one way in which relationships differ from a string of interactions is the way in which expectations (representations) come into play in guiding interactive behavior. In this way, representational models of relationships affect the future as much as they do the present.

Representational models can have an effect on the formation and the quality of a relationship through brief, often subtle qualities of moment-to-moment interaction with children, such as the adult's tone of voice, eye contact, or emotional cues (Katz, Cohn, & Moore, 1996), and in terms of the tolerances that individuals have for certain kinds of interactive behaviors. Thus, adults with a history of avoidant attachment, who tend to dismiss or to diminish the negative emotional aspects of interactions, will behave differently in a situation that calls for a response to an emotionally needy child than will adults with a history of secure attachment, who tend to perceive such needs as legitimate and to respond to them sensitively.

Thus the teacher quoted in the previous paragraph, who emphasized that children neither misbehave nor are needy or demanding, when observed in his classroom, appeared to ignore the subtle requests for contact or for help that children displayed. In one activity, he asked the children to write down or draw a picture about a family activity. One child protested that he did not want to do it if he had to share his product. The teacher indicated that he would not have to share. When the children finished, the teacher asked them to tell each other about what they had done and pressured the child to share. Upset, the child ran from the room to the counselor. The counselor assisted the child in devising a plan to share his feelings of anger and betrayal to the teacher. He did so, in the presence of the counselor, in a mature manner. The teacher said, "I don't see why you got so upset." This teacher almost appeared to have "blinders" on with regard to the emotional needs of the children in his class.

Working with teachers (and other adults) in assisting them to form and maintain close relationships with children requires attention to their representations of adult–child relationships. This involves attention not only to how they represent relationships with children in their class but also to how they experienced relationships with adults as a child. Furthermore, these representations, in the context of this dyadic system, both affect, and are affected by, other components of the system. How people interact can affect what they think of one another or vice versa. Thus it is important, in the context of thinking about intervention, not to see representations as the only avenue by which relationships can be affected.

Feedback Processes

Relationships can also be understood in terms of the feedback processes that involve exchanges between the two individuals (adult and child). These processes are absolutely critical to understanding how a relationship functions to regulate the behavior of the individuals involved. These processes are most easily observed in interactive behaviors but also include other means by which information is conveyed from one person to another. What people do with, say or gesture to, and perceive about one another are also major components of feedback mechanisms (see chapter 2). Furthermore, the qualities of or the way information is exchanged (tone of voice, posture or proximity, timing of behavior, contingency or reciprocity of behavior), as noted earlier, may be even more important than what is actually performed behaviorally; it has been suggested that these qualities carry more information in the context of a relationship than does behavioral content (Greenspan, 1989).

With respect to interactive behaviors, patterns of behavior appear to be more important indicators of the quality of a relationship than do single instances of behavior. It is not the single one-time instance of child defiance (or compliance) or adult rejection (or affection) that defines a relationship. Rather, it is the pattern of child and adult responses to one another—and the quality of these responses. Pianta (1994) has argued that these qualities can be captured in the combination of the degree of involvement between the adult and the child and the emotional tone (positive or negative) of that involvement. Birch and Ladd (1996) pointed out that relationship patterns can be observed in global tendencies of the child in relation to the adult—a tendency to move toward, move away, or move against.

As pointed out earlier, a relationship between a parent and a child is more than the sum of the parent's disciplinary actions and the child's compliance, just as relationships with teachers involve feelings of closeness, sharing information, memories of the others' behavior patterns, and expectations for responses (Hamilton & Howes, 1992; Pianta, 1992). Therefore, observing interactive behaviors and how they are patterned across time, situations, and contexts is a key to understanding a relationship. In particular, observers should note the degree of involvement and responsivity (Do the individuals behave toward one another and is it mutual or reciprocal?), the emotional tones exchanged verbally and nonverbally (warmth, negativity, dismissal), the spontaneity of behavior (Does the child spontaneously approach the adult?), physical proximity (How do the individuals organize themselves physically in relation to one another?), and caregiving (In situations of need on the part of the child, is this expressed and responded to and how?). These are just some of the interactive exchanges that can be observed between adults and children that are important as indicators of the quality of this dyadic system.

Also involved in the exchange of information between adult and child are processes related to communication, perception, and attention. For example, how a child communicates about needs and desires (whiny and petulant or direct and calm), how an adult selectively attends to different cues (e.g., the teacher who did not see misbehavior or emotional needs), or how these two individuals interpret one another's behavior toward each other (e.g., "this child is needy and demanding" vs. "this child seems vulnerable and needs my support") are all aspects of how information is shaped and exchanged between people in a relationship. Perceptions and selective attending (often related to representations of relationships) act as filters for information on the other's behavior. For example, when a teacher reports, "he *never* listens to me" or "this child is *always* demanding my attention," he or she is placing filters or constraints on the information exchanged in this system. These filters can be important in guiding interactive behavior because they tend to be self-fulfilling. Thus, if a teacher feels a child never listens, he or she is unlikely to perceive the child's compliance and may actually respond to ambiguous behavior as if it was noncompliance. Over time, these feedback and information exchange processes form a structure for the interactions between the adult and the child. One aspect of this structure is the tolerances for behavior and expression that are built into interactions.

In one case of parent–child consultation, the two parents described their child as incapable of accepting their help or affection and attention. He (a 9-year-old) was viewed by these parents as rejecting, and they felt hurt by him, isolated from him, and were afraid that they were slowly losing a connection with him. Their response to these feelings was to increase their involvement with the child to the point of being observed as quite intrusive. These perceptions, although very real to the parents, and based on behavior of the child, were nonetheless perceptions and were amenable to change. It was decided that one goal of intervention would be to try and alter these global, rigid perceptions that appeared to dominate these parents' experiences of their son.

In several parent consultation sessions, parents were involved in a process of agreeing to focus their attention on learning something new about their son each week. This learning was to be accomplished in the context of a daily session in which the parents would engage with the child in an activity of the child's choosing. Parents were instructed by the consultant not to ask questions of the child during these sessions, only to respond to the child and not to initiate activities or conversation. Through these carefully designed parent–child sessions, in which the parents' behavior toward the child was highly constrained, the child was given more "room" to play and to communicate with them. It took many consultation sessions, with continual encouragement and reminding, to get the parents to follow these constraints, but over time, the parents began to "see" the child's behavior differently. What was once perceived as a rejection of help was viewed as a wish to communicate independence (and also to ask somewhat controlling parents to back off).

As perceptions changed in these isolated, constrained situations, they were linked to perceptions of the child in other contexts. For example, once it was clear that parents began to perceive the child differently in the play sessions, the consultant asked them about other situations (usually the ones they complained about initially, such as homework). The parents were then asked to notice their behavior and their son's behavior in these (e.g., homework) interactions, using the lens and perceptions they had acquired in the constrained interaction sessions.

Through assigned practice and support in the consultation sessions, the global perception of this child as "rejecting" was transformed. In this way, perceptions that acted as filters for information about a child were changed, and a "new" filter, one that promoted a better connection between the child and the adult, was put in its place.

Clearly, these filters for information play key roles in structuring interactions within relationships. Pianta (1994) has suggested that teachers also have such filters for children's behaviors and that one aspect of interventions with teachers can be to elicit and describe these filters and to begin to work on transforming them (when needed). One important aspect of such interventions is that one understands the value that certain child behaviors have for the adult. Some child behaviors (e.g., aggression, dependency, affection, noncompliance) are "triggers" for certain adult responses because of the way the adult interprets the behaviors. Over time, the combination of adult and child filters and behavioral triggers set up limits for what is "allowable" and "not allowable" in a relationship, which are referred to as *tolerances* in Figure 4.1. In the parent–child consultation case described above, the relationship system neither allowed the child to be independent nor allowed the parents to be less controlling. Tolerances serve an important role in systems, as they keep a system organized and prevent a lot of random behavior and adaptations. However, if based on distorted perceptions or filters or on triggers that do not serve the child well (such as when adults are impulsive or emotionally needy), then what is allowable or not in a relationship may not serve the child well.

Clearly, tolerances are present in children's relationships with teachers. From the teachers' end, there is wide variation in how they perceive and respond to children's affection, how they perceive the idea that children should be pushed to be autonomous, and how they set limits to the amount or degree of disruptive behavior that will be accepted before they become harsh or punitive. In short, teachers, like parents, have an emotional life of their own that is enacted in their relationships with children in their classrooms, the behavioral consequences of which can be observed.

External Influences

Systems external to the child-adult relationship also influence it—cultures can prescribe timetables for weaning, expectations about child rearing, and discipline practices (Sameroff, 1989), which, in turn, interact with the caregiver's developmental history. State regulations mandate standards for student performance that affect what a teacher must teach and, at times, how she must teach it. School systems have codes for discipline and behavior, sometimes mandating how discipline will be conducted. States and localities prescribe policies and regulations regarding the ratios of students-to-teachers, the placement of children in classrooms, the grade at which students move to middle school, or the number of teachers a child comes in contact with in a given day. Teachers also have a family and personal life of their own. All of these factors can affect the relationships that teachers form with children, and the consequences of these factors for relationships can be examined

Regardless of the way in which these features of a relationship (i.e., individual characteristics, feedback or exchange processes) are conceptualized or measured, these qualities, together, capture the flavor of relationships in ways that single instances of behavior do not. Thus relationships are better understood as patterns of interactions, expectations, beliefs, and affects organized at a more abstract level than individual behaviors or events (Stern, 1989). Therefore properties of a relationship must be observed over time, over situations, and from multiple windows.

In sum, relationships are multifaceted, complex systems involving two individuals. They involve features of the individuals, feedback mechanisms, and interactive behaviors. In an adult–child relationship there is an inherent asymmetry that places greater responsibility on the adult for the overall quality of the relationship and its influence on the child's development. The next section of this chapter focuses on two sets of developmental processes that adult–child relationships regulate: emotion and achievement.

Relationship Processes and Mechanisms

Earlier, it was pointed out that child–adult relationships serve as regulatory mechanisms in the development of child outcomes, particularly outcomes in the socioemotional and academic domains. But adults are also involved in the regulation of motor activity and motor control and social behaviors involving conformity to accepted rules for greeting, interaction, and communication (Kopp & Wyer, 1994). Teachers play key roles in the regulation of activity level, communication and contact with peers, formation of friendships, and self-image. This section discusses the role of child–adult relationships in the regulation of emotions and in the development of achievement–academic competencies.

Relationships and Emotion Regulation

Thompson (1994) noted that the child–parent relationship regulates several aspects of emotional development: the production of emotion, the relief of emotional distress, the reinforcement of certain emotional experiences, the interpretation of emotion and emotion cues, and the strategies for self-regulation. There is also evidence that these processes are also influenced by children's relationships with teachers (see the beginning sections of this chapter for a summary of this literature).

The understanding, expression, and control of emotion are major themes in childhood (Thompson, 1994) and are hallmarks of competence in school settings. As discussed in chapter 3, the increased organization, intentionality, functionality, and complexity of emotion regulation processes are often used as markers of the difference between "early" and "middle" childhood, whereas deficits in these skills are viewed as central to the most common behavior problems in children—externalizing and overactive behaviors that are disruptive to adults and to other children in early childhood settings (Greenberg et al., 1991).

Thompson (1991) has defined emotion regulation as the following:

> the extrinsic and intrinsic processes responsible for monitoring, evaluating, and modifying emotional reactions, especially their intensive and temporal features . . . and are necessary both to provide flexibility to the behavioral processes that emotions help to motivate and direct, and also to enable organisms to respond quickly and efficiently to changes in their environments by maintaining internal arousal within performance-enhancing limits (p. 271).

As discussed in chapter 3, the child who is capable of regulating emotions uses and manipulates internal representations to tolerate arousal states and events to respond with behaviors appropriate to a situation and its demands. Relationships with adults provide input to these processes in various ways: They support the tolerance of anxiety and arousal and provide labels for emotional states, models for responses to emotions, and direct instruction in the management of emotion. Relationships with adults also provide experiences for the child that lead to emotions.

Thompson (1994) suggested that neurophysiological processes, attention, interpretation of emotion-related events, encoding of internal emotion cues, access to coping resources, regulation of emotional demands of certain settings, and selection of adaptive response alternatives are all part of emotion regulation, and each of these is influenced by interactions with adults. Greenberg and colleagues (Greenberg et al., 1991; Greenberg et al., 1993) outlined three phases in the development of emotion regulation, each of which highlights the role of child–adult relationships. In the first phase, early in development, emotion is expressed behaviorally by the child, and the child's emotional experience is wholly regulated by an adult caregiver. This phase is critical for establishing the acceptability of emotional expression by the child, establishing a regulated emotional experience for the child, and forming early routines by which the adult caregiver-as-regulator can be integrated into the child's emotion expression and management system. In the second phase, the adult is intertwined in emotion regulation—providing comfort for arousing experiences and labels for the child's affective states—that occurs in the context of the child–adult relationship. Affective labels, first nonsymbolic, then symbolic, form the basis for emerging links among cognition, language, and emotion that are then enacted in various forms in countless interactions between child and adult (parent or teacher). These labels are a critical feature of what is acquired in the context of the child–adult relationship that has consequences for later self-regulation. Not surprising, in the third phase of emotion regulation, communication about emotional states (as one example of emotion regulation outcomes) is a prominent feature of both child–parent and child–teacher relationships that, in turn, is related to child competence. Furthermore, the communication of affective states allows the adult to function as a direct regulator of the child's emotional experience and, in turn, enhances the adult's role as a secure base from which to explore (Cassidy, 1994).

The development of connections between emotion and cognition (labeling feelings, manipulating emotional experience through cognition) is a fundamental theme in early childhood that extends into early adolescence (Cicchetti, Ackerman, & Izard, 1995). Virtually nonexistent prior to the early childhood period, cognition–emotion linkages are functionally operative by the beginning of the middle childhood period. Children begin talking about their emotional experience and using selective attention, problem solving, and other cognitive processes to manage their emotional experience.

Another set of emotion regulation control processes described by Cicchetti and colleagues (Cicchetti et al., 1995) involve links between emotion and behavior. Behavior must be directed toward adaptive goals and must be organized within the larger social context. Children who have difficulties inhibiting links between arousal and behavior are more frequently referred for problems with externalizing symptomatology and are rejected and excluded in the peer group (Greenberg et al., 1991; Rubin, Coplan, Fox, & Calkins, 1995). Children who over control emotion–action links might inhibit expression, might be anxious or depressed, and might fail to benefit from the peer group because of their low initiation and interaction. Relationships with teachers play prominent roles in developing emotion–action links in terms of labeling affect and linking affect with behavior, moderating arousal, providing behavioral support and modeling, arranging supporting interactions between the child and others, and directly teaching coping skills (Doll, 1996).

Child–Adult Relationships and the Development of Academic Skills

Parents and teachers also teach. They are nearly continuously involved in interactions with children that are designed to impart knowledge, to improve skills, and to enhance competencies with respect to academic performance (Rogoff, 1990). As discussed in chapters 2 and 3, the acquisition and performance of academic skills (e.g., literacy behaviors, quantitative concepts, reasoning, etc.) occur within a social context—instruction is provided most often by adults and by peer models. Instruction occurs in the ZPD through interaction with a more skilled performer (Rogoff, 1990), at first in naturalistic contexts such as free play, but then in increasingly formalized and constrained contexts such as a mathematics lesson in a fifth-grade classroom.

Although instruction-oriented interactions with adults have the goal of increasing the child's skills in a particular area, these interactions nonetheless occur in the context of the relationships in which they are embedded—and they are influenced by the qualities of those relationships. Thus, child–mother relationships characterized as insecure or intrusive are also relationships in which problem solving is poor—low quality instruction is provided, timing of hints is poor, feedback is distorted or inaccurate—and children experience frustration and failure. Similarly, a child who feels emotionally isolated and distant from his or her teacher will not learn from interactions with that teacher in the same way as a child who has a close and affectionate relationship. The same qualities of relationships-as-regulators (presented in Figure 4.1) that operate with respect to emotional development operate with respect to instruction in more academic skill-oriented areas of development. Reading and responding to cues, providing accurate, well-timed feedback on performance, and sustaining the child through frustrating periods of problem solving are all processes characterizing well-functioning child–adult systems.

As has been pointed out repeatedly, adult–child relational processes do not only operate in the context of child–parent relationships. Starting in early childhood, these processes are also observable in child–teacher relationships. It is interesting that a feature that often distinguishes "early childhood" education from "elementary" (and elementary from middle school) education is the prominence with which relational processes are featured in the classroom environment as a support to the development of academic skills (Pianta & Walsh, 1996). The construct of "developmentally appropriate practices" (Bredekamp, 1987) is, in part, dependent on the role of child–teacher relationships in cognitive development.

Summary and Implications

Child–parent and child–teacher relationships serve a regulatory function with respect to emotional and academic skill development. In so doing, they have enormous influence on a child's competence in childhood. There is evidence that child–parent relationships provide an infrastructure for these processes and that child–teacher relationships, in turn, operate on and extend this infrastructure. There is also evidence that child–teacher relationships may play a formative role in emotional and academic skills development. Although by the time a child reaches kindergarten, developmental history will constrain child–teacher interactions, the limits of these constraints have not been established, and there is ample evidence that child–teacher relationships can overcome or override early history.

Child–adult relationships regulate development through a set of processes that are characteristic of dyadic systems. Applications of systems theory to adult–child relationships reveal a number of parameters of importance: representations, feedback mechanisms, tolerances, timing of interaction, and contingency of interactions. It is important that these components form a system—all are connected to one another in bidirectional or mutually influencing links. Thus, representations guide behavior, but behavior effects representations. Feedback processes structure interactions but are also influenced by the kind of interactions that take place. This emphasis on the bidirectional connections among the components of a relationship system is important for intervention practices designed to change relationships because it suggests that relationships can be accessed through many possible points and can be changed as a function of creating pressure at any of these points.

Relationships create a Zone of Proximal Development (ZPD) in which children's competencies are extended and enhanced as a function of the adult–child relationship in which they are expressed. Relationships of different quality create ZPDs that are more or less functional with respect to enhancing child competencies. Operationalizing classroom and school environments in terms of relational "affordances" is a step toward policies and practices that recognize that child competence is embedded in relationships.

One contribution of the developmental–systems lens to the practice of psychology in schools, as described in chapter 2, is a theory of how change occurs. However, fundamental to this contribution is the recognition that the adult–child relationships are one of the prime sources of developmental change. Thus, the more known about child–adult (teacher) relationships in development, the more is known about change. Consequently, school-located interventions can be the strategic and intentional use of teacher–child relationship processes toward enhancing the adaptation of the child. In the next chapter, issues regarding assessment of relationships and techniques for observing and describing teacher–child relationships are discussed.

5

Assessing Child–Teacher Relationships

A third-grade teacher has asked her students to engage in an activity in which they are to draw a picture about their feelings and write down some words about the picture. The activity is a blend of art, creative writing, and self-expression. She assures the children that they will not have to share what they put down on the paper. One boy, John, somewhat reluctant to engage in this activity, needs a bit of encouragement. Others in the group just dive right in. When all the children are finished, the teacher then asks them to sit in a circle and share their products with one another. John asks to be not involved in this activity, and the teacher tells him that the group is going to do this. He says he wishes to not share. The teacher pressures him, he starts crying and wishes to go out of the room. The teacher sends him to the school counselor.

How does this teacher's behavior reflect her approach to relationships with children? In what role does she see herself with respect to their emotional and social needs? What are her representations for relationships with children, and how do these representations affect her behavior toward them? Is she just insensitive? How do the children perceive her? Does her behavior affect the quality of her relationships with children? How can children feel comfortable about going to her for help or being vulnerable with her? Will they risk feeling uncomfortable? How will children respond to her when they come from a harsh background? Can she encourage relationships that help them overcome that background?

Answers to these questions link the real-life experiences of children in classrooms, such as that of John above, to the theory of adult–child relationships that has been described earlier. The bridge that completes this link between theory and experience is the assessment of child–teacher relationships. Psychologists often see the fallout of the kind of interactions described above (the counselor already has seen it). Certainly this teacher is neither alone nor unique. Establishing ways for psychologists to understand these relationship processes, to enter into them, and to shape them in more positive directions is the goal of this book. The purpose of assessment should be to serve this goal. The previous story continues as follows:

The counselor sits with child, who by this time is teary and says, "I just don't like telling the other kids about me." After some comforting, the child mentions, "She's always doing that, telling us we don't have to share and then making us share." The counselor spends several minutes talking with the child, working to come up with a solution for his distress. She offers the child the opportunity to tell the teacher how he feels about this whole incident and the feeling of being forced to share. He is reluctant, but the counselor offers to go with him and be present. He agrees. The counselor and John approach the teacher in the hallway. John shares his concerns about the activity in question and about feeling forced to share. The teacher responds, "I am sorry, John. I did not know you felt this way about sharing, and I should have done a better job of listening to you." She offered her hand to John, who grasped it and returned to the classroom with her.

This chapter describes methods for assessing relationships between children and teachers. Although there are literatures that reflect certain aspects of relationships between children and teachers, to date, there have been few attempts to integrate knowledge about teachers' attributions, interactions with children, expectations, and attitudes in the context of a systems-oriented perspective on relationships (Brophy & Good, 1986; Pederson et al., 1978; Zeichner, 1995). Children's feelings about teachers, time spent in contact with teachers, and attentiveness to teacher-directed activities also contribute to an understanding of the relationship and should be acknowledged (Lynch & Cicchetti, 1992; Toth & Cicchetti, 1996; Wentzel, 1996). The study of relationships encompasses interactive behaviors and individuals' cognitive, affective, and motivational attributes (Hinde, 1987). Developing valid measures of teacher–child relationships is one step in a process that can ultimately lead to the better use of these resources.

It is interesting that although there is a large amount of literature on interactions between teachers and children (e.g., Brophy & Good, 1986; Zeichner, 1995), this literature is focused almost entirely on instruction. Recent work has integrated a social component to understanding instructional interactions (e.g., Rogoff, 1990), but in the majority of studies of teachers' behaviors toward children in classrooms, the social, emotional, and relational qualities of these interactions are almost always neglected. As has been argued elsewhere, children's development is not easily carved into academic–cognitive and social–emotional domains (Sameroff & Haith, 1996). Thus, although there exists a fairly large amount of literature on student–teacher interactions, this literature is not integrated with theories of social development. The outcome of this missing link between the educational and the developmental literatures is that educators have not had easy access to understanding the role that relationships between children and adults—in particular, between children and teachers—may play in education. In addition, most assessment devices for examining teacher–child interactions, or instruction, lack a relationship perspective. The reader might find it informative to use the relationship perspective discussed in this book to understand the literature on instruction.

In a unique study that provides considerable impetus for viewing the child–teacher relationship as a developmental context, Pedersen et al. (1978) conducted a case study in which adults were asked to recall experiences with a particular teacher who had an exceptional reputation. This was an attempt to examine (retrospectively) the features of experience associated with an influential teacher. In these recollections, the adults described the impact of a teacher who formed relationships with students that, according to their reports, made them feel worthwhile, supported their independence, motivated them to achieve, and supported them to interpret and cope with environmental demands. This teacher's students differed from their same-age peers (with different teachers) on dropout rates, academic achievement, behavioral competence, and adjustment in the adult world. Thus, this teacher's students had achieved much different (and more positive) outcomes than had the typical students in this school.

The relation between felt security in a relationship with an adult and freedom to explore the world in a competent manner is a hallmark of the parent–child attachment relationship and is present to an exceptional degree in the teacher–child relationships described in the Pederson et al. (1978) data. The stories about this teacher reflect an almost parentlike influence, in which the emotion and the social quality of interactions that children had with her are highlighted throughout. In qualitative form, this case study integrates developmental and educational perspectives— linking cognitive development and academic performance, on the one hand, with emotional experiences and social interactions, on the other hand.

This chapter presents information regarding assessment techniques that can be used to describe child–teacher relationships. Because this is a fairly new field, the number of well-validated techniques are few. In the discussion of instruments, emphasis is placed on those tools that have demonstrated adequate psychometric properties and that have a strong theoretical grounding. First, there will be a brief introduction linking the teacher's classroom role and function to the model of the child–adult relationship presented in the previous chapter. Then, instruments will be discussed in three major sections: (a) child report, (b) teacher report, and (c) observational. Readers are encouraged to view these and other assessment instruments in light of the model of child–adult relationships in chapter 4, specifically in terms of the extent to which the instrument's constructs and methods map onto the many aspects of relationships depicted in the model.

What Do Teachers Do?

Teachers routinely function as prominent adult figures in children's lives. They perform a myriad of functions in response to children's needs, functions that define the nature of the experiences of teacher and child in relation to one another, experiences that ultimately construct the relationship they form. Howes and colleagues (Howes & Hamilton, 1992a) in their analysis of child-care settings, used an activity-setting analysis for identifying key components of the child-care environment that suggest the importance of the care provider as an attachment figure. In their analysis of early childhood teachers' behaviors in the classroom, Howes and Hamilton presented evidence that teachers function as attachment figures, as physical caregivers, as socialization agents, as mediators of peer contacts, and as teachers. From a systems perspective, to cleave these functions into those that are purely instructional–academic and those that are nonacademic is to create an artificial distinction that neglects important aspects of classroom life.

The Howes (Howes & Hamilton, 1992a) analysis examined the constraints on interaction that are present in a classroom setting and the patterns of interactions between children and teachers that reflect those constraints. Admittedly, this analysis was conducted in early childhood settings. Thus, one would expect a stronger emphasis on social processes, the emotionally supportive role of teachers, and the role of teachers as physical caregivers than would be found in a fifth-grade classroom. There is substantial evidence that teachers' roles become increasingly differentiated over time and that the social component may be downplayed. Nonetheless, as one fourth-grade teacher put it,

> I still have a close relationship with Gail, even though she is in sixth grade. She has always tried to be a help to me and on many occasions has gone out of her way to help. We see each other on occasion, and she keeps me informed on how she is doing. About a month ago, her parents went through a divorce, and she came often to talk with me about how she was feeling. I like that she uses me as a support; our relationship is important to both of us.

Thus, relationship assessments must attempt to integrate the various roles and functions that teachers play in the classroom—instructor, socialization agent, caregiver, peer mediator, and organizer.

The most pressing issue, then, is how best to conceptualize, to describe, and to assess teachers' relationships with children. This is a critical step in bridging the theory of child–teacher relationships with applications in the classroom. First, it is important to recognize that relationships are easier to talk about than to observe or describe. They remain something with which most people are familiar (they "know 'em when they see 'em"), but clear descriptions and operationalizations needed for application tend to be difficult to come by and elusive.

Returning to the model of adult–child relationships, in Figure 4.1, relationships were conceptualized as dyadic systems—more than simply the sum of parts—that include interactions, representations, and the characteristics of the two individuals involved. Instead, relationships are a product of the actions of these components over time and over thousands of occasions. As Hinde (1987) noted, relationships are ephemeral; they are reflected in behavior but reside in patterns and history, structuring interactions and perceptions and at the same time being structured by interactions and perceptions. They are processes as well as social structures. Relationships are known from the inside and from the outside, and knowledge is almost always indirect and incomplete. For Sroufe (1989b, 1996), relationships are organized; they follow rule structures in their actions, and their components are rule-governed as well. The patterns and rules in relationships suggest that they can be studied formally, are nonrandom and predictable, and can be reliably described. However, because of their degree of abstractness, our studies, predictions, and descriptions are not always accurate—they are quite literally like the hands of the blind men exploring the elephant.

Description and assessment of relationships is then, by necessity, best when informed by multiple perspectives, by multiple methods, across multiple occasions, and in multiple contexts. In this way, description is like the relationship itself—it is an amalgam of data. There are least two critical perspectives on the assessment of relationships—the insider's view and the outsider's view—both of which have a great deal to tell us about a given relationship.

Assessing Child–Teacher Relationships: The Child's View

Methods for assessing child–teacher relationships from the child's view include interview and questionnaire methods used with children. The reader should be familiar with the limitations of self-report measures, in the sense that they may not adequately correlate with behavior, yet should also recognize that one goal of assessing relationships is to examine and describe representations that each individual has about the relationship and that interviews are one method for accomplishing this goal.

Interviews

Although there are a range of informal interview techniques used to ask children about classroom life, and a question or two about teachers are usually included on structured interviews, there are few, if any, formal interviews that focus on the child's view of relationships with teachers.

Goldstein (1993) described a Clinical Interview Form that includes a wide range of questions pertaining to a child's experiences at home, at school, and with peers. Similarly, Sattler (1997) described an interview with a series of questions about school that elicit the child's emotional experience in that setting. These two interviews are good examples of measures that are fairly generic approaches to interviewing children about classroom experiences. However, certain adaptations can be made to increase the content of these (and other similar) interviews with respect to teacher–child relationships. For example, in the Goldstein (1993) protocol, there is a section on Family that includes questions about qualities the child likes or does not like about his or her parents, punishment and rule enforcement parents use in the home, and both problem and enjoyable activities parents and the child engage in at home. These questions can easily be translated into questions pertaining to the classroom and the teacher.

Interview assessments of elementary- and middle-school-age children related to the child–teacher relationship can include the following suggested questions and topics to gain information on the child's perception of his or her relationship with a teacher. These questions have been culled from several pilot interview protocols used with a large number of children across the elementary to middle school age range. Counselors or practitioners need to be alert to the fact that this task is difficult and that many younger children will simply not be able to perform the requests made in the following:

1. Who is the teacher you spend the most time with?
2. What are some things this teacher does that make you feel good? What does this teacher do that's fun? The interviewer should probe for specific examples and should encourage the child to elaborate on what about these activities make the child feel good. Also, one should try to find out how often and under what circumstances these activities occur.
3. If you are feeling upset, can your teacher help you feel better? How does that happen? Again, the interviewer should probe for details.
4. Does this teacher even make you feel mad or sad? How does that happen? What does she do to make you feel mad or sad? As before, one should probe for specific examples and should encourage the child to elaborate on what aspects of these activities make the child feel mad or sad. Also, one should try to find out how often and under what circumstances these activities occur.
5. Does this teacher ever yell or get mad? Do some kids get punished? Do you ever get yelled at or punished? The interviewer should probe for details.
6. Does this teacher pay much attention to you? What do you do to get her to pay attention to you?
7. Is this teacher a good helper to you? How does she help you? Does she help other kids too?

These are a subset of questions that could be used with children ages 6 through 12 years. Most experienced practitioners could easily come up with additional questions. In interviewing children about relationships with teachers, a few general principles should be observed. First, children may not respond to direct questions about their own experience but may readily respond to the same question if posed about children in general or about other children in their class. Second, once a child has responded, the interviewer should affirm the child's view and should gently probe to elicit specific examples of the experience in question (see above). In fact, one goal of the interview should be to attempt to elicit information on relationships at the level of specific experiences. Recent findings on a relationship-focused interview (e.g., Main, 1996) emphasized that a respondent's ability to recount specific experiences is a good indicator of their willingness to evaluate the relationship and is often a sign of a "healthy" representational model, relative to respondents that cannot or will not recount specifics. Third, the interviewers should approach the interviews as opportunities to gain information about the children's representational models of the relationships they have with their teachers. This model is the children's view of reality, and like representations of other relationships, is based on what the children have experienced and what they have observed across numerous instances. Questions like those above can be framed for the many roles teachers fill (e.g., instructors, socialization agents, caregivers, peer mediators, organizers).

With young school-age children, George and Solomon (1991) described the use of a doll-story technique for eliciting children's representations of relationships with parents that has also been used on a limited basis with teachers, with some success. This technique is a semistructured play-interview in which the child is given a set of props (such as a dollhouse or school–classroom setting) and dolls, and the interviewer poses the task for the child as one of completing the story from the stem the interviewer offers. Thus, the interviewer will hand the child a child doll and say, "The boy's parents have gone to the park and left him alone while they go for a walk . . . what happens next?" Or, the interviewer could say, "One of the kids in the class won't listen when the teacher said to be quiet . . . what happens next?" The interviewer then uses reflective techniques (e.g., saying "so the boy runs after his parents" or "the teacher yells at the kid," following the child's demonstration of these responses in play) to support the child telling a story starting from the separation (or noncompliance) theme. There are a series of stems that reflect aspects of the child–adult relationship that can be used with child–teacher relationships (e.g., protecting under conditions of danger, guiding socialization, facilitating exploration). Interested practitioners could tailor stems to roles filled by teachers.

The George and Solomon technique has demonstrated reliability and validity in small-sample studies of preschool- and elementary-school-age children but has not been subject to large-scale psychometric analysis. In recent years, a range of other similar techniques have proliferated on studies of child–parent relationships as attempts to gain information on children's perceptions of those relationships. These techniques have not been applied or developed for children's perceptions of relationships with teachers but show promise for that purpose. At this point, such techniques must be considered somewhat experimental, although promising.

Questionnaires

There are several sets of questionnaire methods for assessing child–teacher relationships that show considerable promise for use by psychologists working in schools. Like interviews, these methods can also be used to examine children's representations of child–teacher relationships. Well-born and Connell's (1987) Relatedness scale has been used in several studies with children who range in ages and risk level (Lynch & Cicchetti, 1992, 1997; Toth & Cicchetti, 1996). This 17-item child-report scale assesses two dimensions of childrens' relationship experience: "emotional quality" and "psychological proximity-seeking."

Emotional quality refers to the range of emotions (positive and negative) that a child experiences with the teacher in an attempt to capture the overall emotional tone of the relationship from the child's perspective. Questions are rated on a 4-point scale and include items such as "When I'm with my teacher I feel happy." Specific emotions assessed include the following: relaxed, ignored, happy, bored, mad, important, unimportant, scared, safe, and sad. Alpha reliabilities for this scale have been reported in the range of .74 to .84.

Psychological proximity seeking assesses the degree to which children desire to be psychologically closer to the adult. Four-point ratings are made on items such as "I wish my teacher paid more attention to me" and "I wish my teacher knew me better." Alpha reliabilities for this scale have been reported to range from .86 to .88.

The Relatedness Scale has adequate psychometrics, and Lynch and Cicchetti (1992) have described procedures for deriving five patterns of relatedness between children and teachers: optimal, adequate, deprived, disengaged, and confused. Children with optimal patterns report higher than average positive emotion and lower than average psychological proximity seeking. Deprived patterns are associated with lower than average emotional quality and higher than average proximity seeking. These children do not experience positive emotion and want to be closer to the teacher. Children with disengaged patterns report low emotional quality and low psychological proximity seeking. They are insecure and dissatisfied but do not want to be closer to their teachers. Children with confused patterns report high emotional quality and extremely high proximity seeking. They seem very needy despite their reporting feeling secure. Finally, children with average patterns are in the mid-range on both dimensions. These patterns reflect the different organizations of emotional tone and involvement that are very similar to patterns described by Pianta (1994) for teacher report.

It is interesting that Lynch and Cicchetti (1992) have established that maltreated children, as a result of experiences with parents, are sensitized to seek certain relational experiences with teachers—they are less likely to form optimal relational patterns and to seek psychological proximity and support from teachers. Thus, the Relatedness scale provides information on students' representational models of their relationships with teachers that correlate with their experiences in relationships with parents. The scale provides a window on the child's experiences and representations of relationships that can help a consultant gain valuable information regarding both sides of a child–teacher relationship.

Wentzel (1996) reported on the use of two child-report scales that examine aspects of the child–teacher relationship from the child's perspective. Perceived Caring, a dimension assessed with the Classroom Life Measure (Johnson, Johnson, Buckman, & Richards, 1985), is a short (8-item) scale that assesses the degree to which the child experiences social support and concern from the teacher and has high alpha reliability (.86) for such a brief instrument. Questions involve the child's rating the degree to which he or she experiences the teacher as a help or a support in instructional and social situations and the extent to which he or she experiences the teacher as a caring, concerned adult. Children's perceptions of teacher support and caring have been related to a range of teacher behaviors as well as student outcomes (Wentzel, 1996) and appear to tap aspects of students' representations of these relationships.

Finally, aspects of teacher behavior that map onto feedback functions in the model of adult–child relationships can also be assessed from the student's perspective with the Teacher Treatment Inventory (Weinstein & Marshall, 1984). This instrument involves the student's ratings of the teacher's behavior and examines the student's perceptions of the teacher's expectations, individual attention to the student, and nurturance. The items assess the degree to which the child perceives the teacher's expectations as fair, consistent, and accurate; feels the teacher attends and responds to his or her individual needs as a student; and feels the teacher behaves in a caring or concerned way toward the child. These dimensions also show adequate alpha reliability and correlate with a range of student performance outcomes (Wentzel, 1996). Used with upper-elementary- and middle-school-age students, the Perceived Caring scale and the Teacher Treatment Inventory provide a fairly comprehensive picture of the child–teacher relationship from a child's perspective.

Thus there are several child-report questionnaires available for assessing students' perceptions and representations of their relationships with teachers. By and large, these measures tap similar constructs, although they differ with respect to their focus on the child's emotional and psychological experience versus the child's perceptions of teacher behavior. As with most self-report measures, one must take caution in using these instruments with young children, and most of these measures would be inappropriate for children less than 8 years old. It may be possible, however, to adapt these with different response formats (e.g., pictures, structured interviews). Together, this set of questionnaires and interviews embody an approach to examining child–teacher relationships from the child's perspective and offer a valuable window for a consultant who is focused on relationship processes in the classroom.

Assessing Child–Teacher Relationships: The Teacher's View

Assessments of child–teacher relationships with the teacher as an informant are more well developed than those using the child as an informant. These techniques include questionnaire and interview methods and are subject to the same criticisms of self-report measures that were mentioned for child measures.

Questionnaires

The Student–Teacher Relationship Scale. The Student–Teacher Relationship Scale (STRS; Pianta, 1994) is currently the only standardized and validated instrument available for assessing teacher's perceptions of student–teacher relationships and, as such, offers an opportunity for school professionals to focus on this important context for development and school adjustment. This measure blends theory on child–adult attachment with research on the importance of early school experiences in determining the trajectories of children's school progress. The STRS has undergone extensive development and revision in many studies over the course of the last 5 years. It is currently being used throughout the United States in several large-scale national studies, in many smaller scale studies, and by many school personnel in a wide range of applications.

Pianta and Nimetz (1991) developed the pilot version of the STRS in a sample of 24 teachers and 72 children from their kindergarten classrooms. This initial version of the STRS contained 16 Likert-type items and 3 open-ended questions designed for further item development. Two factors emerged from factor analyses of this scale: a Positive Relationship factor, reflecting warmth and open communication, and a Dependent factor, reflecting overdependence and vulnerability in the child. Subscales based on these factors were moderately related to concurrent measures of classroom adjustment in kindergarten, teacher ratings of adjustment in first grade, and retention decisions (Pianta & Nimetz, 1991).

On the basis of the initial pilot study (Pianta & Nimetz, 1991), several items were dropped from consideration and many new items were written to assess negative aspects of the student–teacher relationship as well as other positive aspects. The resulting second version of the STRS contained 31 items and has been used extensively in many large-scale national studies, as well as in more focal regional and local studies, with children from age 3 through 9 years (Saft, 1994). These studies provide much of the psychometric information available on the STRS.

The first of these studies used the STRS with more than 400 kindergarten children and their 26 teachers (Pianta & Steinberg, 1992). Initial factor analyses reported that five dimensions accounted for the teachers' perceptions of their relationships with students: Conflict/Anger, Warmth/Closeness, Open Communication, Dependency, and Troubled Feelings. As expected, the addition of items to the pilot version allowed for the measurement of several new dimensions. The Conflict dimension is measured by items that indicate that the teacher and child are frequently at odds with each other ("this child and I are always struggling"). The Warmth dimension assesses positive affect ("I share a warm affectionate relationship with this student"), whereas the Open Communication dimension measures the degree to which the child and teacher communicate about personal items ("this student shares information about him (her) self with me"). The Dependent dimension measures the child's degree of developmentally inappropriate dependency ("this child is always seeking my help when it's not necessary"), and the Troubled Feelings dimension indicates the teacher's being worried about his or her inability to relate to the child. Subscales based on these factors contributed a significant proportion of variance (between 5% and 15%) to a number of measures of adjustment in the kindergarten classroom and were related to but not redundant with teachers' ratings of the children's classroom behavior. Analysis of these dimensions indicated that they were strongly related (correlations in the .40–.65 range) to children's classroom behavior in kindergarten (e.g., conduct problems, attention to task, peer social skills).

Furthermore, teachers' decisions to retain a child in kindergarten were related to STRS dimensions. Within high-risk groups of children with similar ability and readiness profiles who were predicted to be retained in kindergarten, high scores on the Warmth and Open Communication dimensions were related to promotion to first grade (Pianta & Steinberg, 1992). Children who were retained had relationships that were characterized by higher scores on the Conflict, Dependency, and Troubled Feelings dimensions than had nonretained children, differences that remained even after controlling for the children's classroom behavior (e.g., behavior with peers, noncompliance, etc.).

A subsequent analysis used kindergarten screening data from school entry to identify a group of children who were highly likely to be retained or referred for special education, as predicted on the basis of screening test scores. Within this "high-risk" group, the children who ultimately did get retained/referred were compared with those who, despite being high risk, were promoted or not referred. The children who, despite predictions of retention/referral, were ultimately promoted or not referred had far more positive relationships with their teachers than did their high-risk peers who were retained/referred. It is significant that this successful high-risk group was notable for its lack of conflict and its high degree of open communication. In short, it appeared that the STRS measured the buffering effect of the relationship between the child and the teacher (Pianta et al., 1995).

One study used cluster analysis to describe patterns of kindergarten teachers' perceptions of their relationships with students (Pianta, 1994). As noted earlier, six clusters of relationships were derived: Dependent, Positively Involved, Dysfunctional, Functional/Average, Angry/Dependent, and Uninvolved. Children whose child–teacher relationships fell in different clusters also differed significantly in their adjustment in first-grade classrooms, with the Dysfunctional and Angry/Dependent relationship clusters showing the most problems. Relationships classified as Angry/ Dependent were very high on the Conflict dimension and very low on Warmth. Teachers experienced very high amounts of negative emotion and very little amounts of emotional warmth or personal contact with students in these relationships. Uninvolved relationships were marked by the strong tendency of the child to be uncommunicative about personal information and to not rely on the teacher for help. In these relationships, children made very few emotional demands on their teacher. Positively Involved relationships were characterized by children showing behaviors toward their teachers that were indicative of a secure relationship; they shared personal information, appeared comfortable with dependency but were not too dependent, and displayed positive affect in response to the teachers' interactions or in regard to their relationship with the teacher. In the context of these relationships, teachers felt warm and close to the child. In the first grade, they were clearly the most competent of the STRS cluster groups. Children with histories of Positively Involved relationships in kindergarten showed the fewest behavior problems and the highest levels of competence behaviors in both the social and the instructional areas. Dysfunctional child–teacher relationships represented a group with needs for intervention. Teachers characterized these relationships as filled with conflict and anger, with little warmth and communication. These relationships were emotionally very negative and were also disconnected. Teachers felt troubled by their inability to "reach" these children and thought about them when not at work. Children for whom these relationships were reported were also the least competent in Grade 1, indicating that they were on a path toward continued school problems in both the social and the academic arenas and that some form of intervention was likely to be needed to change the direction of their school trajectories.

It is interesting that these clusters of child–teacher relationships, as assessed through the teacher's perspective, bear close similarities to child–teacher relationships when assessed from the child's perspective. As in the Lynch and Cicchetti (1992) report on the use of the Relatedness Scale with children, the use of the STRS with teachers yields a set of cluster groups that classify relationships into patterns reflecting the emotional tone of the relationship and the degree of involvement or engagement between the child and the teacher. The similarities in these cluster solutions, with two different scales and two different sets of respondents who play different roles in the child–teacher relationship, attest to the importance of the emotional tone and the engagement dimensions as ways to think about differences across child–teacher relationships.

The distribution of relationship groups across the participating teachers provides information on the types of child–teacher relationships in a classroom and the generalized tendencies of some teachers to form certain types of relationships with students, and it suggests a means of screening, at a classroom level, for relationship patterns. Several teachers were reported as having somewhat unique profiles for classroom average scores on the STRS subscales. These profiles, as indicative of general styles of relating, may be useful for the purposes of matching students with teachers. For example, studies suggest that some students with high-risk backgrounds because of maltreatment may benefit from placement with a teacher who would acknowledge and encourage communication and expression of emotion. Such an experience might enable the child to form a relationship that would compensate for relationships with other adults (parents) and would foster the kind of teacher–child contacts and interactions leading to improved classroom performance and enhanced self-esteem. A child with these needs might not do as well with a teacher whose tendency was toward less involvement.

A case-by-case perspective also indicated teachers who may be in need of extra support or teacher-centered consultation. In one classroom, the teacher reported (on the basis of the data described in preceding paragraphs) that 30% of her class was composed of dysfunctional relationships. Thus, this teacher experienced very high levels of conflict and anger and very low levels of closeness and warmth with about one third of the relationships she had with children in her classroom. Although this finding in itself does not indicate whether this rate of problematic relationships is due to the teacher's practices or the children's behavioral tendencies apart from the child–teacher relationship, it very clearly exemplifies someone who, because of either the children's or her own needs, may be "burning out" and in need of assistance.

Recent work with the STRS has focused on refining the factor analyses and the numbers of items associated with each subscale. Work suggests that a three-factor solution is most parsimonious and practical, with respect to the criteria of (a) variance accounted for, (b) alpha reliability, (c) construct validity, and (d) ease of use and interpretation (Pianta et al., 1995; Saft, 1994). The work on which these factors are based includes more than 1,400 child participants and more than 200 teachers (Saft, 1994) from classrooms and preschools across the United States, including Arizona, California, Connecticut, Colorado, North Carolina, Wisconsin, and Virginia. This sample nearly matches the U.S. census in race–ethnicity distributions and reflects a wide range of socioeconomic status, as well as a wider age range, than was reflected in the original sample of 426 children and 26 teachers on which the five-factor solution was based.

The three-factor solution derived from these data included Conflict, Closeness, and Dependency. The Conflict scale very closely resembles the Conflict/Anger scale reported in the original five-factor solution. The Closeness factor (and corresponding scale) is a combination of the Warmth and Open Communication factors from the original solution, and the Dependency factor is identical to the Dependency factor from the original five-factor solution. The two-item Troubled Feelings factor from the original five-factor solution was dropped in the three-factor solution. The three-factor solution replicated across sites, and no site differences or race–ethnicity differences were found for mean scores on subscales based on the three factors or the total score. The three-factor solution has been replicated with samples from Illinois (Birch & Ladd, 1997) and in a multistate study of children in child care (Cost, Quality and Outcomes Study Team, 1995).

Validity studies have indicated that the STRS correlates in predictable ways with concurrent measures of behavior problems and competencies in elementary classrooms (e.g., Pianta, 1994; Pianta et al., 1995), peer relations (Birch & Ladd, 1997), cost and quality of the child-care environment (Cost, Quality and Outcomes Study Team, 1995), and the behavior of children and teachers toward one another (Greene, Abidin, & Kmetz, in press). The STRS Conflict scores are related to observations of child misbehavior, off-task behavior, emotionally negative interactions, and ineffective behavior management. Dependency scores are correlated with high levels of help seeking by children, physical proximity seeking by the child, emotionally negative interacting, and high levels of responding to the specific child by the teacher. Closeness is related to moderate levels of involvement with and responses to the child and strongly related to emotionally positive interactions.

In sum, the STRS appears to be an instrument that is sensitive to teacher–child interactions, teachers' decisions about the child's school career, and the child's current and future school adjustment. Its normative base of more than 1,400 children of varying ages and backgrounds makes it probably the most psychometrically advanced instrument available for the assessment of relationships between teachers and children. However, the STRS is limited by the fact that it assesses relationships from only the teacher's perspective and therefore should be used in combination with other measures that assess behavior as well as the child's perspective.

Index of Teaching Stress. The Index of Teaching Stress (ITS; Greene, Abidin, & Kmetz, in press) has been developed as a teacher-report measure of teacher–child compatibility. This 90-item scale is composed of 2 main subscales, Teacher's Response to Student Behavior and Perceptions of Interactions and Self Efficacy, which in turn are composed of 12 smaller scales, all derived from factor analyses of responses from a large, diverse sample of teachers. Greene et al. (in press) reported low-to-modest correlations between ITS scales and teachers' psychiatric symptoms and modest correlations between ITS scales and STRS scores. Future work will be needed to confirm the factor structure of the ITS and its validity; however, it does appear to have promise as a measure that includes some aspects of the child–teacher relationship. The ITS, as it is further developed and validated, should prove to be an important tool in the consultant's assessment battery because it directly examines the teachers' experiences that are related to their own efficacy and emotional health in the classroom. Although it does not assess child–teacher relationships per se, the dimensions and constructs assessed are related to relationship processes.

Interview Methods

Just as there are interviews that elicit children's descriptions of their relationships with adults that can be adapted for relationships with teachers, so are there analogous interviews for eliciting adults' representations of their relationships with children. Although primarily validated and used with parents, these interviews have recently been adapted for use with teachers (Pianta, 1997c).

On the basis of work with the Parent Development Interview (Pianta et al., 1993), Pianta (1997c) and colleagues developed the Teacher Relationship Interview (TRI). This interview is presented in Exhibit 5.1 and is designed for use with an accompanying scoring system. Together, they are a system for scoring teachers' representations of their relationships with their children and of themselves as teachers. These representations are elicited in a semistructured interview format.

Exhibit 5.1.   Teacher Relationship Interview

Instructions to Interviewers:

It is important that the teacher be as comfortable as possible during the interview, so don't push them to respond if they don't want to. Also, always refer to the child by NAME during the interview. Your style should be conversational but stick to the questions on the form. When possible, probe for particular experiences or examples of a teacher's response.

Instructions to Teachers:

For the next hour or so, I will be asking you some questions about your relationship with *name of child* and about other relationships in your life. You may find some of the questions to be personal. Just let me know if you don't want to answer, and we'll go on to another. We are interested in your story about your relationship with *name*. As you know, we know a lot about children, but we'd like to know more about teachers' relationships with children and other significant people in their lives.

A. *Relationship with child*

1. Please choose 3 words that tell about your relationship with *name*. Now, for each word please tell me a specific experience or time that describes that word. (Re-ask the question twice to get specific experiences. If needed, say "like for 'fun'; tell me about a time when your relationship with *name* was fun".) Go through each word separately.

2. Tell me about a specific time you can think of when you and *name* really "clicked." (Probe if necessary: tell me more about what happened.) How did you feel? How do you think *name* felt?

3. Now, tell me about a specific time you can think of when you and *name* really weren't "clicking." (Probe if necessary: Tell me more about what happened. How did you feel? How do you think *name* felt?)

4. What kind of experiences with other people do you feel have been particularly difficult or challenging (hard, tough) for him/her?

5. Teachers wonder about how much to push a child to learn what is difficult (hard) versus how much not to push. Tell me about a time that this happened for you with *name*. How did you and *name* handle this situation? How did you feel in this situation?

6. Tell me about a time recently when *name* misbehaved (probe for a specific situation). What happened? Why? What did you do? Why? How were the two of you feeling? Is this the way things typically work out?

7. Tell me about a time when *name* was upset and came to you. What happened? Why? What did you do? Why? How were the two of you feeling? Is this the way things typically work out?

8. What gives you the most satisfaction being *name's* teacher? Why?

9. Every teacher has at least occasional doubts about whether they are meeting a child's needs. What brings this up for you with *name*? How do you handle these doubts? Do you ever think about *name* when you are at home? What do you think about?

10. How do you and *name* communicate about his/her need for independence or for help? What does *name* do to communicate his/her need? What do you do?

11. What is your relationship like with *name's* family?

Exhibit continues

Exhibit 5.1.   *Continued*

B. *Adult relationships*

Now, I'd like to ask you about your adult relationships. First, I'll ask you about your relationships in school.

12. How would you describe your relationships with the adults at (*name of school*)?

13. Tell me about your relationship with one of your teachers when you were a child.

The TRI is based on other interviews that elicit representations of relationships, such as the Adult Attachment Interview (Main & Goldwyn, 1994). It contains questions regarding a teacher's general description of his or her relationship with a particular child, followed by questions on specific topics or themes—situations, such as discipline—socialization, facilitation of achievement, efficacy, and affect. Like other interviews that elicit representations, teachers are probed throughout the interview to provide examples for their characterizations of the relationship and for their thoughts and feelings associated with these examples or episodes. The scoring system used to code interview responses is designed to be sufficiently flexible to be applied to almost any semistructured interview of adult perceptions of relationships and to be used in applied and research contexts.

In the present scoring system, adults' representations of their relationships with target children are assessed with respect to three areas: (a) the content or themes represented, (b) the way the teacher views him- or herself in relation to the child (process representations), and (c) the affective tone of representations. Together, these three areas provide a fairly comprehensive view of representations with respect to a given teacher—child relationship from the teacher's perspective. Responses are coded on 4-point rating scales. The Content area includes scales such as Compliance, Achievement, and Comfort and reflects the degree to which these themes are present in the teacher's responses. The Process area includes scales such as Perspective-Taking and Avoidance of Negative Emotion, reflecting the stance the teacher takes vis-à-vis the child's expressed or perceived needs. The Affect area includes scales such as Anger, Pleasure, and Burden. The scoring system is open ended in the sense that questions could be added to the interview and scales could be added to the scoring system.

Overall, the system is designed to provide as comprehensive a description as possible of teachers' mental representations without sacrificing detail and to provide maximum flexibility in analysis and research. In one study of more than 150 parents using the parent-analogue measure of the interview and scoring system, with all interviews coded by two independent coders, reliability was above acceptable levels, with kappa figures exceeding .65. Validity analyses have shown that parents' responses to this interview are moderately related to their behavior with their child in a feeding situation, a play/problem-solving situation, and a separation—

reunion situation. For example, scores on the Achievement scale are related to children's age and skill level and to parents behaving in a controlling manner in a play situation. Scores on the Perspective-Taking scale are highly related to observations of parental sensitivity, whereas scores on the Burden scale are related to observations of disengagement and parental negative affect.

Presently, the TRI is being subjected to psychometric analysis in a sample of kindergarten teachers. Pilot results have demonstrated that teachers find the questions acceptable and not intrusive. They are willing to discuss their relationships with particular students, and their responses reflect a range of positive and negative experiences. The TRI, at this stage of its development, would not be useful for educational decision making but can be a tool used by psychologists who, in the context of a consultation process, require a structured means for eliciting teachers' perceptions of themselves in relation to a particular child. Evidence suggests that the TRI elicits a wide range of individual differences and that it is a method that can be used by practitioners to facilitate a discussion of relationships when working with teachers. As with other methods of assessment discussed in this chapter, I should emphasize that the TRI is only one piece of an assessment package and is focused exclusively on child–teacher relationships from the teacher's perspective. As such, use of the TRI (and other methods) should be embedded in a battery of measures that assess aspects of classroom behavior, such as instruction and behavior management (see Goldstein, 1995).

Observations of Child–Teacher Relationships

There are a range of tools available for observing interactions between child and teacher that reflect the quality of their relationship. These include omnibus classroom observation systems as well as more focused systems. It should be noted that many systems for observing classroom behavior contain items for teacher–child interactions that are relationship salient and that most systems can be interpreted with the relationship-focused perspective discussed in previous chapters.

Classroom Observation Systems

Many classroom observation systems contain codes for teacher–child interaction (e.g., Ladd & Price, 1987; Laparo & Pianta, 1996), and these systems can be used to glean information from the classroom environment that is relevant for the interpretation of teacher–child relationships. Goldstein (1995) provided a succinct discussion of many of these observational systems, as does Walker (1994). (The reader is referred to those and related references for more detailed discussion of classroom observation systems.) These omnibus observation systems, however, typically do not focus exclusively, or in a targeted fashion, on the relationship between child and teacher. The disadvantage of this is that the systems tend not to be very comprehensive or detailed with respect to this relationship. The advantage, however, is that usually these systems contain codes for instruction, child performance, setting of the interaction, and emotional quality of the interaction that provide information on the context of relationship-related interactions. This information can be of help to the psychologist, for example, when attempting to understand when and how a given relationship difficulty is arising in the classroom and whether it is occurring in group settings only or as the consequence of attempts to perform academic tasks.

Relationship-Focused Observations: The Teacher Attachment Q-Set

The Teacher Attachment Q-Set (Howes, Hamilton, & Matheson, 1994; Howes, Matheson, & Hamilton, 1994; Pianta et al., 1997) is an adaptation of the Attachment Q-Set (Waters, 1987; Waters & Deane, 1985), which was designed to assess attachment organization in young children with their mothers. The Attachment Q-Set consists of 90 descriptions of child behaviors derived from attachment theory and research that are thought to reflect different aspects of the child's attachment (e.g., "when upset, the child seeks physical contact from parent"). These 90 items were derived from extensive observations in home environments.

In using the Q-set methodology, an observer spends considerable time in the home or the classroom setting making notes of the child's behavior. Length of observations vary but are typically several hours. After such observation, the observer sorts the 90-item Q-set deck into a forced distribution, such as 9 piles containing 10 items each. The items are sorted into these 9 groups on the basis of the degree to which they are "highly characteristic" of the child or "not at all characteristic" of the child. The end product of the sorting is a forced distribution of 90 behaviors on a 9-point scale of *most* to *least* characteristic of the child. Each behavior (or item) is then assigned a point value (1–9) indicating the group into which it was sorted, reflecting the degree to which it was characteristic of the child. These are Q-item scores that can then be transformed in various ways to profile a relationship.

The Q-set methodology has been used mostly with child–teacher relationships in early childhood settings (Howes, Hamilton, & Matheson, 1994; Howes, Matheson, & Hamilton, 1994; Pianta et al., 1997). Usually, the Attachment Q-Set is adapted by eliminating items that only have relevance to a mother–child relationship and not to a teacher–child relationship, such as "child often cries or resists when mother takes him to bed for naps or at night." Remaining items are rewritten to apply to teachers. Howes has used this methodology with several hundred teachers and several thousand children in her research on child-care and early childhood education settings.

Q-set methods use what are termed *criterion sorts* to derive scores for participants on relevant constructs. Experts knowledgeable regarding a particular construct (e.g., child–teacher security) are asked to sort Q-set descriptions according to their view of what an "ideal" child would receive as a sort—in the case of the aforementioned example, a child who was ideally secure in relationship to his or her teacher.

In several studies (e.g., Howes et al., 1994; Pianta et al., in press), criterion sorts were developed to describe children in "ideal" relationships with teachers: for example, a child in a secure relationship, a child in a conflicted relationship, and a child in a dependent relationship. Interrater reliability for these sorts tends to be high, suggesting that two observers' impressions of characteristic behaviors for individual children can agree. Also, correlations between sorts of teacher–child relationships are strongly related to similar sorts of parent–child relationships for constructs such as security, indicating a high level of consensus among various reporters on the behaviors reflective of a secure child–adult relationship.

Recent applications suggest that teachers can self-administer the Q-set. This option, requiring that teachers sort the 90-item deck according to their views and observations of their relationship with particular children, takes no more than 30 minutes and is correlated with classroom observations of their behavior (Pianta et al., 1997).

Although Q-set methods have been used in research on child–teacher relationships, they are not well suited for use in applied settings. They tend to be fairly complex, and the ways they are scored are not easily learned or practical. However, once scoring is completed, interpretation is fairly straightforward—scores reflect a given child's characteristic behaviors in a relationship. This information could be quite helpful for consultation in a specific case, although the procedure can be cumbersome and time consuming.

Summary

The available measurement systems for child–teacher relationships are less well developed than those for parent–child relationships, but several are at stages of development in which they can be used in school settings. Observational studies have used adaptations of the Attachment Q-Set (e.g., Howes, Hamilton, & Matheson, 1994), but the validity of these systems has simply not been subject to the kind of tests that would establish these methods for more practical use. Teacher self-report instruments have been widely used (e.g., Greene et al., in press; Birch & Ladd, 1997; Pianta, 1992; Taylor & Machida, 1996) and have shown considerable promise with respect to reliability and validity, and new studies have begun to examine their use. The Student–Teacher Relationship Scale (STRS; Pianta, 1994) is the most well developed of these. The Teacher Relationship Interview shows promise but is in a development stage. Child-report questionnaire methods for both child–parent and child–teacher relationships appear promising for elementary-school-age and older children (Lynch & Cicchetti, 1992; Toth & Cicchetti, 1996) but are likely to present validity problems for young children. Although some child-informant methods are available for child–parent relationships (doll-story para-digms), they require considerable training for reliable coding and are likely to prove impractical in applied settings (George & Solomon, 1991). The measurement technology for child–teacher relationships has only be-gun to be developed and will require considerable attention if the benefits of this research are to be realized in applied settings.

Teacher–child relationships are an important "context" for develop-ment and learning in the school setting. The implications of this for school policy, teacher training, and educational practice are substantial. Opti-mizing the relational "fit" between teachers and children could contribute to enhanced relationships and school success, especially for high-risk chil-dren. Observational, child-report, and teacher-report methods of assess-ment provide the kind of multi-informant package of instruments needed for assessment of relationships. It is important that validated instruments exist in all of these categories and can be combined with existing instru-ments or can be used as a comprehensive package to assess child–teacher relationships. Applied child and adolescent psychologists could use any or all of these techniques for a variety of purposes.

At a global level, teachers can be trained to observe relationship pro-cesses and to enhance their relationships with children in ways that could facilitate the preventive effect of relationships. Instruments such as the STRS (or its short form) or some of the child-report questionnaires can be used in screening whole classrooms to identify teachers who may need supportive help or consultation to deal with individual children, to im-prove their interactive style, or to prevent teacher burnout. Once engaged in a consultation with a teacher, the psychologist can use a mix of obser-vation or teacher interview techniques to provide in-depth information re-flecting the richness of the relationship experiences of the teacher and information leading to subsequent planning and behavior change. Fur-thermore, the more standardized of these techniques (such as the STRS or standardized observations) can be used as outcome measures for con-sultation and intervention. As work on teacher–child relationships contin-ues, these policy and practice implications can be field-tested and evalu-ated. It is important that many of the assessment methods described in the chapter are well developed enough for use at the local level, with local norms and procedures developed to enhance their use in those contexts.

6

Examples From Life

This chapter presents brief case descriptions of three different child–teacher relationships. These descriptions were drawn from consultations with teachers as well as from interviews conducted with teachers (the TRI) at the end of the school year as part of a longitudinal study of the school experiences of high-risk children. The descriptions were selected to characterize features of the discussion on child–teacher relationships presented in chapters 1 through 5 and to link the theoretical base provided in those chapters to the actual experiences of teachers. These cases provide a gateway to the discussions of relationship-focused interventions in chapters 7 through 9.

With teachers' own words and observations of their behavior, these cases reflect issues and challenges faced by psychologists in relation to assessing and intervening with child–teacher relationships. In some sense, they reflect the "attitudinal" context in which psychologists work in schools (Hughes, 1992; O'Keefe & Medway, 1997) and in which consultations with teachers are performed. In other ways, these cases capture the system of relationships in which teachers are involved, of which relationships with children are but one component.

The three cases vary in terms of the relational style each portrays, yet each depicts aspects of how a child–teacher relationship functions in relation to a child's ZPD or, in other words, as a context for development. The first case depicts a close, warm, involved relationship between a teacher and a young boy. It presents many aspects of a relationship between an adult and a child that are characteristic of secure attachment. The second case, drawn from a consultation, presents an overinvolved style of relating between child and teacher. In this case, presented mainly from the teacher's perspective, the reader will note the similarities with the kind of ambivalent–preoccupied attachment style described in earlier chapters. The consultation process is also described. The consultation, in this case, addresses the teacher's relational style in general and his relationship with one child in particular, targeting both the representational aspects of child–teacher relationships and his interaction with a particular student. The third case illustrates yet another style of adult–child relationships, described as avoidant–disengaged. This case depicts the consequences of this style for students whose emotional needs conflict with the teachers' stance toward child–adult relationships.

"Secure Base"

Laura has been teaching kindergarten for 1 year. A woman in her late 30s with two children, Laura went to junior college after high school and then raised her family. After working as a classroom aide for 3 years, she went back to school and earned a degree in education. This school draws primarily students from a rural area; Laura has 17 students in this year's class. She also has a classroom aide 3 hours per day.

Elliott is a 6-year-old boy in his first year of school. He is the oldest of two children who are being raised by their mother, and they live in a modest home. His father and mother divorced soon after the birth of Elliott's younger sister; Elliott has frequent contact with his father, who lives in the same community and is an involved parent. Elliott's developmental history is unremarkable. His mother has described him as a fairly easy child to raise, and she describes her relationship with him as close and affectionate.

A research assistant administered the TRI to Laura about her relationship with Elliott. The following material reflects how the interview elicits teachers' representations of a relationship with a particular child and, at the same time, provides examples of the aspects of the model of adult–child relationship systems presented in chapter 4.

Laura was first asked to describe her relationship with Elliott using three words. "Three words! For a person who's very verbose, that's difficult. Let me see. I think trusting, admiration on both sides, and caring."

She was then asked to explain why she chose these words.

> Let's start with trusting . . . Elliott's uncle died this year. And he was really upset about it and didn't want the whole class to know about it . . . he was definitely out of sorts for awhile. I think he felt he could tell me in confidence, and he trusted me to keep confidentiality until he was ready to share his experience with the class. We spent a bunch of time talking about it one on one, mostly quick check-in type of conversations, and one day he said he wanted the class to know.

This teacher's representations of child–teacher relationships include a belief that adults are a source of emotional support for children and that children should be able to confide in and trust adults. Also, she appears at ease with the topic of the interview (Main, 1996); her narrative quickly and easily moves to a specific description of her general characterization of the relationship, indicating her willingness to examine and to evaluate this relationship—a sign of security.

She went on to tell why she chose "admiration" to describe this relationship.

> Well, I think in some ways he seemed to admire me because I was able to have something neat for him to do, and in a child's eyes that is

important. He was always like, 'Well, how do you think up all this stuff, and where does all this stuff come from?' And he'd say, 'If we finish something early, you always have something else to do.' At the same time, he had to deal with the death of his uncle who was very close to him. I admired the way his parents presented it to him and the way, a couple of days later, he presented it to the class. The way he chose to share that information with friends was very mature; I remember feeling a lot of respect for this little child who was trying to come to grips with such a loss.

In this anecdote, the teacher reveals other aspects of her representations—an emphasis on mutuality and reciprocity (they both admire and respect one another), a belief that teachers are stimulating for children and that social–emotional processes (e.g., coping with a loss) affect how a child is performing in school on academic tasks.

Then she described why the relationship was "caring."

> That's easy. He knows that I care about him. I mean he knows that if he is unhappy, he can come up and get a hug or talk if he needs to. That's absolute in my book . . . kids got to know they can get support if they need it. It's interesting with Elliott because he's a real boys' boy and not the type of kid that always needs that extra touch. Many of the other kids are always wanting to be touched, not Elliott. But I have an unconditional rule in my class that if somebody was upset about something that they could always come up and get a hug without any questions asked and if they needed it, that was fine. And he knew during that time his uncle died that he could come and get it. And I think that was important to him. He would just come up and sit in my lap and hold on. He was very fond of that uncle and had a difficult time adjusting. I think it was important that he knew I cared enough about him. . . . You know, it was just a reciprocal thing that we could do for each other.

Again we see the emphasis on reciprocity, the emotional support by the adult, the belief that children should be accepted and should experience care unconditionally, and a respect for the child's autonomy. It is important to note the teacher's emphasis that children can come to her for a hug, that Elliott is sometimes reticent, and that she waits for him to seek a hug rather than indiscriminately giving a hug to him. As before, she easily describes an experience at a specific level, and there is little or no inconsistency in her specific description and general characterization; that is, these specific descriptions are good examples of the adjectives she used.

Laura was then asked to describe a time when she and Elliott were really "clicking" together.

> Boy, that would be a time during math at the end of the year. Addition and subtraction: He just couldn't get it. He'd look up at me and shake his head or sometimes get frustrated and refuse to try. I took him out in the hall during independent work time (my aide was in the room). We worked on the skill together, and he got it. Makes you feel good

> when that 'light bulb goes on.' He was ecstatic! He came in and announced it to the whole class at the top of his lungs.

She went on,

> Or like in reading. He's got a lot more ability than he seemed to think. Wouldn't take a risk to go to the next step. Every time I challenged him with a new set of words, he got frustrated. So one day, instead of doing a lesson, he and I just went to the corner and read together. He liked it. So I then got out the sound board, and we took words from the book we had just read and started to work with them. He hung with me for awhile, and it seemed to give him some confidence.

These two anecdotes are rich descriptions of the ZPD—how Laura's relationship with Elliott supports his learning and mastery. It is important that these descriptions are very different from those in which teachers may describe their ideas of good teaching or their approaches to teaching/interacting with children in general. This is a very personalized description, indicating that Laura has in her mind a clear representation of her relationship with Elliott—that Elliott is an individual and that his feelings and experiences are recognized. She also communicates aspects of the tolerances she attempts to infuse in her relationships with students—she encourages risk taking, and intensifies her approach in response to student passivity.

Then Laura spoke of a time when she and Elliott were "not clicking" and emotions were more difficult. "Elliott had a best buddy and the two couldn't sit next to each other. They just couldn't stay in their own seats ... always had to see what the other one was doing. It would exasperate me."

Laura tried to have the boys take responsibility for the situation.

> I'd approach them with "What can you two do about this?" instead of me, as the teacher, putting them in time-out. Elliott would come up with really good strategies and they'd last about 30 seconds, and I'd come over, "Elliott, what's going on?" It drove me nuts because he's a very bright kid and he knew what he had to do. . . . It's frustrating. One time he wouldn't come in from recess and had to give up some of his free choice time. He was angry, and I was impatient. He can make better decisions than that.

This anecdote is critical to understanding Laura's representations of relationships and her relational style. Again she is at ease with the topic, but this time the topic is misbehavior. She does not deny, downplay, dismiss, or avoid the topic, as was the case for the teacher described in an earlier chapter who responded to the same question, "Children don't misbehave in my classroom. . . . I don't see kids as misbehaving," and who then trails off and offers only very vague and general responses to probes. Laura stores all information about a relationship—both the positive experiences and the negative ones—and she evaluates all aspects of her experience with a child in making characterizations. She is equally at ease in presenting both the positive and the negative information, lending credence to her assertions that she attempts to respond unconditionally to children.

Laura then turned away from talking about Elliott.

> Children are at so many different levels in public school, and there are some kids who really can't understand what you're trying to get across to them at first. So it makes it frustrating to me when kids do understand but don't act. But I have to remember they are just kids. . . . I think boys are impulsive sometimes and they think, "Well, I can get away with it this one time." I think sometimes, if, if he hadn't tried some of the things when there was an opening, I would have wondered what was going on because I think, you know, "I gave you that opportunity and you didn't try it."

As in a previous response, Laura also indicates here that some of her representations conform to stereotypes of boys' behavior (e.g., impulsive), yet stereotypes or generalities do not pervade her narrative. She also hints at how these stereotypes may affect her tolerances for certain behaviors and interactions.

Laura's classroom was visited in April of the school year. The children seemed quite social and appeared to enjoy each other. Laura allowed children a fair amount of freedom to interact with one another. Children were engaged in a variety of social and exploratory activities throughout the morning and they were talkative. At the general level, this classroom appeared to be consistent with what Laura had described in her interview —stimulating and active, she was accessible to all the children, positive, and very involved.

Interactions with Elliott were observed systematically with a comprehensive instrument designed to capture many aspects of classroom functioning (Laparo & Pianta, 1996). During the first half hour of this 3-hour observation (a set of activities the children are free to perform at the start of the day), Elliott particularly manipulated Laura's attention and seemed to want to be in charge of activities. After a few minutes of nagging Laura and not getting his way, Elliott moved to a far section of the room and started taking peers' materials and poking them. It was clear he knew Laura would not approve, as he carefully monitored her. Laura noticed some noise from that section of the room and made eye contact with Elliott; he left that area and started to read a book.

As Laura began directing the children to more formal activities, Elliott was attentive and followed directions. It was as if his initial encounter with Laura earlier in the morning had reestablished equilibrium and balance in their relationship, reorienting Eliott to the nature of the classroom structure and process. Elliott's language arts group was the first to be called to work with Laura, while the aide worked with the remainder of the class. Elliott enthusiastically approached Laura and was allowed to sit closest to her as she led the activity. He was attentive and responsive, his gaze frequently on Laura.

Summaries of the observations made that morning were remarkable for the level of visual contact between Laura and Elliott, their frequent contacts for short intervals, and the very positive overall emotional tone of their interactions.

In responses to another set of questions, Laura described the school as supportive. She reported that although *some of us share more than others,* she felt comfortable and at home there.

> The principal is approachable and has been helpful to me as a beginning teacher. But I really don't feel like a total beginner. Raising my own kids and relating to them, knowing how you have to back off sometimes and encourage at other times, has been a real help to me in the classroom. I just haven't had to get used to that stuff on top of trying to teach them.

Finally, Laura was asked a series of questions about her own family.

> I was the second of four kids. My mother didn't cut us any slack, but we always knew we could count on her. She and Dad were there when you needed them, that's for sure. Dad worked a lot, and I was more distant with him than with Mom. The toughest times between us had to do with how they treated my younger brother and sister. It always seemed to me that they had it easier . . . didn't have to work as much around the house; they had pretty strict rules for me. I kind of rebelled when I was a teenager, didn't go to college right away, ended up getting married early and having kids of my own. I don't think they wanted it to happen that way. But it worked out, and no matter what, even though I knew they didn't approve of some of what I did, I knew I could count on them. They stayed involved with me. I see them now most every week . . . they live in the next county.

This anecdote reveals something of the origin (perhaps) of Laura's representations of relationships between children and adults. Similar to her representations of her relationship with Elliott, Laura notes that growing up there was an emphasis on high expectations of adults, available support, and unconditional acceptance. She is comfortable sharing both positive and negative aspects of these relationships and appears to have come to an understanding of how relationships involve compromise and reconciliation. She seems to enact many of these themes in her relationships with the children she teaches.

Thus, the case of Laura reflects many elements of relationship systems in which teachers are embedded. It is easy to see the parallels between how Laura describes her relationship with Elliott (and what she seeks with other children) and how she was raised by, and still relates to, her parents. Consistent availability runs as a theme throughout this interview and is evident in her interactions with Elliott. Even when Elliott tests limits, Laura remains steadfast in her own sense of how she wants the relationship to be. When confused by Elliott's inconsistency, Laura does not personalize this, instead, she seeks explanations for Elliott's behavior (and her feelings about it) in terms of what she knows about him and about children. In doing so, Laura demonstrates a certain fresh perspective or a willingness to evaluate relationships and her role in them. These qualities characterize individuals with secure attachment histories who, in turn, tend to facilitate security in their relationships with children (Main & Goldwyn, 1994).

Having a relationship with Laura is an added resource for the children in her classroom. All children, whatever their risk status, can benefit from contact with Laura. She very clearly understands the role that this relationship plays in the lives of these children, and she uses it skillfully as a teacher. She "draws on" this resource when children are stressed or challenged, and as evident in the example above, Laura's relationships with children provide the sense of security they need to explore and to master these challenges.

Vulnerable

Barbara, a teacher with 5 years of experience, is considered an above-average third-grade teacher by her supervisor, who describes Barbara as "struggling this year." Barbara is not married and has no children. She is active politically in progressive causes. She works in a school in which a large number of "at-risk" children are served; one year, there were several children in her class with whom she perceived herself to have a "dysfunctional" relationship. The histories of these children's relationship experiences demonstrated the social impoverishment and moderate neglect that characterizes the form of risk described in earlier chapters. Barbara completed the STRS on all the children in her classroom, and her averaged score on the Conflict scale was above the 80th percentile, indicating that she experienced a considerable amount of anger and conflict across all her relationships with students in the classroom. She looked harried and stressed most of the time. Her high classroom-level STRS scores were a signal to the supervisor to provide support and assistance to Barbara although Barbara refrained from contact with the supervisor, with whom she had been in conflict in the past.

During this school year, the school staff had invited a psychologist–consultant to meet with them biweekly for 2 hours. This fairly small school had a staff of 35. The staff was hoping to use the consultant's expertise to understand more about the causes of some of the behavior problems the children presented and how they might respond to these problems. The consultant took a strong stance for empowering the teachers to solve problems using their own expertise and knowledge and using the group to devise solutions. She did focus on encouraging teachers to safely express their emotional experience of the classroom and to provide information on the relationship-based perspective described in earlier chapters as a means of understanding teacher and child experience. This plan for the consultant's involvement was devised jointly with the teachers in the first couple of meetings.

During one session toward the middle of the school year, Barbara began to talk about a situation that she faced in her classroom regarding compliance. This issue was pervasive among the school staff. The specific precipitating incident was that a child would not hang up his coat when asked by Barbara. She noted his inconsistency: "Some days he's fine with this, other days it's a defiant 'no,' and I can't figure out why this is the case . . . why one time and why not another. . . . Is it something I am doing? What should I do?" Barbara was also very concerned about the consequences for her standing with other kids if she allows this child to have control and said, "I don't want them to see him running the show; otherwise, I'll lose the rest of them."

Barbara described how disheartened and guilty she felt when she got into the "consequence" cycle with her students.

> It feels punitive to me. . . . I'm just getting after them for one thing or another. . . . I admit sometimes it feels good to "get them," but I know it's not constructive and probably hurts my connection with them. One day I was feeling stressed . . . it seemed they were all worked up; it was a holiday or something, and I was thinking also about some stuff that was happening in the school that I did not like, and I asked Henry to put away some materials we were working with. He refused. I went through the usual warnings and "name on the board" consequences, but he kept on going. We got into it. I ended up putting him in time out, and he ran out of the room. I thought to myself, "Now what do I do?" I ran after him, grabbed him as he went up the hall and took him to the office. He screamed the whole way, spitting at me and trying to hit me. Yuk.

Clearly, this teacher was very involved with her students, but the emotional quality of this involvement was very low. She appeared depressed as she spoke. This anecdote was revealing of Barbara's awareness of the difficulties that she was having with Henry, that this was, in part, an interactional or relational problem, and that at times, these problems were exacerbated by her own emotional state. Nonetheless, she does not seem to be able to use this awareness to pull herself out of these situations and to respond more neutrally to the child involved. She is looking for ways to understand and prevent these situations and to repair some of these relationships, especially with Henry.

Henry is a 9-year-old boy who had been retained in kindergarten. His risk profile is high. His father is unknown to him, and his mother has had a series of fairly violent and dangerous relationships with men over the past several years. Henry, his mother, and two little brothers (by different fathers) live in a housing project that is frequented by drug dealers. There is no playground, and children play in the street. Henry's mother is intermittently employed, and is on and off welfare. Currently, she is working as a nursing assistant at the local hospital and has hopes of going to community college. Social service agencies have been involved with the family for many years; at one point when Henry was 4 years old, his mother was investigated for child neglect when the children were left alone in the home for several hours and were found wandering around the apartment complex. Observations of Henry with his mother, during a home visit conducted by Barbara, showed Henry to be quite noncompliant and hostile toward her, often using profane and threatening language. His mother appeared equally hostile and emotionally distant. Their interactions were not positive.

Henry has few age-appropriate developmental skills. He does not yet read at a first-grade level and he seems impulsive and aggressive with other children, although he has friends in the class that seem to genuinely like him. He is an attractive boy with an engaging smile.

A teacher of high-risk students, Barbara is at risk herself of leaving the profession of teaching. Her relationship with Henry indicates her feelings about teaching in general. Discussions with the supervisor and the psychologist in this school indicate that they think Barbara can be a very effective teacher, but this year it has been hard. They are at a loss as to how to help her. The consultant suggests to Barbara that they try to work together for a few weeks to see whether they can devise a plan for interacting with Henry (and others) that she finds helpful. She agrees, saying "just these group sessions have been helpful already; at least I know someone is listening."

The consultant conducted a series of classroom observations over the course of a 2-week period. On the basis of the first week's observations, it was apparent that the needs of the children in Barbara's class were beginning to overwhelm her. Predictable routines were not apparent in the morning. The children entered the room and milled about with little direction, and this was a time when some of them seemed to get into trouble. Barbara noted that she displays rules for the children to follow. At the start of the day, Barbara spent little or no time with the children in which there was an opportunity for extended (even 30 seconds) interaction. Barbara's time seemed to be spent moving from one child to another, almost moving constantly about the room, or sitting at her desk feeling and looking tired. She remarked, "I have to be everywhere at all times or things can break loose." No wonder she felt tired. The patterns evident in the first week became even more clear and extreme in the second week of observations, when the news was shared that the mother of one of the boys in the classroom had been murdered. Barbara also shared that she was worried about the health of her seriously ill mother, who lived alone in a nearby state.

During the observation periods, Barbara and Henry frequently engaged in cycles of negative interaction that were usually initiated by either Barbara's request for Henry's compliance or what appeared to be Henry's baiting of Barbara. In these instances of baiting, which often occurred while Barbara was at her desk, Henry would gaze frequently in Barbara's direction and then become involved in an altercation with another child over toys or materials. Barbara would approach Henry, Henry would claim that he was not involved, and Barbara would often blame Henry and start the cycle of consequences. However, on many other occasions, most often during structured instructional time with Henry and Barbara in a small group, Henry was attentive and compliant and engaged with Barbara in a more positive manner.

These observations confirmed the negative cycles of interaction between Barbara and Henry that were initially reported in the staff consultation. They also indicated that despite Barbara's interpretation of Henry as "always after me," there were moments of fairly positive interaction between the two of them. The observations also indicated Barbara's tendency to escalate the negative cycles with a somewhat inappropriate use of consequences and, more important, her tendency to nag Henry (and other students) and to make comments indicating to the children that she felt hurt or betrayed by their disobedience and noncompliance. These were often subtle comments, but nonetheless revealing.

During the period of observation and information gathering in the consultation, the consultant administered the TRI to Barbara about her relationship with Henry. She reported,

> I don't really like teaching this year, and I'm seriously thinking about leaving at the end of the year. I don't seem to be getting anything out of it anymore. The kids are demanding, and I'm having a tough time getting on top of what's going on in the classroom. I miss having a special connection with the kids like I had with a bunch of my kids last year. I think those connections energized me a bit. That's what it's like with Henry, why I said my relationship with him is disappointing. It takes too much out of me.

In reflecting on Barbara's experience and situation, the following questions may be helpful:

1. In what particular ways do Barbara's statements map onto the model of teacher–child relationships presented earlier?
2. What role do her relationships with students play in Barbara's model of herself as a teacher?
3. What are her representations or beliefs and feelings about relationships with children, and how are these affected by experiences with particular children?
4. Can Barbara perceive these relationships and their effects on herself and on her students? Can she discuss elements of relationships like feedback mechanisms? Or is she so caught up in her experience, or defensive about it, that she does not indicate an awareness of relationship processes?

It should be clear that relationships are important to Barbara, as noted earlier; but they are almost too important. One should note some of the differences between the way that Barbara discusses relationships and the way that Laura discussed them in the first case study. Barbara portrays herself as needing and wanting emotional support from the children, to some extent. She engages in interactions consistent with this—she calls attention to her emotional needs and how the children's behavior is connected to her emotional state. This contrasts with Laura's focus on the children's autonomy and a sense of clarity regarding the roles that she and the children have in relation to one another. In Barbara's case, the asymmetric nature of the adult–child relationship has been somewhat compromised. This creates a difficult situation for her in that she does not have good control over the class; at the same time, she requires the emotional support (that she defines) to be present when children comply. These difficulties also undermine her role as an instructor, adding to her sense of ineffectiveness and neediness.

After the consultant had shared some information regarding the patterns of interaction observed in the class, particularly with respect to her and Henry, Barbara requested individual consultation sessions. It was soon clear that Barbara felt emotionally "squeezed," as she put it, by her work with the children in her class as well as in her relations with supervisors and other staff. In addition to problems with children, she felt isolated from staff and suspicious of her supervisors. She told the consultant after the first 20-minute meeting that she felt relieved to have discussed these concerns, especially those regarding the supervisors.

Barbara's supervisors, predictably, asked the consultant to help her cooperate in some of the team problem-solving meetings that they were using; they spent a great deal of time trying to convince the consultant that the problems Barbara was having were due to her mistaken approach to the children. The consultant listened to these impressions but did not agree, framing the concerns in terms of the need for supportive relationships within the entire system. The consultant noted the nature of the agreement with Barbara and indicated that the problem-solving meetings were a separate matter.

The consultation plan involved individual sessions with Barbara, classroom observations by the consultant, and two instances of videotaping classroom interactions for later review by the consultant and Barbara. Although Barbara often focused on children in general, the consultant used Barbara's relationship with Henry as the focus of their work together, with the overall goal of improving this relationship—reducing negative emotions in their interactions, increasing asymmetry (e.g., helping Barbara regain her role as teacher, helper, socialization agent), increasing Barbara's sense of autonomy and emotional independence, helping Barbara understand the role her emotions played in cycles of negative interactions, and identifying strategies for her to address emotional needs separate from the children.

In the individual sessions, the consultant focused Barbara's attention on the role that her emotions played in situations with Henry. This entailed some discussion of the different ways that Henry reacted to her, and that she felt, depending on her own needs at the time (tired, rested, etc.). These discussions often involved references to classroom observations made by the consultant and were also stimulated by the review of the videotapes of classroom interaction. When reviewing the tapes, Barbara made several comments indicating her awareness of the inappropriateness of some of her comments to children regarding her needs for emotional support from them, especially Henry. Infused in these discussions was the consultant's support for Barbara's perceptions of herself in relation to Henry, and affirmation of her desires to help him. Barbara was angry at Henry's mother. She said, "I don't understand why she neglects him. . . . How can she do those things." She empathized with Henry in the following: "I guess I really like him; I'm frustrated that I don't seem to be able to take care of all his problems; maybe I can't and that's ok . . . maybe I can be helpful by just being his teacher."

It soon became clear that Barbara's desires to help created situations in which she "overempathized" with the children, especially Henry, among others. Barbara felt so deeply about the hurts that Henry had experienced that she "took on" his hurts as her own, making it difficult to sort out where he stood emotionally, especially in situations in which Henry (one of these "damaged" children) would attack her physically or verbally. Thus, Barbara was often confused by emotionally charged situations in the classroom, and as would be expected, she acted inconsistently and unpredictably toward Henry. In the same episode, she would try to approach Henry as calm and supportive and then struggle with him when this support did not work; finally, the struggle would escalate to the kind of situations requiring physical restraint and time-out.

These consultation sessions were very similar to individual therapy in the sense that most of what was involved was talking, and the "intervention" often involved the consultant's offering interpretations of Barbara's behavior and impressions. However, there is a very notable difference between these sessions and psychotherapy: the very clear focus on teacher–child relationships. In this consultation, the consultant clearly focused on these relationships, connecting most of what Barbara shared with her emerging understanding of how these relationships worked. In one sense, the "client" of the consultant was Barbara's relationship with Henry. Having this focus, informed by the theory described in earlier chapters, allowed these sessions to be targeted at classroom processes and problem focused.

Once the patterns of her relationship with Henry were identified, the consultant and Barbara planned several changes. One was to help her distance herself emotionally from Henry's "hurts" so that she could actually help him. This was accomplished through a series of observations that Barbara conducted of Henry's behavior. The consultant asked Barbara to observe a set of behaviors in several different situations in which Henry was involved. The behaviors included many competencies that the consultant had observed. Barbara made three such observations and remarked, "It's interesting to see how well he does with some of the other kids; he also seems to do better in structured situations—like in small groups. I wonder if large groups or less structure don't offer him enough support . . . makes sense knowing what home is like." Barbara slowly began to have a more differentiated view of Henry's development—one that included both competencies and vulnerabilities and, also important, a view that acknowledged the connection between situational support (e.g., affordances) and his competence. This emerging view of Henry allowed Barbara to see him less as "damaged" and more as "complex."

A second change was to develop a script for situations that typically led to emotionally charged interactions between the two of them. Having an awareness of situational affordances for Henry's competence, it was now important that Barbara experience her relationship with Henry as one of those affordances. The script involved Barbara's use of physical proximity and attention to Henry early in sequences that often led to problems and more proximity and contact throughout the day, even at predictable intervals. This was combined with her de-emphasizing verbalization and verbal problem-solving approaches that she often used with Henry (e.g., saying "you are making a bad choice now, Henry; can you tell me what a better choice would be?"). Barbara and the consultant rehearsed the script while viewing videotapes of her in the classroom, testing alternative approaches and projecting responses to a variety of scenarios. This strategy gave Barbara a clear mental image of her goals for interaction with Henry as well as a set of strategies for interaction that could be easily accessed because they had been rehearsed and linked to her classroom context. Barbara took this on with enthusiasm, and it was clear that some early successes were empowering to her. She began a book-reading ritual with Henry and some other children right after lunch each day (formerly at time of some disorganization). Henry sat with her and listened attentively as she read, and the rest of the class worked in "centers" or on projects; soon, other children asked to join the group. Barbara interpreted this very positively. She noted,

> I feel more clear about who I am with them now, and they seem to want to be with me. . . . Henry eats up our time together . . . he doesn't even seem too bothered by the other kids wanting to join the group . . . it's now a real ritual for a lot of kids, and the contact with them is positive for me and for them, I think. It's amazing too how I don't seem to be getting into it with them as much; lots of time I just try to come by and be next to them. . . . I feel like I have some influence just by being there.

The third change was to become less involved with supervisors until she became more confident in her interactions in the classroom. Barbara mentioned to them that she did not see a need to attend the problem-solving meetings while she was involved in the consultation, and after several weeks of work with the consultant, she invited her immediate supervisor to observe in the classroom. Finally, Barbara initiated a plan to engage in brief, short-term supportive counseling outside of school.

Once this plan had been initiated, the consultation lasted 6 weeks. A post-consultation STRS administered to Barbara for her relationships with Henry and four other randomly chosen children revealed a drop in her Conflict score (averaged across the five relationships) to approximately the 50th percentile. She indicated an interest in terminating the consultation but wished to have some form of follow-up. The consultant, who spent 2 half-days in the school each week, checked in with Barbara weekly for a couple of minutes for a period of 6 more weeks, reminding her often that change happens slowly and that sometimes things slip back a bit. There were no other concerns about this class for the remainder of the year, and Barbara actively participated in the ongoing group consultation sessions with the whole staff.

This case reflects many aspects of the developmental systems view of relationships described in the previous chapters. As suggested by the questions presented above, Barbara's representations of relationships with children, especially Henry, challenge her ability to be a stable and secure emotional figure in the classroom. As in the systems perspective, Barbara's representations are influenced by her interactions with children and also by her interactions with other adults—supervisors—and her worries about her own attachment figure. Understandably, these circumstances confused Barbara, and the first step in the consultation process was to elicit these feelings, experiences, and representations. Once elicited, problem solving to improve relationships could proceed.

Barbara's behavior in and discussion of important relationships was consistent with a pattern of mild-to-moderate overinvolvement, dependency, and preoccupation with others' emotional experiences. This pattern of overinvolvement made her vulnerable to the emotional vicissitudes of her surroundings—"damaged" children, harsh supervisors, and inadequate parents. Instead of having an anchor in her own emotional world apart from others', Barbara was buffeted by others' emotions. Understandably, she felt angry a lot, in part because it was hard for her to understand her feelings and their intensity. It is important that she was not so angry as to be closed off from examining her feelings and her role in the relationships that produce these feelings. Consistent with research on adults' representational models of attachment, in which a pattern of overinvolvement and preoccupation has been described, Barbara's relationships with children tended to produce similar feelings of anxiety, vulnerability, and dependency in the children.

This consultation differed somewhat from "problem-focused" consultation in the sense that there was a time of eliciting Barbara's emotional experience of the "problem," as she defined it. (The group consultation followed by administration of the TRI provided the impetus and the structure for these expressions.) Thus, the period of "identifying the problem" involved fairly extensive discussions of emotions, beliefs, and attitudes that were experienced by Barbara in a range of relationships that were important to her.

Throughout the process, the consultant viewed her role as one of working with Barbara's system of relationships toward the end of enhancing the quality of relationships she had with the children in her class, with a particular focus on Henry. This case clearly demonstrates the need to consider the system of relationships experienced by teachers and how patterns of representation and interaction in this system can affect representations and interactions at the teacher–child level.

"All's Well"

This case presents a third relationship pattern or style. In contrast to the cases involving Barbara and Laura, Wendy tends to form relationships with children that lack attention to emotion or dependency; her relationships are characterized by low involvement and a degree of avoidance of close emotional contact.

Wendy has taught fifth grade for 8 years and taught above the third-grade level for 13 years. She now teaches fifth grade in an affluent suburban school district bordering an urban area. She is described by other staff as a "nice person . . . keeps to herself . . . don't really know her that well."

Wendy's general tendencies toward perceiving children's emotional needs were to diminish or to dismiss relationship needs or dependency. Her beliefs were very strongly oriented toward encouraging independence in the children in her classroom. She firmly believed that child autonomy was a function of not reinforcing children's dependent behavior. Wendy often spoke in very glowing terms about different children in her class— she always seemed to have a favorite, and, in fact, it was tough to get her to speak in negative terms about anything related to teaching. To most observers, Wendy's classroom seemed like an inviting place for fifth graders; she seemed to treat her students with respect.

When an STRS profile was done in Wendy's classroom, three patterns were very clearly represented. The limitations of self-report are evident here, in that these scores reflect only Wendy's perceptions of her relationships. Relationships with one group of children were characterized by average scores for all three scales (Conflict, Closeness, and Dependency) at or near the 50th percentile (a Functional/Average profile), whereas another group was characterized by average scores on Closeness near the 80th percentile. The third group was consistent with a disengaged pattern, in which scores were very low on all three STRS subscales (see Pianta, 1994, regarding disengaged pattern, STRS subscales). These results indicated that Wendy believed relationships were fine with most children in her class; the fact, though, that she reported such low engagement with one group of children suggested the need for a closer look. If asked whether she had any concerns about these relationships she had characterized as disengaged, Wendy responded, " I really like them all very much."

Wendy was administered the TRI concerning her relationship with a particular girl in the class, Deborah. Wendy's relationship with Deborah was of interest because this relationship fit the disengaged pattern above; that is, it appeared that Wendy was not particularly close to Deborah, although no overriding problems or concerns were noted either.

When asked for two words to describe her relationship with Deborah, Wendy used the words "fun" and "encouraging." Wendy described her enjoyment in encouraging Deborah to expand her academic skills. "Deborah and I had just finished reading a book together. She did a very good job with her reading and when I complimented her, she asked me if she could go and read the book to one of her classmates. I was really proud of her."

Wendy felt that she and Deborah really "clicked" right from the start.

"On the very first day of school, Deborah came into my class with a wonderful attitude, a smiling face. She seemed very relaxed and ready to work." When asked whether there was ever a time when she and Deborah really were not clicking, Wendy shook her head and said, "None that I can think of. She's always a happy child and well behaved." When asked whether she ever doubted that she was meeting Deborah's needs, Wendy again shook her head and said, "No."

The interview lasted 12 minutes. Wendy's pattern of responses is similar to the responses of adults who downplay the significance of emotions. In fact, the emphasis on uniformly positive characteristics of a relationship, in the absence of details supporting these characterizations, as well as the tendency toward neutralization or veering away from questions pertaining to negative affect closely parallel the behavioral and narrative profiles of adults whose representational models of attachment and parenting would be characterized as somewhat idealizing or dismissing. One should note the contrast of this pattern of responses with that of Laura, who spoke positively about her relationship with Elliott but could also acknowledge negative experiences and integrate them within an overall picture of the relationship as positive. Furthermore, Laura also provided detailed, specific descriptions of her positive characterizations, something Wendy does not do even when probed. Wendy's interview suggests a lack of collaboration with the interviewer and a tendency not to be at ease with the topic.

Wendy's responses to the TRI are of interest because of their consistency with the pattern of responses usually shown by adults who have similar tendencies to downplay the significance of emotion, relationships, and vulnerability. In interviews concerning attachment-related experiences and representations, these adults often respond with very short answers, lack memory for significant events, and have difficulty providing evidence for their characterizations of relationships; when they do respond with detail, it is typically positive in tone. Thus, there is often an overriding inconsistency between the global characterization of the relationship in positive terms and the evidence for that characterization, a pattern described as "idealizing." In relationships and interactions with children, these adults tend to focus on tasks and materials rather than on emotional signals and to actually ignore signals of mild or even moderate distress (Main & Goldwyn, 1994), leaving the children to fend for themselves. The developmental histories of individuals with these response styles indicate that close relationships were often not available and that attachment figures stressed independence. There may also be evidence of somewhat rejecting or neglecting parenting, especially with respect to situations in which the child expressed dependency.

It is not clear whether this style of representing relationships posed problems for the children in Wendy's classroom in the same way that Barbara's relational style posed some problems. At face value, Wendy's approach to forming relationships with children in her class seems to serve most of them well. The class, by and large, was orderly and appeared productive. On the basis of Wendy's own report, her relationship with Deborah was positive, and Wendy provided little reason to believe otherwise.

Yet Deborah's relationship history suggested clear difficulties with establishing a sense of trust in adults to be responsive under times of distress. Deborah was one of four children. Her highly successful parents were very focused on their work, with little time for Deborah or for the other children, who were primarily cared for in a string of formal child-care settings that were notorious for high staff turnover rates and large group care. Both parents stressed achievement, and Deborah reported that it was "real important to get good grades and behave . . . mom needs me to do that." Deborah loved her third-grade teacher, Yvonne, who by Deborah's report was "great, she gave hugs all the time, sometimes I could even spend time with her by myself. She liked to see my drawings and listen to me read." When asked about Wendy, Deborah reported, "She's ok, but I'm not sure if she likes me . . . I just try to do my work." On the Relatedness scale completed by Deborah, she scored high on psychological proximity seeking (indicating a need for contact with adults) and low on emotional quality, endorsing feelings such as scared, sad, and nervous in relation to Wendy.

Deborah was made vulnerable by Wendy's tendency to steer away from affection and emotional contact. Although Deborah could keep to herself in the classroom, getting her work done and rarely interacting with Wendy (except to show her things she had done well), it was clear that on many occasions, Deborah required an adult's assistance and did not appear confident in the possibility of obtaining Wendy's help. Academically, Deborah was in the middle of the class, and her parents were putting pressure on her. Wendy agreed with Deborah's parents that she could work harder. She worked hard and was temperamentally an easy child to get along with, but her performance was generally poor. Nonetheless, she almost never asked for help nor did she show indications of distress, at least not around Wendy. Instead, Deborah almost appeared to mask her poor performance, and her interactions with Wendy at times had an "overbright," almost staged quality to them, as if the two were performing a script. When stressed, Deborah seemed to withdraw, not engaging peers or Wendy. During the classroom observations, Deborah could appear at times to be quite self-reliant and content in her activities, confidently approaching Wendy when she completed an activity. On these occasions, they exchanged many smiles, and Wendy praised Deborah. However, when Deborah struggled with a task, she would look at Wendy but not approach. If Wendy noticed Deborah's struggles, she would offer mild, firm encouragement, usually from a distance and usually verbally.

Thus, the emphasis in this classroom on not seeking adult resources when needed had consequences for Deborah's performance and probably for her self-esteem. The situation is made more complex because Wendy's relational style is reinforced by the fact that independence is highly valued in schools (especially by the fifth grade). This almost ensures that Deborah, in this and in many other classrooms, will not find it easy and comfortable to get close enough to an adult to ask for and to receive the support she perceives that she needs.

Sroufe (1989b) and others have written about the mistaken notions of independence, autonomy, and self-reliance that pervade cultural values and perceptions of adult–child relationships. Instead of viewing self-reliance as some trait acquired by the child and manifest in terms of "not needing" adult help, Sroufe argued that self-reliance is a relationship-level construct. That is, the child is secure enough in him- or herself, and in the context of a relationship with an adult (teacher or parent), to confidently explore his or her environment and to master challenges, but when challenges exceed their resources, the child comfortably and appropriately seeks the adult's assistance.

This negotiation between the child and the adult over exploration and assistance does not end when the child enters school, nor can one predict success by whether assistance seeking was reinforced. Rather, developing self-reliance in the context of adult–child relationships is a process that continues through young adulthood and almost paradoxically, the truly self-reliant children and adults are usually those whose bids for help have been responded to consistently and sensitively by adults.

Thus, the case of Wendy illustrates a paradox for the consultant interested in promoting child–teacher relationships that enhance self-esteem. Wendy's relational style downplays children's dependency at the same time schools value independence. In this case, the consultant will have great difficulty "getting the message across" to Wendy to be more responsive and, for example, to seek out Deborah and to offer help. Work with parents with similar profiles suggests that progress is quite slow. Perhaps the best solution in Deborah's case is to identify adults in the school context who can provide the kind of emotional security that she needs and to encourage those relationships.

Summary

The relationships that teachers form with children, although important sources of support or stress to the children, affect teachers' sense of themselves and, in turn, are affected by the teachers' current and past relationships. Thus, teacher–child relationships are embedded in a system of relationships that itself has a history and a developmental trajectory. In this way, child–teacher relationships cannot be easily reduced to the interactions one might observe in the classroom, and no single assessment device adequately describes such a relationship. Influencing child–teacher relationships involves entry into this relationship system. The first step in this process is listening to teachers describe their relationships in their own words, listening to children describe relationships with teachers, and observing relationship-related interactions and processes. This approach to understanding relationships is informed and aided by the assessment procedures presented in chapter 5. Results obtained from those procedures were evident in the cases just discussed.

Furthermore, these case studies portray how child–teacher relationships function to support (or to inhibit) a child's movement through a zone of proximal development (ZPD). As was noted earlier, the extent to which a child will perform at an optimal level depends on the extent to which his or her immediate context affords, or provides resources for, performance through a blend of support and challenge. The child–teacher relationship is clearly one of the important parts of this context. In viewing how child–teacher relationships function with respect to the ZPD, readers should keep in mind some basic principles related to the developmental model described in chapter 3.

First, functioning in the ZPD is best understood in terms of the developmental model described earlier. In this model, child competence is understood as encompassing broad qualities of adaptation with respect to phases or key developmental challenges or themes (e.g., attachment, self-reliance, etc.). It is important that organizations or strategies that are useful in adapting to early themes remain latent, and available, to the child, even in response to later themes; these will be mobilized in response to those themes or challenges if there is insufficient support to meet that challenge. Thus, when viewing a child's functioning in the ZPD, one should observe the ways that the child's functioning varies with different contexts or with changes in a particular context (e.g., child–teacher interactions).

Second, evidence of the child's use of strategies that are successful in "early" themes (e.g., avoiding a challenge, seeking physical or personal contact in the face of a challenge, using aggression or defiance as a means of self-assertion) can be interpreted within the developmental model as a signal for more support (or less challenge). A child's use of these signals requires that the context recalibrate itself to the child's perceived needs or state and either reduce challenge or increase support.

Finally, in the context of child–teacher relationships, teachers can provide support when they respond to children using strategies that functioned as supportive for those "early" modes of adaptation or developmental challenges. Thus, when the child seeks proximity because of perceived stress, the teacher (and thus the relationship) responds supportively by accepting proximity and providing comfort (probably in different forms for 5-year-olds and 9-year-olds). Aggression or defiance is interpreted as a signal of self-assertion and is responded to with appropriate limits (to define the boundaries of the self) and support for the intent of the action (recognizing and validating the self). In many of these interactions, responses that are gestural (using calm, warm tone of voice; proximity; predictable routines), contingent, and well timed (sensitive) will function most effectively as support. Responses that have a high representational load (verbal problem solving, encouraging too much choice or discussion) will add challenge to the situation.

These ideas about the ZPD now carry into a range of intervention strategies that can facilitate building and maintaining teacher–child relationships that function as developmental resources for children. The examples of child–teacher relationship functioning depicted in the three case studies presented in this chapter set the stage for the next three chapters, which more specifically address ways of intervening, at multiple levels, to enhance child–teacher relationships.

7

Supporting Teachers: The Key to Affecting Child–Teacher Relationships

> Ms. Thomas is an experienced teacher. With 22 years in the classroom, she is the most senior of the five first-grade teachers in this school. In her years of teaching, all in the same school division, she has witnessed a dramatic change in the student population, a change that worries her. She is concerned that 16 of the 18 children in her classroom live with a single adult in their home and that many of her students lack attention to basic needs such as clothing, food, or hygiene. Although considered a good teacher by her supervisors, Ms. Thomas admittedly is losing interest in trying to teach children who, she views, are not taken care of by the community or family. She voices a feeling of being "tired and frustrated" by these circumstances. The most bothersome issue faced by Ms. Thomas, according to her report, is the increase in disruptive and "disrespectful" behavior on the part of children in her classroom and her feelings of simply not being able to reach children and connect with them. She feels that this makes the management of her classroom very difficult and that she has to spend too much time on behavior management and not enough time on instruction. She reports considerable concerns with several specific children who "push my buttons." She is getting to the point with some students that she is convinced they cannot be helped—she feels they are intentionally targeting her with their misbehavior. She is thinking of taking early retirement and leaving teaching.

This is an all-too-frequent example of an experienced teacher at the end of her rope. This veteran teacher is tired. She watches as cohorts of children come to school less and less prepared to take advantage of what she feels she has to offer. She feels as if her classroom is saturated with risk. Like many of her peers, she will either leave teaching altogether in the next few years or will slowly disengage from her students and from the school. Although this particular teacher has 22 years of service behind her, many of her less experienced peers have the same feelings.

The focus of this chapter is on practices that are designed to enhance the relationships that Ms. Thomas and her peers form with individual students in their classrooms. These practices target several aspects of the experience of teaching. They provide (a) a means of helping teachers understand their relationship experiences with children and (b) a set of intervention techniques that can be used to establish effective relationships with particular students with whom a teacher feels especially frustrated. Chapters 8 and 9 target classroom and school-level practices that enhance relationships.

Working With Teachers: A Focus on Relationships

The challenge for the psychologist working with Ms. Thomas and her peers is to find ways of reestablishing her psychological connection to her work: her motivation and her emotional investment. This could take many specific forms, but one assumes here that teachers teach, fundamentally, because they are motivated, in part, by their relationships with children. They wish to feel connected to and to influence the lives of children. Thus, the psychological connection of this teacher to her work is through her relationships with her students.

Think of the typical inservice activity—you are the presenter. Half the school staff (teachers and aides) is sitting in the school library after school. They are tired. You wonder if they will listen to you. The principal goes through the list of announcements. Now it's your turn. What can you tell them about relationships with children?

In one of my attempts at this task, I launched into a discussion of the phases of the development of self-regulation, the role of relationships with adults in the developmental process, and some techniques for enhancing relationships—with a sidebar discussion of how contingency management fits in. It was abysmal, and I wanted to leave after about 5 minutes.

In my second attempt at this task, with the other half of the school staff, I started with what makes them feel good and bad about their experiences with different children. I tried to engage the staff in something like a "group" TRI. Almost immediately, we launched into a discussion of the teachers' feelings about working with the children in their classes—what they found rewarding and frustrating. The discussion was interactive and flowed rapidly from one experience to another. In the course of the discussion, it was easy to tie these experiences to the model of self-regulation, relationships with adults, and classroom practices that had been the outline of the earlier inservice.

What differed across these two inservices? One might argue (convincingly) that the second session simply reflected good teaching practices—starting with a focus on the learners' experiences and using those to make a conceptual point. To a large degree, that was true. But the topic—teachers' experiences of relationships with children—was a big factor in creating the energetic discussion that took place, because it was the focus of the teachers' emotions. It is interesting that allowing adults (teachers or parents) to freely voice their experiences of relationships with children—in other words, to allow them to reveal or to narrate their representational model of the relationship—is an opportunity they welcome and approach enthusiastically (Pianta & Button, 1997). In a recent project using the TRI discussed in chapter 5, research staff were quite reluctant to ask teachers to narrate their feelings about relationships with children. As the project progressed, it became clear that teachers really enjoyed these interviews, even the ones that could be perceived as difficult, and found them rewarding and often the source of new insights. Again, relationships with children are clearly on the minds (and often hearts) of teachers.

My point here is that relationships with children are a very relevant and salient feature of teachers' experiences, in and out of the classroom. Allowed the opportunity to examine, reveal, and discuss these experiences, teachers will engage. These experiences are often critical determinants of teachers' own feelings about their worth in the classroom (and their efficacy) as well as influences on their behavior toward the child.

One can recall Ms. Thomas in the anecdote with which this chapter began. She was emotionally tired, and her experience of relationships with children was not consistent with what she wanted, and probably needed, from those relationships. She finds herself increasingly in "lock-up" with children—feeling angry at them and knowing that they also feel angry and isolated from her, neither being able to move out of this negative pattern. Her classroom average STRS Conflict score increased over the course of the last couple of years and was now above the 60th percentile. Yet Ms. Thomas is a valuable resource to this school division, school, and classroom—her years of experience are sources of wisdom and guidance for children and staff.

The present chapter describes ways to work with relationship experiences and teachers' representations of these experiences, as is the case for Ms. Thomas, and to strengthen relationships between teachers and children. In this way, these interventions attempt to harness the preventive influence of child–teacher relationships for all children, in part, by better using these relationships in relation to supporting children in the ZPD. The following sections discuss three ways of working with teachers to affect their relationships with children through (a) giving teachers information, (b) working with their representations of relationships, and (c) interacting directly with a child.

This discussion of the practice of child and adolescent psychology in the schools assumes a problem-solving orientation with respect to the role of the psychologist vis-à-vis the concerns noted (e.g., Goldstein, 1993; Knoff & Curtis, 1996). That is, the psychologist explicitly views his or her role to be one of applying psychological theory and techniques to enhance the capacity of children and teachers to perform competently in the classroom environment. Primary professional concerns are not regarding whether children should or should not be referred for evaluation, what particular diagnosis they might have, how their family treats them, or even why they behave the way they do.

Using the version of a problem-solving orientation advocated here, the psychologist is to approach the case functionally—how best can knowledge of child–teacher relationship systems be applied to enhance the functioning of a teacher and a child? This approach involves interpreting current classroom practices (e.g., instruction, grouping, behavior management) from the perspective of child–teacher relationships, understanding what the child and the teacher bring to their relationship with one another (e.g., individual characteristics that affect their relationship), applying the model of development and relationships with assessment approaches to gain new and fresh perspectives on the relationship, and, finally, using the techniques described here to develop a strategy for improving and strengthening the relationship or relationships. Thus, the philosophy underlying the application of theory is a problem-solving orientation in which the school psychologist is expected to assume a consultant role or to intervene directly with a teacher, generating hypotheses and possible solutions based on the theory of relationships as dyadic systems (Goldstein, 1993; Gutkin & Conoley, 1990; Meyers et al., 1979; O'Keefe & Medway, 1997). Within the present focus on teacher–child relationships, in few cases will the psychologist work directly with the child or the family.

One should recall the model of child–teacher relationships as a dyadic system. The present chapter focuses on the teacher (and indirectly on the child) components of that model. The chapter discusses interventions that target teachers' knowledge about relationships with children in general; perceptions, feelings, and biases that teachers may have about specific children's relationship behavior toward them; and ways that teachers can implement practices to alter relationship interactions with specific children. By focusing on the teacher, several aspects of the child–teacher relationship system will be affected. One principle that becomes apparent in this discussion (and in subsequent chapters) is that the separate practices discussed with respect to strengthening teacher–child relationships are not isolated from one another; applying these practices in concert or in combination strengthens the possibility of changing the overall quality and functioning of the relationship in a way that can be self-sustaining. Although the goal of the set of interventions described in this and in the next two chapters is to change relationship systems, this chapter targets the teacher as a means of accessing these systems.

Giving Teachers Information

There is a need to inform teachers of the developmental perspective on children and relationships that has been outlined in earlier chapters. Most teachers have taken only one or two courses in child development, most often at the undergraduate level more than 10 years ago, and their classes were frequently focused on cognitive, not socioemotional, development (Goodlad, 1991; Pianta & Walsh, 1996). Thus, their knowledge of development is limited to a somewhat distorted (by others) interpretation of Piagetian theory—what Walsh (1991) called "vulgar Piagetian" theory. To the extent that teachers understand children's social development, their understanding is informed by a combination of Piagetian theory (e.g., this child is at concrete operations), behaviorism (children's behavior is a function of reinforcement), and a view that the family is somehow implicated in school adjustment. Recent training in early childhood education has emphasized Vygotsky's perspectives on learning, although other than noting the social nature of instruction, this perspective does not specify features of interaction or social relationships that support or inhibit child performance in the ZPD.

What are not well understood, even by teachers trained in recent years, are the social processes inherent in instruction and learning (Resnick, 1994; Rogoff, 1990) and the wide variety of ways in which children acquire and display competent forms of skill production. With respect to the central thesis of this book, teachers have not been systematically exposed to an understanding of the role of relationships in social development (and the acquisition of other skills), the meaning of children's relationship-oriented behavior toward them, and the role that their own relationship biases and tolerances may play in relationships that they form in the classroom. If their understanding of these processes was more thorough, teachers would have more tools to make informed "local" decisions in the classroom.

In this way, there is a role for delivering information to teachers that can help them better understand the behavior of children in their classrooms. The theoretical base provided in earlier chapters is a set of knowledge that can be transmitted to teachers. Core elements that can be included are (a) the key themes of socioemotional development, (b) the role of relationships in socialization, (c) the definitions of relationships and their components, (d) the recognition of relationships in trouble, and (d) the idea that instruction and learning are mediated by social processes.

Key Themes of Socioemotional Development

In chapter 3, it was suggested that emotion regulation processes and relationships between children and caregivers are themes of development in early childhood and in the elementary school period. This knowledge is by and large unavailable to many teachers, yet it is often helpful to them in understanding their experiences with and their observations of a particular child or children and has direct implications for classroom practice.

For example, one can look at practices related to behavior management and self-regulation for children in a third-grade classroom in a highly diverse, and somewhat high-risk, neighborhood school. For the teachers of these children, finding ways to manage the activity and the attention of the children and to focus their social behavior toward competent ends are tasks of enormous importance. Believing that children's self-regulation is enhanced by discussing social problems and feelings, making informed choices, and evaluating those choices, teachers (counselors and psychologists) focus a great deal of attention and intervention on verbal processes and on the use of language to mediate social and emotional experience. These are fundamentally representational processes that are being used to intervene with children whose behavior indicates that they are stressed by challenges present in this classroom environment.

Representational functioning is the hallmark of competence at this age; however, for many children, particularly those for whom the relationship experiences that give rise to the development of representational functioning (see chapter 3) have been impoverished, stressed, or inadequate, language is not the medium through which social conflict and difficult emotional experiences can be negotiated. As described in the discussion of key themes, in this classroom, symbols will not accomplish what caregiving behaviors or gestures will. Thus, the highly verbal nature of classroom discussions, class meetings, or one-on-one interchanges with teachers about "the choices you are making" may indeed confuse and overwhelm the child. For children whose relationship history has not provided the relationship infrastructure to make the connections among emotion, cognition, language, and behavior, it is helpful for teachers to learn to understand their social behavior as a function of their previous developmental history in relationships and in the current relationship environment—not just a matter of whether they are in "concrete operations." In turn, teachers can then understand the child's need for caregiving or gesture in these situations and can respond through using physical proximity, monitoring tone of voice, establishing routine contact, practicing contingent responsiveness, and decreasing transitions and increasing predictability. (See the case of Barbara in chapter 6 for an example of these kinds of interactions.)

Thus, teachers can come to understand the phases of socioemotional development outlined in chapter 3 (Greenspan, 1989; Sroufe, 1996) and can calibrate their behavior toward the child in terms of support and challenge, emphasizing the following principles. First, these phases are not stages in the sense that they reflect the child's functioning across all domains and situations involving social and emotional behavior. Nor do all children move through these phases in a specific sequence. Instead, children's functional capacity to process social and emotional experience varies as a function of the type of information and experience and of the resources available to them in the context. Thus, experience or information of a stressful nature (anger or conflict) in situations with little support (only peers available or teacher is nonsupportive) are likely to be met with a lower level processing capacity—in other words, with strategies that were successful for the child during earlier developmental challenges or themes. Words or symbols may not function for the child in these currently stressful situations in the same way they would if their experience were different (e.g., experiencing success or support) or the situation were different (interacting with aggressive peers on the playground vs. interacting with peers during circle time). This reflects a general rule that challenges or stress (of a social or emotional nature) in a situation are likely to induce a lower level processing response or a previously successful adaptation strategy from the child.

Second, children's processing of emotional–social experience is most sophisticated (i.e., most representational in form) in the context of a secure relationship with an adult. In this relationship, the adult is available and accepting, values the child's perspective, sets appropriate limits, and responds contingently and with warmth. Children will use words to process and to understand difficult emotions and, as a result, may display impulse control when the adult supporting them to do this is one with whom they feel close. How the child responds to difficult social experiences will depend on how safe, secure, and trusting he or she feels with the people present.

Third, it may be important to address teachers' ideas about how children's socioemotional competencies change over time. For many teachers trained in the behavioral tradition, change is a function of contingencies placed on discrete behaviors. From the relationship-systems perspective, the foci of change typically are not isolated, discrete behaviors but patterns and qualities of interactions that, in turn, create pressure on systems. Although changes in discrete behaviors are often desirable and important aspects of change, most teachers seek change of a more developmental nature—more stable across situations and time (Diaz & Berk, 1995). One can recall that the change of complex systems is a function of the interaction of these systems with one another; this interaction demonstrates principles of differentiation, integration, self-stabilization, and self-reorganization, with the relational context playing the central role in inducing change. Again, the focus is on the level of patterns of behavior. Thus, when multiple relationship systems (e.g., peers, teacher, family) are brought "on-line" to consistently challenge (and support) the child–teacher relationship, change of this form is more likely.

The Role of Relationships in Socioemotional Development

The role of relationships in socioemotional development has already been discussed in many ways; it is a key component of understanding that bridges the child's home and school experiences and his or her capacities. Information on the role of relationships in development provides the basic support for any further discussions of techniques to enhance child–teacher relationships.

Building on a discussion of the importance of relationships per se, one needs to clarify the particular components of relationships as they pertain to social and emotional functioning of children. The model for dyadic systems described in chapter 4 provides the detail for this knowledge. At the most basic level, teachers can come to understand how their relationships with children involve (a) qualities and experiences that each individual brings to the relationship (e.g., skills and abilities, developmental history), (b) representational models of adult–child relationships, and (c) feedback or exchange mechanisms between the teacher and the child. Each of these components can be described in ways that link to teachers' experiences with children and that illuminate these experiences in terms of the model of dyadic systems and development that has been described here. Examples of each have been provided in chapters 4 through 6.

Relationships in Trouble

To better harness child–teacher relationships as a preventive intervention, one should understand how important it is that teachers be given information about how to recognize relationships that are in trouble—by observing their own behavior or the child's behavior, or by examining their own representations (what they think and feel) about a relationship. This would be important for Ms. Thomas in the example at the beginning of the chapter. Teachers typically are not encouraged or permitted to engage in this kind of self-examination. It is important that such an examination should occur in the context of attempts to enhance relationships and with exposure to a theory. Similar to the anecdote of the inservice meeting described earlier, teachers need to have permission to explore their feelings about children, to examine their own relational styles and needs, and to recognize those markers of relationships in trouble. This is best done when the teachers themselves feel supported by relationships with colleagues, supervisors, or consultants. Schools can provide consultants to teacher discussion groups or make consultants available to individual teachers as part of a program of teacher support. Principals can also encourage and allow discussion of teachers' feelings and self-examination.

These markers for relationships in trouble often involve an experience of feeling "stuck" or "locked-up" in relation to a child, such as was the case for Ms. Thomas, or similarly, when a relationship fits one of the problematic relational patterns described in chapters 4 and 5 (Lynch & Cicchetti, 1992; Pianta, 1994). Thus, when assessed from either the teacher's or the child's perspective, a relationship is in "trouble" when either participant reports predominantly negative emotions regarding the relationship, a pattern of over- or underinvolvement, or both. Lock-up occurs when a teacher and child have certain scripted roles and interactions that produce negative feelings and experiences, such as when teachers feel that they cannot help but respond in certain (negative) ways to children, when their perceptions of children seem uniform (negative) and resistant to change or variation across situations, or when teachers find themselves expecting negative responses from children regardless of their own efforts. Other signs of relationships in trouble involve high and persistent conflict, disengagement, despair, and a sense of helplessness in affecting the child's behavior.

For teachers' self-examination to occur, the process needs to be valued in schools. Then, teachers need supportive relationships that permit discussions of their relationship experiences and their perceptions in a free and noncritical manner. Also, they need a theory for understanding their experiences in relationships. Thus, the psychologist working in a school can initiate ongoing, informal, consultation groups with teachers that are aimed at establishing these discussions among teachers and, at the same time, can offer a conceptual framework for the interpretation of their experience.

Finally, the psychologist may use an assessment tool, such as the STRS, asking teachers to complete the scale for all children in their classrooms (to gain a sense of relationship patterns in the class) or for one or two children about whom they are most concerned. This information will be helpful in describing the teachers' concerns and in elaborating on their nature. Interviews, such as the TRI, can be used to elicit greater detail on teachers' relationship experiences. Again, these activities fit best in the context of an accepting, supportive group consultation.

Social Processes Mediating Instruction

Educators often do not recognize that all or most of instruction involves social exchanges and emotional experiences—in the present case—between adults and children. Information for teachers can be helpful to understand these social processes, the way they change over time, and the role they have in inducing change. In imparting this information, it is important to label teachers' experiences and observations as consistent with a theory and knowledge base (see chapters 1–6) and to recognize the ways that risk can be understood in terms of these social, relationship-based processes.

Teachers' Representations of Relationships

Another major focus of psychologists' work with individual teachers, in an effort to improve their relationships with children, is on teachers' representations of relationships with children (individuals or children in general). For Ms. Thomas at the beginning of this chapter, helping her understand her experiences with children, how she represents these experiences, how her beliefs and expectations may affect her behavior, and how these experiences may be tied to her experiences in other relationships can be an important focus of re-energizing her work with children.

In several studies of elementary school teachers, involving more than a thousand teachers and many thousands of children, one item from the STRS, "Dealing with this child drains my energy," typifies the teacher who is frustrated and has a conflict with a child. Teachers endorsing this item often have high scores on relationship conflict. Ms. Thomas had several relationships in her classroom that were typified by this STRS item. This specific item and others on the Conflict dimension signal a teacher who is feeling out of control and ineffective in this relationship, probably for a variety of reasons. These are teachers for whom teacher–child relationship feedback or exchange processes with specific children are not functioning well. These teachers feel they cannot communicate with the child, and their feelings, beliefs, and perceptions about the child's behavior are often narrow, negative, and fixed. This feeling is exemplified when a teacher believes as follows: "He is *always* trying to make me angry . . . why does he do that? I wonder sometimes if he actually tries to get me going, almost like he knows that I'll be upset . . . like the other day when he tipped over a paint bucket . . . there *always* seems to be trouble around him . . . I talk about this to my husband so much he's tired of hearing it."

In this quotation from a TRI, the emphasis is on all exchanges with the child, the negative emotional tone, and the locus of blame in the child. In this context, even if the child did change his behavior, the teacher's expectations for negative interactions are ingrained in ways that make it difficult for her to perceive the child's more positive intentions or behaviors. In these cases, there is a need for intervention at the level of the individual teacher's representations of her relationships with children or with this child; these interventions are similar to those applied in the case of Barbara in chapter 6.

This situation is not at all unlike incidents with many parents, in which the adult's perceptions of the child's behavior is related to a variety of negative behaviors by the adult—nagging and repeating commands, using a harsh tone of voice, overcontrolling, blaming, and perhaps even baiting. The child, however, often contributes to these perceptions by displaying noncompliance, resistance, or passivity. This combination of mutually reinforcing negative behaviors and perceptions is characteristic of a relationship system in lock-up. Although there are many avenues for intervention in this relationship, one means of addressing lock-up is through the perceptions of the adult.

Teachers' perceptions of children, like other strongly held feelings and beliefs, do not change easily, especially if they involve "problem children." In the case of Ms. Thomas at the beginning of the chapter, her experiences had given rise to some fairly strongly held beliefs about the incompetence of the "at-risk" children in her class—some might call this stereotyping. Ms. Thomas would argue that her experience with lots of children tells her that she could expect little in the way of competence from "those kids." Teachers, like parents, feel defensive about having their perceptions changed or attacked, and rightly so. Representations of relationships are the product of experience (feelings, behaviors, information) accrued over thousands of data points. Unlike psychologists who interact infrequently with children, teachers are there every day all day—collecting lunch money, teaching reading and social studies, putting on coats, monitoring peer behaviors, watching kids in the halls and at recess, all with, at least in part, an agenda to promote socialization and skill performance. Over these thousands of interactions, certain invariants appear (Stern, 1989)— certain feelings are triggered on a predictable basis, and certain behaviors or reactions can be expected. Thus, a teacher's representational model of children (or a child) is based on the reality of his or her experience (and of the child's experience). These representations guide the adult's behavior toward the child as well and reinforce themselves over time in a self-fulfilling way. These become representations of self and other that can be very constraining on behavior and highly stable over time.

How can these representations of self and other be altered? Psychologists know little about this in terms of actual empirical research on teachers and children. But there is a literature on how to change (or not to change) parents' representations of and behaviors with their child (e.g., Stern, 1989; Zeanah et al., 1993), so this discussion primarily relies on that literature. Anecdotal applications of the parent-based literature to teacher–child relationships, as well as the literature on behavioral consultation, provide the most direct evidence of effective applications with teachers. For example, in Goldstein's (1993) book on managing children's classroom behavior, in several of the intervention chapters, especially in the chapter on consultation, strategies used for intervening with teachers reflect some of the intervention strategies used with parents. Is is important that there are different formats in which teachers' representations can be altered: group consultation, individual consultation, and even through forms of self-evaluation.

Regardless of the format, the consultant should note that the goal is to create representations that (a) are more flexible and differentiated, in which there is evidence that the adult sees and interprets the child's behavior in a range of ways, both positive and negative, and that these representations are contextualized (i.e., tied to the child's actual behavior and not global characterizations); (b) are more positive in tone or at least reflect positive and negative emotions in a more integrated manner, and thus, if the teacher does have negative beliefs or feelings about the child, these will be balanced by positive experiences or by an understanding of the child's needs that give rise to the behaviors that the teacher characterizes as negative; and (c) reflect the teacher's belief and experience that her behavior affects the child, and thus there will be an absence of blaming the child for the entirety of relational problems and observations of instances in which the teacher felt effective and could link the child's behavior to his or her own behavior.

Together, these features would characterize a representational model that is more open to new information, more responsive to the child, and more integrative and balanced. These changes, independent of efforts to change behavior (through coaching or behavior management), have been shown to result in increasingly positive patterns of interaction between adults and children (see Stern, 1989).

The available evidence suggests the following methods for consultants who are working with adult representations of relationships with children:

1. It is necessary to help the adult narrate the representation. This is the first and most important step in this intervention form. Semistructured interviews, such as the TRI, can facilitate this step and, in many cases, will accelerate intervention. The key concern at this point is to have the adult put words to the feelings and beliefs they have regarding the relationship, in a group or a one-to-one setting.
2. It is important to label narrations and to observe patterns in the representations. The consultant helps summarize the teacher's narration of relationship experience in more general terms.
3. It is helpful to identify and to understand connections among beliefs, feelings, and behaviors toward the child (e.g., "it's hard to respond positively to him or her when you're feeling like he or she intentionally makes you angry," "you two seem to interact a lot even though it's not fun," or "he actually seems to like being close

to you although he seeks you out in negative ways"). The consultant can help the adult begin to understand that the child's behavior toward them is in part dependent on the setting and the teacher's own behavior. This goal can be accomplished through discussion and can be facilitated either through reviewing a video of the classroom or by observations conducted by the teacher, the consultant, or both.

4. It is useful to introduce new information or frameworks for understanding the child and the interaction with the child. This follows from the strategy above and, in part, depends on the consultant's use of theory when labeling narrations and observing their patterns. Armed with a capacity to observe themselves in relationships with children, and to understand the child's behavior in terms of the phases of socioemotional development, teachers can then apply the systems theory view of relationships to interpret and to hopefully change their interactions with the child.

In many, or even most, cases of working with teachers regarding representations, the format of the work involves irregularly scheduled consultation sessions between the psychologist and teacher usually involving verbal exchanges about the situation in question. This format can undermine the probability of success in altering representations because the teacher and the consultant find it difficult to form a relationship between each other. Thus, it is essential that the consultant strive to emulate good relationship building in terms of interactions with the teacher.

First, the scheduling of sessions on a regular basis is necessary for any change to take place. Some form of rhythm must be established so that contact with the consultant is predictable.

The use of verbal exchange is problematic because it is easy, and understandable, for the teacher to become defensive. In this context, it is often the teacher's job to recount and recall certain experiences—or in circumstances in which the consultant has observed in the classroom, it is the consultant's role to present observations that again can be reacted to defensively. Relying on recall or even observations (typically of short duration) can limit the information available for processing in the consultation.

One very helpful tool to use in intervening at the level of a teacher's representations is a videotape, which is used as a source of feedback to the teacher. The use of a videotape addresses two needs in consultations of this sort: first, the need to have accurate, "third-party" (neutral) feedback on teacher and child behavior to introduce as an information source to the teachers' representations and second, the need to allow for the targeting of very specific interactions under the control of the viewers and thus not subject to selective recall or lack of memory. There are several ways in which videotaped feedback can be arranged and used within a teacher consultation.

In one set of approaches, the teacher and the consultant arrange to videotape in the classroom during a period of time that suits the nature of the concern. This could involve a reading group time in which the target child participates, a seatwork time, or some other arrangement. In nearly all cases in which it is arranged to have taping done, it is a good idea to videotape the period of most concern and a time in which the teacher reports that things go fairly well (one should note the goal of a differentiated view of the relationship). One of the strategies of intervention noted above is to provide new sources of information to the teacher's representational model of the child—if there are times in which the child does not behave as expected or predicted, these are good times to tape.

Once there is footage of relevant periods, the consultant and the teacher arrange a meeting to review the tape. In viewing the tape, the goal is to use the information on the tape as a source of input to the teacher's representations. This input can be in the form of the child's behavior, the teacher's behavior, or the feelings that the tape triggers for the teacher. The initial approach to the tape must be as neutral as possible for it to have the desired outcome; consultant and teacher need to understand the tape viewing as a means of jointly learning about and understanding this teacher's relationship with a particular child. Under these circumstances, review of the tape will be enhanced if the consultant has administered the TRI as an initial assessment so that both consultant and teacher have a somewhat shared set of information about the relationship under consideration.

Consultant and teacher then view the tape together. The consultant may ask the teacher to narrate the tape and to label an impression of his or her behavior and the child's. For example, the consultant may ask for the following: "Just tell me what you see going on between the two of you— what you are doing, thinking, and feeling, and the same for him. Let's not focus on whether you or he did the right or wrong thing, but just help me understand what's going on."

The consultant may then ask the teacher to identify critical episodes on the tape—situations that went well or poorly, in the teacher's view, and then to recall his or her perceptions during those times. For example, the consultant might say the following: "ok, now that I understand a bit more about what was going on, let's find the spot on the tape that shows things at their worst, and then find one where things are at their best, and tell me again what's going on, what you and he are thinking and feeling." These discussions might easily involve what the teacher was thinking or feeling at a particular moment or in response to a child's behavior, or they may involve what the teacher identified as the links among his or her perceptions, his or her behavior, and the child's behavior.

In subsequent sessions, the consultant might begin discussions with the teacher of his or her tolerances for children's relationship behaviors, her attitudes and feelings about these behaviors, and her responses to these behaviors. For example, the consultant might say, "You know, it seems to me that he actually does seem to comply once in a while, and it seems to happen mostly when it's a request he can do, and when you and he have not been going at it for a while, sometimes it happens when you're physically close to him."

Over a couple of sessions of observation and discussion, consultant and teacher might draw up a list of patterns (similar to those in the above paragraph) that emerge across observations. Following this, they can then generate a list of teacher responses to these patterns and follow-up plans. These follow-up plans should be in the form of hypotheses to be tested— different forms of responses the teacher might try, situations the teacher may create, or settings for the teacher to observe. These hypotheses are ultimately used to target representations; that is, they are ways of changing representations. In an earlier chapter, I described the parent consultation in which the parent was asked to not try to teach the child during play sessions. During this consultation, the parent noticed the child could play on his own, information that altered the parent's perceptions (representations) of the child. Thus, teacher and consultant should approach this task as an experiment. What is important in this is a flexible, observant stance, informed by the model of relationships described earlier. Variants of this form of consultation can include one-on-one work, group consultation, and the use of other teachers as observers.

The interventions just described are aimed not at a teacher's behavior toward a child or children but at his or her representations of behavior. The interventions were not explicitly intended to have the teacher do anything differently but to have the teacher observe and understand differently. To the extent that behavior was altered, it was altered to test hypotheses about what the child might do, how the child might respond, and how the teacher might feel, toward the goal of introducing new information to the representational model, information that would create pressure to reorganize this model. Admittedly, the ultimate end of such an intervention would hopefully be an alteration of interactive patterns between child and teacher. However, improvement in a relationship can take place when someone experiences a relationship more positively once they have understood the perspective or the behavior of the other, without making a great deal of change in behaviors per se. The introduction of new information, of changes in the representations of the relationship, actually alters the relational experience of the partner.

In the case of Ms. Thomas, benefits of the work just described might be that she comes to an understanding of her experience with children that allows her to tolerate or to enjoy her classroom experience in ways that help her feel effective as a teacher. It could mean that she has renewed motivation to reach certain children or to now learn and attempt new techniques (see below) for addressing the needs of these children in her classroom. It might also mean that she approaches children more flexibly and responsively, enabling them to better use her skills as a teacher.

Direct Interventions in Teacher–Child Interaction

Unlike the interventions just discussed, in which the stated aim is to alter teacher's representations—an internal phenomenon—the interventions discussed in this section specifically pertain to interactive behaviors: external, observable phenomena. These interventions are targeted at the interaction of teacher–child dyads. Two intervention strategies are discussed: *Banking time*, an intervention prescribing specific forms of teacher–child interaction, and *contingency management*, in relation to its role in improving child–teacher relationships.

Banking Time

As was the case for the interventions aimed at teachers' representations of their relationships with children, these more direct interventions have their roots in work with parents and children (e.g., Barkley, 1987). A review of the literature on parent–child intervention reveals a range of intervention techniques that frequently contain a component that involves the parent and child spending time together in a nondirective, child-centered session of play or other activity. Greenberg and colleagues (see Greenberg at al., 1991) have described problem adult–child interactions as involving difficulties in the adult "following the child's lead" in play, learning, or semistructured activities. Not surprising, research on child–parent relationships has frequently demonstrated that parents of children with behavior problems (noncompliance or resistance) are observed to be very controlling, dominating the child in play sessions (Greenberg et al., 1991, 1993). This form of overcontrolled or even intrusive style of interaction by the adult is a very common correlate of dyadic relationship problems (e.g., insecure attachment, noncompliance, emotional negativity, and adult ineffectiveness). These features characterize teacher–child interactions when teachers report high scores on the STRS Conflict scale (see chapters 5 and 6).

The remedy used to address these relationship problems, which are also correlates of problem behaviors that cause children to be referred for intervention in the first place, is a set of procedures designed to help the adult interact nondirectively with the child, thereby creating a different set of relationship feedback processes and tolerances. In the case of Barkley's (1987) parent consultation program, for example, parents are directed to spend up to 20 minutes daily with the child in an activity chosen by the child. These sessions occur regularly each day, regardless of the child's behavior or misbehavior, and they require that the parent adopt a much different role than is typical for adult–child interaction. They are instructed not to teach, elicit information, ask questions, or direct or control the play—instead they are to narrate, observe, and label (not interpret). In short, as Barkley noted, the adult is to act like a "sportscaster."

It is interesting that this type of time is one of the first skills prescribed in the Barkley behavior management system, before the use of a token economy (reinforcement) or a time out. It is viewed as a foundation on which to build the child–parent relationship, which, in turn, can facilitate the effectiveness of behavior management techniques by promoting increased value of the adult's attention to the child, better child–parent communication, and more positive emotional experiences and motivation to change.

This technique has been adapted for use in schools in the Banking Time intervention. In Banking Time (Pianta, 1997b), the teacher works with a consultant and implements a daily (if possible) regimen of between 5 and 15 minutes of individual time with a target child. The intervention is called Banking Time because of the metaphor of saving up "positive experiences" so that the relationship between teacher and child can withstand conflict, tension, and disagreement without deteriorating and returning to a negative state. Thus, the child and teacher can draw on their accrued relationship capital and can "withdraw" from the relationship resources that enable them to interact effectively in times of stress.

For example, one second-grade teacher had been practicing Banking Time with a child for two weeks because she felt that she was unable to "break through and communicate" with this child, which troubled her, and the child was not doing well in the classroom. After the two weeks (five banking time sessions), one afternoon the child was in a conflict situation with peers that usually led to his breaking of classroom rules. The teacher approached the child and touched him with her arm (he did not recoil as was the case before); she then asked him to look at her (he made eye contact) and asked him to stop (he stopped). She and the child walked to the side of the class and discussed the problem situation, and the child verbalized his version of the experience and engaged with the teacher in some problem solving. The teacher reported this was a completely new pattern; prior to the banking time intervention, this would have inevitably resulted in a deteriorating situation, with the child noncompliant and angry and the teacher feeling frustrated and ineffective. In this case, the teacher–child relationship afforded resources to the child in a challenging situation and enabled the child to function in a more advanced or developmentally mature (e.g., representational) manner than he would have previously.

Specifically, Banking Time involves the prescription of a set-aside time between child and teacher (or other adult with whom he or she has frequent contact, such as an aide). The following prescribed dimensions are important:

1. Children are told that the time (5–15 minutes) is theirs to do with what they wish; teachers will follow and participate as children direct.
2. The sessions, if at all possible, should occur on a regularly scheduled (or at least predictable) basis. Most important, occurrence is not contingent on the child's behavior. This is a critical issue. One of the more common practices undermining relationships between teachers and students are teachers' views that giving attention to children who misbehave will reinforce the misbehavior. This is only true when the teacher's attention is contingent on the misbehavior and occurs in sequence with, or in the same situation as, the misbehavior. In the Banking Time protocol, sessions are not typically coincident with misbehavior because they are defined

ahead of time in the daily schedule, and teachers' approval of behavior (rewarding or punishing) is not part of Banking Time.

3. Teachers' behaviors and verbalizations to children during Banking Time should be as neutral and objective as possible and should not focus on children's performances of skills. Teachers should refrain from any teaching, directing, selective attending, or reinforcement. Statements such as "let's read a book" or "let me show you how to do that" are directive and to be avoided. Statements such as "you read well" or "how does that work," although conveying a positive message (approval and interest), are also not neutral and, if possible, should be avoided. Teachers can be coached by a consultant to adopt a more neutral tone in which behavior is observed (e.g., "you like reading," "you put that whole puzzle together," "I can help you if you wish," or "you aren't asking for help on that, you want to do it by yourself"). If at all possible, children should be allowed to choose, to lead, and to direct the activity (within limits established for the classroom).

4. Teachers can convey several "messages" to the child through Banking Time. In this way, Banking Time can help children and teachers define their relationships, which, in turn, can facilitate children's knowing how to use teachers in classroom interactions. To the extent that teachers would like to call attention to aspects of their role vis-à-vis the child, they should do so in very simple terms, and these terms should be used consistently across Banking Time and other classroom interactions.

It is recommended that teachers identify no more than three such messages. These can include messages such as "I am interested in you," "I accept you," "I am a helper when you need or ask me," "I will try to be consistent and available," and "I am safe." The teacher can choose these messages on the basis of interpreting assessment information from the child, such as when a Relatedness scale reveals that the child feels disengaged from or anxious with the teacher. Or they can be gleaned from observations that the teacher and the consultant make in the classroom or from the child's responses to interview questions about the child–teacher relationship. The important point is that the messages chosen should actually disconfirm the child's expectations of or beliefs about the teacher and, like the interventions on teachers' representations (see Teachers' Representations of Relationships section), these teacher messages should provide new information to the child's representations of the child–teacher relationship.

By and large, messages involving the teacher as a helper, a person who is unconditionally available and predictable, a source of safety and comfort, and a resource for problem solving are common to most child–teacher relationships in childhood. Depending on the actual nature of the child–teacher relationship and the child's perceptions of adults, these messages can be tailored. It is important that these messages be limited in number and in complexity—simplicity is a key and consistency of expression and enactment of these messages (in and out of Banking Time sessions) is important. Thus, teachers can communicate consistent availability as a helper in Banking Time when the child expresses a need for help (e.g., "sure I can help you with that, teachers are helpers, I'm here to help kids") or during classroom instruction or recess periods during which help is needed (e.g., "I wonder if you need help on that ... I am here to help"). Because the child in Banking Time sessions has actually experienced what these messages mean in actual interactions, the messages are a powerful means of helping the child understand what the teacher–child relationship can afford him or her. These messages then become like "relationship themes" that the teacher and child can work on together. Even more important, these messages begin to pair words with meaningful experiences for the child so that eventually, words can begin to substitute for these direct experiences.

5. Behavioral standards during Banking Time sessions are the same as those observed during other classroom periods. That is, the rules for behavior do not change during Banking Time. If cursing is not allowed during reading instruction, it is not allowed during Banking Time. If classroom rules are violated during a Banking Time session, the typical consequence should be delivered following the session. The session should not be terminated and instead, can be used as a means of understanding and extending some of the themes or messages previously mentioned.

6. Banking Time, as noted above, is not a reinforcer, nor is termination of sessions a punishment. Use of Banking Time as a reinforcer (e.g., "you now have earned your session with me") or as a punishment (e.g., "you lost your time with me today") will eliminate its effect on the child–teacher relationship and most likely damage the relationship.

Banking Time, as an intervention, is usually necessary because the child–teacher relationship needs to change. Banking Time introduces a systematic challenge to the relationship system toward the goal of requiring that system to reorganize. Because it is used with relationship systems that are usually in some form of difficulty, one should prescribe the time in the way it has been described above. That is, it is important to constrain teacher–child interactions. Teachers can find this difficult and may need support and instruction (e.g., review videotapes) from the consultant.

There is also the problem of making time for Banking Time, something that teachers can find difficult. But the "where and when" of Banking Time is very flexible, and if teachers have been exposed to some of the information about relationships that has been described, they are much more receptive to implementing Banking Time interventions. Teachers often work it into their schedule during transitions to gym, music, art, or free time (e.g., when the class goes to lunch) and sometimes during actual instructional time, even doing Banking Time in small groups. It is important that Banking Time be taught not as an end in itself but as a way to introduce new interactions, perceptions, and feelings to a relationship. The interactions, on the part of the teacher, that accomplish these ends in the context of a Banking Time session can also accomplish these ends in reading group, recess, circle time, or a science lesson.

The Banking Time technique acts on nearly every component of a relationship between a child and adult, and thus it is a powerful source of pressure on the relationship system. First and foremost, it constrains the behavior of the adult—in so doing, it creates a variant of interaction between child and adult that typically is viewed as different, novel, and better by most child and adult participants. This constraining of adult behavior in turn frees up the child to display behaviors (and competencies) that are typically not seen in routine interactions between teacher and child. The child often explores at a higher level, shows interest in the teacher and the teacher's attention, and, in turn, the teacher's perceptions (representational beliefs) may change or at least be subject to reexamination. The "difficult child" becomes easier to get along with and is viewed more positively (with experiences to back up these beliefs). It is this pairing of emotional experiences with the other person and the accompanying changes in belief and perception that can have a large effect on both the child's and the adult's representation of the relationship. This typically results in one's having a more integrative, positive view of the other person that is carried into other situations when banking time is not being implemented.

Feedback and exchange processes between teacher and child are altered as well—especially if the teacher used Banking Time sessions to impart a particular message to the child. These messages (availability, responsivity and acceptance) are not just words but, in fact, are tied to the experiences that the child has—a teacher that follows the child's lead, consistently gives time to the child, and helps when asked. Banking Time sessions allow the teacher to build credibility that supports these messages, so that his or her words have meaning for the child. In this way, new pathways or dimensions of feedback and communication between teacher and child become possible as Banking Time is implemented. As always, interactions outside of Banking Time sessions should be used to practice these new feedback mechanisms.

Troubled relationships between teachers and children often consist of uniformly negative perceptions in which all aspects of the others' behavior are channeled, such as is experienced when someone feels that "I can't do anything right in her eyes." Emotions tend to be negative, and engagement is around negative experiences or is absent altogether. These relationship systems have lost the flexibility they need to respond to the challenges produced by classroom demands. In so doing, the adult's resources are not available to the child, and the child is likely to display less and less competence over time (unless some other resource is available) or will seek other resources (such as peers). In these circumstances, Banking Time interventions help "loosen up" these rigid, frozen, inflexible, stuck relationships and help the partners practice alternative behaviors and perceptions. When linked with experiences in the classroom outside of the Banking Time session, this produces a powerful effect on the relationship between teacher and child.

To the extent that these relationships can be altered, they may provide an avenue for addressing children's emotional and behavioral problems in the classroom. Strengthening child–teacher relationships in situations such as this can prevent referrals for special services and can function as a protective factor for children in the development of serious behavior problems (Pianta et al., 1995).

One format for Banking Time implementation involves a screening–intervention format. Using the STRS or another assessment device, psychologists screen the population of teachers. To start the screening, they ask teachers to complete the STRS on all children in their classroom; subsequently, they identify those relationships or teachers that cause the most concern. Similarly, psychologists can ask teachers to complete the instruments on a selected subgroup of children about whom they have the most concern. Psychologists can also cull referrals from teachers who are concerned about children with whom they have a relationship. These children could also be involved in more formal referral systems in the context of "prereferral interventions" or as part of the special education referral–assessment–intervention process. Regardless of the particular path by which individual children and dyads are identified, the common thread in this screening-for-intervention pathway is that "high-risk" dyads are identified on the basis of some referral or assessment process. Specific high-risk dyads are then targeted for intervention in the hope of improving relationship functioning, interrupting what is likely to be a sequence of negative classroom outcomes for the child, and preventing more serious problems from developing.

A second delivery format is more oriented to primary prevention, and the nature of the Banking Time intervention is altered somewhat. Assuming that it is unrealistic for most teachers to set aside 10 minutes of time for each child in their classroom on all or most days (although some teachers with small class sizes, aides, or special circumstances might find ways of accomplishing this), the delivery of the Banking Time intervention must be incorporated into normal classroom routines and interactions. This format is discussed briefly in chapter 8.

Paramount to the Banking Time intervention is the notion that if the adults (and hopefully the children) invest in their relationship with one another, this investment pays dividends in the long run in situations in which stressors are introduced to the relationship. In this way, the relationship is a resource to be built and to be strengthened in opportunities as they present themselves in the classroom. Thus, teachers have to be alert to relationship-salient opportunities, and they have to have an idea of what they would like to accomplish in those opportunities. These opportunities are present in classroom interactions—teachers' requests for compliance, children's requests for help, or teachers' and children's working together on a task.

Behavior Management and Child–Teacher Relationships

Behavior management, or contingency management, is a form of constraint on child–teacher interactions that has implications for the quality of the child–teacher relationship. In positive form, operant conditioning principles emphasize several aspects of interaction that can be beneficial to the child–teacher relationship.

First, when behavioral goals (e.g., the target behaviors identified for change) have been communicated clearly to the child, as is the case in a well-administered approach to contingency management, the child understands clearly the expectations and tolerance for behavior in that relationship. Thus, the regulatory role of the teacher–child relationship can be supported by behavioral approaches that take this form.

Second, good behavior management stresses the need for contingent responses to both positive and negative behaviors. When children's behavior is contingently reinforced, the teacher responds positively and predictably to the child's behavior, something that can be part of a larger pattern of sensitive, responsive interaction. To the extent that the teacher uses these reinforcement episodes as opportunities to call attention to relationship themes or messages (see the Banking Time section above), these interactions can be used to provide the child with information about the child–teacher relationship, and the reinforcement can exemplify a larger pattern of interaction that the teacher is trying to promote. Contingent interactions promote a sense of predictability, availability, and structure in child–teacher relationships.

Third, effective, well-designed and administered behavior management systems communicate to teachers that they play a strong role in regulating the children's performances and increases their sense of effectiveness. Thus, such systems, especially when designed for an individual child with whom the teacher is struggling, can teach the teacher that he or she plays a role in the ZPD and, in fact, can inform him or her about the level of support a child needs to function in the classroom. For example, the teacher may learn that the child needs goals communicated clearly, particularly in the form of individual, face-to-face contact, and that tangible sources of feedback and progress (e.g., tokens, chips, stars, stickers) are most effective, indicating the child's prerepresentational nature. The progress that behavior management systems can produce as a function of the teacher's interactions with the child are important sources of information about the salience of the teacher's interactions for children. Thus, it is useful for behavioral consultants to frame the development and implementation of contingency management systems in terms of the relationship-systems perspective presented in chapters 1 through 5.

Contingency management can also be counterproductive to child–teacher relationships, pointing to the need for such systems to be implemented under the guidance of a consultant. This counterproductiveness occurs when, for example, teachers remove rewards earned previously, do not allow the child to experience rewards earned because of some intervening behavior, or engage in negotiating rewards and punishments.

These practices, no strangers to classroom applications of behavioral interventions and classroom management, place the teacher in the position of taking away earned rewards or tokens. To the extent that this is true, the child may experience the teacher as capricious, unpredictable, and inconsistent. When teachers negotiate contingencies on the fly, change consequences for behavior across situations and episodes, and confuse rewards and punishments, fundamental qualities of the child–teacher relationship (consistency and trust) will be undermined.

Conclusion

In this chapter, the relationship-based perspective outlined in earlier chapters has been brought to bear on the task of improving relationships between teachers and children in elementary classrooms. The applications described in the chapter focus on practices related to individual teachers and children, and they embody the notion that relationships between teachers and children are a valuable resource for child development that can be intentionally harnessed to enhance developmental outcomes for children and for teachers like Ms. Thomas.

When educators understand child–teacher relationships, and have tools to improve them, they can deliberately shape the classroom context in ways that harness the value of these resources. This is of importance for many children who enter classrooms having experienced relationships with adults that are confusing, unpredictable, or negative in some form. For many children, the idea that an adult can be unconditionally accepting, safe, trusted, consistent, and available violates their expectations of relationships with adults. Although these new ideas are likely to be explored and tested by children, they nonetheless use the relational environment of the classroom to induce change in the child's representations of relationships with adults. If carried through consistently across the many adult-child interactions in which the child engages, these messages can form a powerful intervention. The interventions discussed in this chapter can strengthen a child's connection to an adult in the school and can begin to nurture beliefs that relationships with adults are important and helpful resources. As noted earlier, when children have these perceptions of teachers, they are less likely to drop out of school, less likely to engage in high-risk behaviors, and more likely to succeed academically and socially.

8

Enhancing Relationships Across the Classroom

It is the first week of school in this combined kindergarten/first-grade class. The children file into the classroom well scrubbed and ready to start. There are 18 children in this class, 10 of them first graders. The children come from diverse backgrounds—some from upper-middle-class golf-course communities and others from farm communities, trailer courts, apartment complexes, rural hollers, and subdivisions. No single social class dominates. The teacher, Ms. Zahnd, is an experienced kindergarten teacher, respected by staff and liked by parents. Her room is stimulating.

The school struggles to meet the needs of the children. One solution it has used with increasing frequency over the past few years is team-teaching. Teachers are paired, and the children switch from a "home classroom" to the partner teacher's room for some subjects. Ms. Zahnd's class is paired with the classroom next door, and there is considerable movement throughout the day. Minimally, the children in these classrooms interact with four adults (two teachers and two teachers' aides) as well as the other 37 children that populate these classrooms (they have gym every day with another teacher).

For one particular child, Jason, this situation is exacerbated by his academic and behavioral needs. (This is true for roughly one third of the children in these classes.) Jason sees several other adults during the day—the speech–language pathologist, a Chapter One reading specialist, a classroom volunteer who helps with reading on a regular basis, and the guidance counselor. Although not all these specialized adults see Jason on a daily basis, on any given day, he can expect to have to interact, in a formal learning situation, with at least five adults. Furthermore, in order to have these interactions with different adults, Jason either travels to a different place in the school or is worked with in the classroom in a small group—all of which requires a transition in and out of an activity.

This situation is replicated throughout every single elementary, middle, and junior high school in the United States. Heterogeneous grouping of children and the realities of instruction collide in the face of the highly diverse (academically and behaviorally) groups of children that sit in these classrooms (Graue, in press; Pianta & Walsh, 1996). Ask any teachers to

147

identify the greatest challenge they face in trying to teach, and many will respond with comments reflecting how hard it is to teach a group of children who are so different in their needs. These within-classroom differences frequently are addressed by between-classroom grouping of children with similar needs, or through some form of pull-out program for children with higher levels of needs. These "solutions" to within-classroom heterogeneity destabilize the relational environment of the classroom by inducing numerous transitions and changes. In one second-grade classroom (in a different school from that attended by Jason above), a child made 14 transitions during the course of a typical Tuesday—and this was one of the children designated as a "high-risk" student.

There are many reasons to wonder whether the frequency of these changes is helpful to the education of students, regardless of their level of risk. Earlier, I argued that the children most typically designated as "high risk" are those for whom high levels of consistency and stability are needed for a variety of instructional and social reasons. These children come to school often lacking the social (e.g., relationship) experiences (Pianta & Walsh, 1996) that enable them to adapt well in the classroom context. In turn, as well-intentioned attempts to respond to their needs, schools implement locally designed practices that have the potential to create more instability. These grouping and teaming practices, as identified with respect to Jason above and as discussed in terms of larger contexts (Pianta & Walsh, 1996), have the potential of actually undermining the value of child–teacher relationships as a resource for children as well as the relationship-forming capacity of a school.

Classroom-level practices related to relationships between teachers and children are the foci of this chapter. The discussion concerns decisions made at the classroom level—how classrooms are organized and the structures put in place to facilitate interactions and socialization in the classroom. The classroom practices discussed in this section affect child–teacher relationships classroom wide, in contrast to those interventions discussed in chapter 7 that addressed primarily particular child–teacher dyads. Classroom-wide practices have the potential to function as preventive interventions—when implemented, they can reduce the rates of relationship-related problems (or sequelae of those problems) that might occur if not implemented and can improve relationship (and related) outcomes for a large number of children (risk and nonrisk). Used in concert with the practices discussed in chapter 7 (e.g., Banking Time), classroom-wide practices are part of a more comprehensive approach to relational processes that can then target particular dyads with more serious relationship problems as well as the entire class.

For the most part, what is discussed in this chapter is an approach to analyzing current classroom-level practices from the perspective of relationship–systems theory described in chapters 1 through 4 and the techniques of relationship assessment discussed in chapter 5. Although there are very few classroom-level intervention practices that are specifically designed for and targeted at relationships between children and teachers, many classroom practices currently in widespread use have considerable implications for relationships between children and teachers and the extent to which these relationships function effectively to promote development. This is also the case for school-level practices and policies, which are the foci of chapter 9. In the absence of well-tested classroom (and school) interventions, an important role remains for applied child and adolescent psychologists working to enhance child–teacher relationships at the classroom level. This role is largely concerned with psychologists' using the relationship–systems perspective as a framework for analyzing and organizing current practices that have been derived from theories of instruction or behavior management.

I describe a few more points concerning classroom-level practices here. Psychologists working in schools typically have little to do with classroom-level processes—that point has been made repeatedly here and elsewhere (e.g., Gutkin, 1997; Gutkin & Conoley, 1990). Whether psychologists should work at this level can be debated. However, when one considers the range of professionals working in schools, and the needs of children attending those schools, it is clear that psychologists have much to say about classroom-level (not just individual-level) practices with children. This is particularly true with respect to practices that affect social development and social behavior. Although it has been argued that the processes involved in educating children (e.g., instruction or socialization) are composed of social behavior and interactions (with other children and with teachers), practices that relate to social behavior and enhancing the developmental impact of these social interactions are frequently not well informed theoretically or from a research-based perspective. Classroom grouping or the informal behavior management systems used by many teachers are just two examples of the widespread use of classroom practices that may collide with theory.

In this context, there is a clear role for the school professional (psychologist and counselor) who is knowledgeable about theory and research in social development and who implements that knowledge in classrooms. That knowledge is sorely needed, especially given the tendency for decisions about classroom-level practices to be a function of local norms, local culture, and local practice in contrast to being based on intervention research that is directly applicable to the situation that a given teacher or principal faces. Even when research is available, it still may not penetrate local culture. The present chapter specifically addresses implementing knowledge about child–teacher relationships at the classroom level. The practices discussed in this chapter affect the entire classroom, not just targeted individuals. In this respect, the psychologist must see the classroom system as her or his "case" or target for analysis and inquiry.

Although many teachers' complaints and experiences related to relationships with children emanate from interactions with individual children, there are nonetheless distinct differences in relationship patterns across classrooms (Pianta, 1994). In the study of approximately 30 classrooms and more than 400 children described in chapters 4 and 5, Pianta presented a typology of relationships between teachers and students. Relationship groups were characterized by distinct patterns of the degree of teacher-reported involvement with students and whether that involvement was experienced as emotionally positive or negative. It is interesting that when looking across classrooms in this sample, classrooms differed (sometimes dramatically) in the modal form of child–teacher relationships. One can recall from chapters 4 and 5 that some classrooms were characterized by low or high levels of involvement combined with highly positive or negative emotions. Some teachers (in the angry and dysfunctional groups) reported high frequencies of involved, highly negative relationships with students, a pattern that was associated with their leaving teaching within the next couple years.

This research pointed out for the first time that there are classroom-level features of relationships between children and teachers. Whether these features were primarily a function of the teachers or the children in these classrooms was not studied. Although this issue poses an interesting question from a research–theory perspective, the absence of data on it does not in and of itself obviate the need for considering classroom-level interventions that affect child–teacher relationships. Clearly, when a teacher reports high levels of conflict and negative emotion in relationships with a substantial proportion of students in her classroom, a classroom-level perspective is warranted.

In working to improve child–teacher relationships at the classroom level, several strategies are appropriate. In most strategies, the teacher (e.g., his or her behaviors and representations) is the focus of the work, but it is also possible for consultation to address classroom-level practices, such as organization of the day, scheduling, and behavior management. For example, a goal of affecting classroom-wide child–teacher interactions could involve working individually with a teacher (such as Ms. Thomas in chapter 7) to address feelings and beliefs about relationships with children (not individual children but children with respect to the teacher's role). Classroom-level applications usually involve concentrated work with the teacher and assessment of the entire classroom (through child report, teacher report, and observation) integrated within a classroom-level view. Although a lot of data can be gathered from individuals within the classroom, it must be interpreted at the classroom level. This type of work is not unusual for many practicing child and adolescent psychologists (Goldstein, 1993; Gutkin, 1997; Gutkin & Conoley, 1990; Meyers et al., 1979; Ysseldyke & Christensen, 1987). However, the focus of the work—relationships with children—may be unique. Questions such as "What is the typical way that children relate to this teacher?", "What are the tolerances for relationship behavior between children and this teacher?", and " What is the emotional quality of how this teacher and children relate to one another?" are all valid ways of bringing the relationship perspective to a classroom-level focus.

In approaching the task of analyzing classroom practices with a relationship perspective, there will inevitably be pushes and pulls to focus on one child or another within a given classroom. Thus in working with Ms. Zahnd on her approach to teaming, one may be pulled to focus on Jason. This is not unlike work in family system interventions when a particular individual is brought to attention in the context of family sessions (Molnar & Lindquist, 1990). As has been discussed, individual relationships between teachers and children are a legitimate focus of a number of interventions—and, at times, these interventions can then affect the classroom. However, the consultant should not confuse individual teacher–child relationships with strategies that have the primary goal of altering how child–teacher relationships are formed and maintained at the classroom level. With this in mind, the discussion now turns to analyzing the implications of practices at the classroom level for child–teacher relationships.

Stability-Enhancing Interventions

This set of practices are best characterized as decisions that set in motion policies for organizing the scheduling and management of time and personnel resources to which children are exposed. These decisions have a fundamental impact on organizing social interactions and relationships in a classroom and affect the stability of contact between child and teacher, a factor that is important for the development of a relationship (see chapters 3 and 4). Embodied in practices such as instructional grouping, team teaching, scheduling, and behavior management are decisions that address the academic needs of the children in the class. These decisions also can define the number, the form, and, at times, the quality of social interaction between children and adults (such as is the case in Ms. Zahnd's class). As has been argued elsewhere (Pianta & Walsh, 1996), it is often difficult to tear apart social processes from learning or instructional processes. It is interesting that data suggest that the effect of practices related to grouping and teacher–child ratios on academic performance is, at least in part, attributable to the way in which these practices organize social interaction and exposure to adults (e.g., Bourke, 1986; Thurlow, Ysseldyke, Wotruba, & Algozzine, 1993).

There are many reasons for how time is scheduled and a given classroom is organized. Sometimes these reasons are overtly stated; other times they are not easily recognized or understood. In Ms. Zahnd's classroom, these practices were related to school policies regarding child–teacher ratios and how aides were counted in that ratio, space allocation, the "pullout" model for delivery of support services to children, and school-level decisions that team teaching was the best way to respond to diverse needs of students. It is safe to say that when these practices were discussed before they were implemented, relationships between teachers and students were not a central focus of the debate.

Examining practices related to the stability of adult resources for children leads to a couple of important questions: To what extent does a practice (or decision) increase or decrease transitions in relationships between children and adults? Relatedly, does a particular practice (such as having aides in classrooms) affect the stability of contact and interactions between those children and an adult? This question goes to the heart of the definition of a relationship because, for the sake of argument, if a child has 100 contacts or interactions with an adult in a classroom environment per day, it makes a difference if those 100 contacts are with one person or distributed across three or four. For close relationships to form between children and adults, hundreds or thousands of interactions need to take place so that a history or a predictable pattern of interaction can form the structure for the emotional investment of the child (and the adult). This combination of predictable, reciprocal interactions and emotional investment then has the potential to organize experience and to provide a regulatory function to development (see chapters 3 and 4).

As stable, predictable interactions with a particular adult are compromised, the formation and maintenance of an effective child–teacher relationship is undermined. Without this regulatory influence of a relationship, development is less directed, and less optimal outcomes can be expected. In this sense, practices that stabilize interactions between children and adults afford children (and teachers) the opportunity to develop relationships that serve this organizational function. Likewise, practices that divide adult resources across many individuals, or introduce frequent disruptions, may undermine the possibility of developing an effective child–teacher relationship. As has been discussed, this is particularly the case for children whose histories of relationships with adults has been compromised in some form (see chapter 1).

Optimally, classroom-level practices can be designed to maximize contact between a given child and a particular adult. In the example of Ms. Zahnd's team-taught classroom, although a great deal of adult resources were available to children, these resources were organized in such a way that children were required to interact with several adults during the course of the day. This was not simply the case of requiring perfunctory interactions between children and another, different adult but of requiring that children make meaningful progress in the development of valued skills in the context of interactions with several adults. This practice can be viewed as "fractioning" adult resources and can compromise the extent to which there is a relationship available to support performance in the ZPD. Instead of one full-time-equivalent teacher meaning that one adult serves as a consistent and stable figure for a given child, that full-time equivalent can actually be the result of summing across four adults—the resources of one person are fractioned across four.

In-Class Grouping and "Functional" Teacher–Child Ratios

Teacher–child ratios affect the stability of adult–child interactions by influencing the frequency or rate of interactions between a single adult figure and a child. By and large, evidence suggests that when the class size of a teacher is smaller, children receive more frequent and individualized feedback, resulting in better performance and behavior (McGiverin, Gilman, & Tillitski, 1989). Thus, the opportunity for a child to have more frequent interactions with a single teacher results in better functioning feedback–exchange processes in the child–teacher relationship. With the increasing use of team teachers, paraprofessional aides, volunteers, and other adults, there are many ways teacher–child ratios are manipulated in any given classroom. From the perspective of using classroom-level practices to enhance child–teacher relationships, it is important to examine these grouping strategies to determine the "functional" ratio—that is, the frequency of contact between a given child and particular adult in a small group or dyadic setting.

In the pair of classrooms housing 38 children described at the beginning of the chapter, there is a commendable adult–child ratio of approximately 1:9. However, this ratio masks the relationship challenge facing the children: getting to know four different adults and interacting with them in meaningful ways throughout the course of the day. Thus, a ratio of 4:38 is not the functional equivalent of 1:9; adult–child ratios cannot be reduced to lowest terms.

In this classroom context, what is designed and intended as an organization of adults and children that produces flexibility in instructional programming may also produce instability and confusion for some children, while at the same time benefiting others. There may be a fairly large percentage of children in this classroom whose relationship experience with adults has been compromised; to that extent, those children need considerable stability in interactions with teachers. In this respect, it is important to gather information related to the relationship needs of children in classrooms and to make programming and staffing decisions accordingly. Thus it is possible, in the interest of meeting a range of academic needs, to have a classroom organization that is so flexible that children float from experiences with one adult to another without the opportunity to engage in the kind of close, intimate relationship with an adult that can have considerable developmental benefit.

As noted above, the class-size literature suggests that lowered child–teacher ratios are associated with greater success for children (see Bourke, 1986; McGiverin et al., 1989; Thurlow et al., 1993). It is important that this literature indicates that the processes by which ratios affect child achievement and competence involve teacher–child interactions. Across different grades, and across both special and regular education classrooms, when teachers have fewer children to teach, there is evidence that teachers respond more frequently and positively to children, interact with them in a more individualized manner, and can monitor their progress more carefully. Thus, the teacher functions more effectively within the ZPD when there are fewer children in the class; in particular, child–teacher relationship feedback processes (see Figure 4.1) are greatly influenced by these ratios.

In addition, although there have been few rigorous empirical tests of these practices, there is also considerable theoretical and some anecdotal support (see Graue, in press) for other practices that affect the degree to which a child interacts with a stable adult figure, such as *looping*, in which a child remains with the same teacher for more than 1 year (see chapter 9 for a more thorough discussion).

Exits and Entries

Another practice that can disrupt child–teacher relationships is the use of "pull-out" models of service delivery, such as is embodied in the many "exit and entry" transitions that characterize the school experiences of high-risk children like Jason in the example above. These models of service delivery affect the stability of child–teacher interactions by introducing discontinuities in the adult with whom the child has to interact and the situation (classroom setting). These practices fraction the child (Pianta & Walsh, 1996) to the extent that overdifferentation may occur—too many teacher–child units, each with different expectations, interaction patterns, and tolerances, that cannot be integrated by one child. Thus, the forms of intervention help (e.g., special education or counseling) that require children to be removed from the classroom to interact with another adult potentially undermine the stability of child–teacher interactions by introducing new persons with whom the child must interact in a functional manner. They decrease the likelihood of a child's interacting with the same teacher over time or over situations.

This "pull-out" model of service delivery can affect the quality of teacher–child relationships in another way by requiring the home classroom teacher to interrupt the child's activity and to ready them for the exit as well as to integrate them back into the classroom flow on reentry. These entry–exit transitions can introduce increased numbers of compliance and monitoring-type interactions that challenge child–teacher relationships.

For example, Jason leaves for speech three times a week. This appointment is scheduled by the speech–language pathologist at 9:30 in the morning, during the language arts period. Typically, Jason leaves toward the end of the period and does not miss a lot of instruction. Nonetheless, Ms. Zahnd has to monitor Jason's activities in language arts to ensure he is instructed well in that program, and, on any given day, she has to ask him to complete what he is working on or end what he is involved in and walk (usually accompanied) to the speech room. Depending on Jason's state and the activity in which he is involved, he may or may not comply with this direction, may resist, and may require several reminders. Depending on Ms. Zahnd's state and the activity in which she is involved, her reminders to Jason can take the form of a supportive request or a sequence of nags. With Jason, who leaves the room at least twice a day, these "exit–entry" sequences can dominate his relationship with Ms. Zahnd. Then on his return to the classroom, Jason has to receive instruction in the ongoing activity and often some support for joining that activity—again with the same kind of relational consequences that were described for the exit sequence.

Multiply the above scenario by 4 to 5 (children) to project the "tax" levied on adult–child relationships at the classroom level by delivering supportive services to that number of children on a "pull-out" basis. The sheer numbers of entry and exit sequences in a classroom can have a marked effect on the emotional and relational quality of that classroom environment. For the student with an identified special educational need, who may be receiving services for academic needs, speech—language, and counseling, the services offered can undermine the quality of the relationship that can be developed between him or her and their "home" classroom teacher. This effect on the relationship has consequences for many forms of adjustment and for many educational goals.

By and large, there is no easy solution to the dilemma posed by the scenarios just described. However, Pianta and Walsh (1996) have pointed out the tendency toward overdifferentiation (fractioning) of children's educational programs as a response to the challenge of educating a highly diverse set of children, many of whom have extraordinary levels of need. This tendency toward overdifferentiation can be countered with a flexible approach to the delivery of support services (a school-level intervention) through the use of consultants. A consultation-based approach (see Goldstein, 1993, Meyers et al., 1979; Molnar & Lindquist, 1990; Wang & Kovach, 1995) immediately reduces the likelihood of exit and entry events that destabilize relationships and, in some cases, has the added indirect benefit of increasing the number of regular education teachers available for the goal of lowering child—teacher ratios. There are few substitutes for consistency, stability, and predictability in child—adult relationships— they are the foundations of a relationship that takes form in a sense of "knowing each other."

> By the fourth week of school, Ms. Zahnd was troubled by the way she felt some children were not benefiting from the time they spent in her classroom. She had invested a great deal of time and energy in designing stimulating and interesting lessons, assessing the children's instructional levels, and grouping them for instruction in the most flexible manner possible. Her team-teaching with Mr. Katz was an extension of this approach, and she believed it was "the way to go" with respect to meeting the needs of children in her classroom.
>
> Nonetheless, she was feeling ineffective, the children seemed to not be responding to her approach as they had in years past, and one day she voiced to the psychologist that she was getting "down" on this group of children and it surprised her. The psychologist, who knew Ms. Zahnd to be a very effective teacher, also knew that she tended to focus more strongly on children's academic needs than on their social or emotional needs. The psychologist offered to come and observe her classroom in an effort to offer a fresh perspective on the problem, and Ms. Zahnd readily accepted this opportunity.
>
> The psychologist's observations are similar to the description of Ms. Zahnd's classroom at the beginning of this chapter. In the record of her observations, she noted the arrangement of children (how they were grouped and with what teacher they worked) throughout a 1-hour block in the morning and the qualities of their interactions with Ms. Zahnd and the other adults. The psychologist noted the fact that the children were rotated frequently from teacher to teacher and were rearranged on average four times in the 1-hour period and that most often, these transitions involved changing teachers. She also noted that the adults started each "session" within the 1-hour block with many prompts to

the children for attention and that by the end of each session, the children seemed better focused, only to have their attention interrupted by the next activity. She also noted how many of the children seemed very focused on wanting to be in close proximity to the adult with whom they were working, and they nearly invariably smiled or were enthusiastic when they made physical or other forms of contact with the teacher. She also noted that Ms. Zahnd spent a great deal of time managing transitions in the block of time, and the majority of her interactions with children involved management or arrangements of children's attention.

The psychologist shared these observations with Ms. Zahnd, along with an interpretive framework based on the relationship perspective discussed in chapters 1 through 4. The psychologist offered the impression that it was possible that this group of children may be more "needy" in terms of relationships than were classes in the past, that the frequent shifting in the classroom was not allowing them to "settle in" and form a relationship with one adult who they could count on predictably and get used to, and that their inattentiveness and proximity seeking may be signs of this "need" for a relationship figure. Ms. Zahnd reported being a bit surprised by the fact that the children were not stably involved with one adult, although on reflection she agreed. She was interested in the psychologist's impression regarding the children's needs and how those needs matched her typical style of arranging classroom experiences.

They designed a modification of the morning routine that brought the average number of shifts (of adults) down to under two for each child, allowing the children who appeared more "ready" to shift to have more frequent opportunity to do so. Thus, children were less fractioned. The modified routine retained the same number of "sessions" of instruction; it just reduced the number of different adults to whom the child was exposed. After 1 week, Ms. Zahnd reported feeling better about how things were going: "I'm really getting to know these kids better. . . . I don't have to nag them all the time to attend . . . the other adults seem to like it too . . . and it's added to the class feeling more organized."

This brief vignette describes a consultation-based intervention at the classroom level that affected many aspects of child–teacher relationships. Primarily, it addressed concerns with (a) the "functional ratio" in the classroom, transforming the grouping arrangements so that the 4:38 ratio of adults to children functioned more like a 1:9 ratio and (b) the number of transitions across different adults with which children had to cope. In so doing, the intervention stabilized the child–teacher interactions in this classroom—the adults even felt things were more relaxed and predictable. In this context, the opportunity for the child–teacher relationship to develop and flourish was enhanced by changing grouping patterns.

Behavior Management Systems

One set of classroom practices that can affect child–teacher relationships in either positive or negative directions is the system for behavior management that is present in the classroom. When they are well designed and implemented appropriately, on the one hand, behavior management systems support the development of a positive child–teacher relationship by strengthening the feedback functions of the relationship and by contributing to a sense of the teacher's effectiveness and influence (Epanchin, Townsend, & Stoddard, 1994; Goldstein, 1993; Walker, 1994). On the other hand, behavior management systems, if not implemented or designed with a relationship perspective in mind, can erode child–teacher relationships.

On the positive side, well-designed behavior management systems support child–teacher relationships in several ways. First, they provide limits for student behavior and clear tolerances for the nature of child–teacher (and other) interactions in the classroom. These limits and tolerances can help regulate students' behavior and can provide a sense of safety and security for children, especially for those whose relationship histories have not provided similar constraints (see Greenberg et al., 1991). Second, most recommendations for designing behavior management systems emphasize the contingent nature of the teacher's response to positive (or negative) behaviors. This emphasis on contingency (as was discussed in chapter 7) helps support the perception (and experience) of the teacher as responsive, available, and predictable. Third, because behavior management systems help facilitate teachers' effectiveness and control in the classroom environment (Brantley & Webster, 1993; Epanchin et al., 1994; Goldstein, 1993), they can affect teachers' representations of their role with children. Teachers can see themselves as affecting children through how they behave with and respond to them, thereby innoculating against a sense of passivity and helplessness. By affecting teachers' control of the classroom environment, behavior management systems support the asymmetry of the child–teacher relationship and highlight the role of the teacher as a figure for attachment, regulatory, and role-modeling functions.

Fourth, effective behavior management systems create opportunities for positive feedback to the child. Systems that are built on operant conditioning principles (see Epanchin et al., 1994; Goldstein, 1993) will focus on noting and rewarding the competence behavior of children in classrooms. Teachers' responsibilities in these systems are to note, to record, and to acknowledge (using rewards, tokens, etc.) the desirable behavior of the child. In enacting these responsibilities in the classroom, teachers have the opportunity to link behavior, affect (the child's experience of being acknowledged and the teacher's own positive expressions), and language (labeling of the situation). These situations mirror the role that parent–child relationships provide in the development of self-regulation (see chapter 3).

A fifth and important way that effective behavior management supports child–teacher relationships is by affecting the child's behavior in the classroom. Successful behavior management systems reduce the child misbehavior that is related to teacher–child relationships characterized by conflict (Pianta et al., 1995). In these types of relationships, teachers' negative affect is high and involvement is either too great (leading to dependent or angry relationships) or too little. By enhancing child competencies and by decreasing the likelihood of child misbehaviors that are related to negative relationship experiences, behavior management systems can have the effect of increasing rates of positive child–teacher relationships through the way that they structure child–teacher interactions and affect child and teacher perceptions of self and other.

Thus, consultation that focuses at the classroom level on implementing effective behavior management systems can function not only as a preventive intervention for child misbehavior but also as a means of enhancing child–teacher relationships. In many ways, good behavior management techniques can be seen as compatible with a relationship perspective, and, in fact, such techniques can be seen as a more intentioned, goal-directed, overt, and focused way of improving the feedback functions of a relationship. In this sense, behavior management can be organized within the relationship systems model described in earlier chapters.

However, behavior management systems can also undermine the quality of the relationship between teacher and child, especially if misunderstood or misapplied. This is done in one of two ways (a) if "response–cost" practices in token economies are used incorrectly or (b) when teachers adopt the idea that their attention to children is part of a reinforcement paradigm (in behavioral terms) and they become concerned that individual attention to children can reward their misbehavior. These concerns are elaborated in the subsections below.

For many applied child and adolescent psychologists, these misapplications of behavior management often occur without their knowledge. Teachers are trained that it is important to have a system for managing behavior, but training is usually not very thorough, nor are such systems always well monitored by supervisors or principals (Christenson & Ysseldyke, 1989). It is not at all unusual for a psychologist, once called in to consult with a teacher or to evaluate a student, to notice the misapplication of behavior management. Thus, although one may read the examples below and note, "well this is just not the way to do behavior management," the examples reflect how behavior management is often applied in schools (Christenson & Ysseldyke, 1989).

Mixing Reward and Punishment: "I Have to Take Away Your Points"

As noted above, relationships may be negatively affected when a teacher misuses a system in which reward and punishment are included, such that the child may "earn" a reward (or tokens) for positive behavior and "lose" the reward or token for negative behavior. Although this type of practice has been shown to increase the effectiveness of behavioral interventions over and above the "reward only" approach (Walker, 1994), when analyzed from a relationship perspective, the practice carries the possibility of undermining the relationship between teacher and child by "taking away" points or rewards that have already been earned and by focusing the child's emotional experience of the teacher on the reward–punishment dimension.

> Ms. Bowers started a system of rewards for children in her fourth-grade class. She decided to award points to children for any of a set of positive behaviors that included "getting along with others," "following directions," and "completing your assignments." Furthermore, negative behaviors such as fighting with peers, not listening to Ms. Bowers, and failing to complete assignments resulted in the loss of points. Points were tallied and exchanged at the end of the week for rewards. The system was to be administered at the end of the morning and then again at the end of the day before the children went home.
>
> Ms. Bowers typically did not use a behavior management system but felt one was needed because the class was starting to get on her nerves, especially a few children who were particularly unruly. These three boys, plus a small group of girls, were loud, demanding, not keeping up with work, and inciting the rest of the class. Ms. Bowers frequently found herself angry with these students, and although she did not express her anger directly, she was beginning to resent the time these students took away from her teaching the rest of the class and the fact that she felt these students were rejecting her efforts to bring them into line.
>
> It was easy to explain the system to the children, and during the first couple days they seemed to be "on board." Sometime during day three or four, the testing of the system began. The room felt like it had before the system was implemented—there was lots of noise, Ms. Bowers periodically felt somewhat out of control of the class, and there was not as much productive activity as Ms. Bowers would like. She reminded the students that they would not earn points for their behavior and pointed toward the chart on which she was keeping track of points for exchange for rewards of free time, extra recess, and so forth. Ms. Bowers noted that she was going to have to take away points for negative behaviors.
>
> Henry, a boy in the difficult group, had earned three points that morning for cooperation. During recess, he had a fight with another student that the teacher did not see. On hearing of this, Ms. Bowers told Henry that one of his points would be removed. He got angry and spoke loudly at her (his point total was actually fairly close to earning the weekly reward). She ignored Henry at first, reminding him that listening was important, at which point he threw down some papers and books off his desk, proclaiming "I won't do this work, make me!" and Ms. Bowers told him he had just lost another point. The class watched as Henry got angry at Ms. Bowers: "You can't take away my points for that! You never told me to do work." The argument continued, with Ms. Bowers getting more and more angry, feeling that Henry was escalating the fight, and Henry feeling that Ms. Bowers had acted arbitrarily—never warning him that she was taking away points. Finally, she started threatening Henry with taking away points he had earned yesterday and he started crying; Ms. Bowers asked for him to be taken to the principal's office.

What damage was done here? Why did this well-intentioned implementation of behavioral principles go awry, leaving child and teacher at odds with one another? The damage was twofold. First, Ms. Bowers and Henry ended up angry and resentful of one another. Henry's trust in Ms. Bowers was shaken, and he likely does not see her as a resource for him, especially in this time of stress. Ms. Bowers had her suspicions confirmed—that kids like Henry always push and never let up, draining her of time and of emotional resources. She's tired and does not feel like dealing with this—both child and teacher are estranged from one another. In addition, the rest of the class observed Ms. Bowers lose her cool, and they began to question her resolve in implementing this behavior management system.

Damage was done to the relationship between Henry and Ms. Bowers that was, in part, related to her application of behavior management. However, behavior management is central to good teaching (Walker, 1994). How can principles of good and effective behavior management and classroom structure be reconciled with a relationship-oriented perspective? Specifically, how was the damage in Ms. Bower's classroom contributed to by the design of the behavior management system and its implementation?

The nature and design of this behavior management system may have contributed to Ms. Bower's faltering during a period of uncertainty for two reasons. First, by "taking away" earned points, the behavior management associated unpleasant emotional consequences with being part of the management system. This practice can erode motivation for a child to participate in this system, especially if the child knows he or she is likely to be among the point losers. This damage can be minimized by the careful selection of target behaviors, rewards, and costs (Goldstein, 1993; Walker, 1994). But more important, this system places the teacher in the position of the arbiter of rewards and punishments. She is the agent that takes away rewards. Often, the escalation, anger, and resentment by students, the negotiating and bartering by teachers and students that can follow response–cost procedures, can affect the consistency of the teacher and her value as a resourceful figure for the child. To minimize this risk, teachers using response–cost methods have to be very careful to ensure that children understand the system and the consequences ahead of time and to remain as neutral and consistent as possible.

Second, many elementary school children are not able to adequately understand the rationale for the giving and the taking away of rewards, and they see their teacher in a confusing light when she is in the position described above. Think of Henry's sense of Ms. Bowers. If the child has a conflictual relationship with the teacher to begin with (such as Henry), the relationship between the teacher and the child is likely to further erode when behavioral procedures are misapplied, such as above. In extreme form, the taking away of rewards can be used punitively and can be an outlet for the teacher's anger and resentment. In these cases, intervention is needed in many forms, not the least of which is to support the teacher's emotional state and to provide an outlet for anger.

There is a clear role for a consultant in the situation described above. Preventive measures, at the classroom level, can include the consultant's providing training in principles of behavior management and its application in classroom management systems. Included in such training can be information on the relationship perspective and the ways in which management systems can enhance or can undermine the relationship between child and teacher. As has been discussed above, it is important to note that positive and negative reinforcement play a role within the context of the child–teacher relationship and its function in the socialization process. This role calls attention to a desired outcome, and when paired with labeling and praise, it identifies and defines for the child the experience of self-regulation and what the child did to achieve this experience. Like other types of feedback, this feedback is best and most effective when it is clearly understood and is consistent. It is also best when the emotional experience of being rewarded is clear and can be connected to events and verbal labels.

The Reinforcement Fallacy

One of the great points of conflict between a behavior management perspective of child–teacher interactions from the view of reinforcement and punishment and a relationship perspective of child–teacher interactions from the view of emotional regulation and social systems is that if teachers spend time unconditionally with students (especially those in trouble), they are reinforcing the child's bad behavior. Teachers who are stressed by conflictual interactions and are becoming emotionally disengaged from children can have difficulty accepting children's needs for time with them.

> In one long-term consultation in which a clinical child psychologist was involved, a 9-year-old boy with serious emotional disturbances was enrolled in a full-time special education class with five to six other similarly troubled boys in a suburban elementary school. This child had been severely maltreated from birth until the time he was removed from the home to foster care when he was 5 years old. His foster mother was loving and caring to him, although she struggled with implementing certain procedures (e.g., time-out), seeing him as already a victim of mistreatment and being afraid of hurting his emotional development further. The boy was engaging and social, liked by many, and a bit of a character. He also could be aggressive toward adults, belligerent, and easily incited by more malicious children to misbehave and was a frequent visitor to the principal's office. Nonetheless, he had survived K–3 fairly well.
>
> In this fourth-grade special education class, the teacher was in his second year. He received little support from school administrators, who were mostly satisfied if they had little or nothing to do with the children in his classroom. The school psychologist in this school was almost completely involved in assessment and eligibility. The teacher had implemented a fairly complex behavior management system, involving the addition of points for many behaviors and the loss of points, time-out, and removal from the class in a series of escalating punishments in response to different forms of misbehavior. He believed he had all the bases covered for misbehavior and reward.

The child had substantial relationship needs, particularly for helping him experience a regulated and predictable emotional state and for clarifying the connections among emotional states, actions, and words. He had few resources for these skills himself and was very dependent on adults and his environment for these resources. His experience in this classroom was a struggle. Almost invariably, he would start the day well, earning points and heading toward "free time" as a reward at midday. He really enjoyed spending his free time at the class computer. Just as invariably, he would be "set off" by something late in the morning—another child, a frustrating activity—and his behavior would escalate as the teacher frequently responded with "you just lost your morning points." This invariably set off a sequence of events that landed the child in the principal's office, at which time his mother was usually called to come and pick him up.

A meeting was called among the child's mother, teachers, principal, lead teacher, and the clinical child psychologist who worked with this child in therapy. At this meeting, the teacher was angry and tired and seemed uninvolved, although he sincerely wanted things to improve. During the course of the hour-long discussion, the therapist raised the question of what the child liked to do and of what the teacher liked about the child. The teacher responded perfunctorily to the question of what he liked and then noted the child really enjoyed time at the computer, to which the clinical child psychologist responded, "I wonder if the two of you could spend some time together each day—maybe 10 minutes—doing something he likes, like the computer." The teacher thought awhile and then noted, "But that would be reinforcing his bad behavior—what if he loses his points, then I go and spend time with him at something he likes?" The principal and lead teacher agreed. Changing tacts, the therapist wondered whether there were other ways the teacher might spend time with the child on a regular basis, regardless of his behavior—perhaps letting him sit closer to him, maybe reading together in the morning when he came to school. The response was the same. No, it would reinforce him for bad behavior.

Although this story involves an individual child and a teacher (whose relationship is in conflict), and many aspects of the story are relevant to the previous chapter's discussion of strategies focused at individual teacher–child relationships, it is nonetheless relevant to this discussion of classroom-level interventions. It suggests an aspect of teacher beliefs that pervades classroom interactions across a range of children and often is reflected in the implementation of classroom-level practices. In particular, this story indicates a mistaken understanding of reinforcement in a situation in which the teacher–child relationship needed strengthening and repair. When teacher–child interactions are seen only through the lens of reinforcement, teachers are prevented from engaging in the kind of relationship-strengthening activities of Banking Time; their use of language will typically flow from this perspective and thus not call attention to the affective or relational components of interaction with children (thus their messages to students may not reflect their value as a relational figure), and their interactions with students are constrained and inflexible.

Thus, at the outset, it is important to communicate to teachers that behavior management should not conflict with building a relationship (Epanchin et al., 1994).

In the example above, it was not clear to this teacher how to understand his interactions with the child from a perspective other than behavior management. When teachers view child–teacher interactions in reinforcement terms (e.g., Goodlad, 1991), they impose a narrow view on child–teacher interactions; in so doing, they are removing the possibility that these relationships might serve other developmental functions and are viewing the child as someone to be controlled or managed. This particular case involved a sincere and well-intentioned beginning teacher whose special education training emphasized behavior management of the form he was practicing, albeit not well. He was greatly stressed by this class of acting-out boys and increasingly felt lonely, isolated, and unsupported in the school. He was also anxious about asking for help. In this context, he was doing (seeing) what he knew and believed to be correct and true.

A consultant was introduced in this case at the suggestion of the principal, who was concerned about losing the teacher and the increased class disruptions with which he was having to deal (that involved children other than the boy described). The consultant spent three mornings in the class observing patterns of teacher–child interaction, the use of language and reinforcement, grouping strategies, and time use. She also videotaped one hour-long session and met with the teacher on three occasions. On the first occasion, she administered a modification of the TRI (that focused on relationships with children in general), talked informally with the teacher about his goals, and assigned the teacher to complete the STRS on all the children in his class. During the second meeting, the consultant introduced a relationship perspective as an adjunct to his behavior management perspective. The relationship perspective (embodied in Figure 4.1) was connected to the teacher's sense of what he wanted to be for the children in his room, on the basis of what he had shared in the interview sessions: a father figure as well as a teacher.

Once this link was made, in the third meeting, the consultant helped the teacher test out different grouping strategies that concentrated his time with individual students, and alternative forms of interactions with the children that allowed him to experience more of this role and greater closeness with the students. The teacher and consultant designed a modification of Banking Time for the classroom—working with the class schedule to identify at least 5 to 10 minutes per day that the teacher could spend individually with each child. They also discussed the use of affection, positive attention to the children's interactions toward him, and a streamlined version of his previous behavior management system that was focused on positive consequences and consistency.

This "package" of classroom interventions was put on paper, and a timeline for implementation and follow-up was discussed. The consultant and teacher agreed to meet weekly for the next month to discuss implementation and to review videotapes of the classroom. After a month, a second classroom-wide set of STRSs was administered, with the consultant noting a considerable drop in the classroom average for Conflict and a rise in Closeness. In the 4-week follow-up session, the teacher reflected on the changes he was experiencing in the class; in particular, he noted a sense of effectiveness and the value that his attention had for the children.

Banking Time at the Classroom Level

In terms of building and maintaining relationships, there is no substitute for children receiving attention on an unconditional basis from the teacher. Although many children receive individual attention as a reward for positive behavior, it is not usually the case that time is built into the day so that each child is attended to by an adult in an unconditional manner. This goal is challenging, yet examples exist in which teachers build this time into the flow of the day. Most take small snippets of time: During instruction, teachers will take a child aside for a couple minutes, they will take a small group of children and work on an activity of their choosing, or they will use "downtime" like recess, lunch, or gym to make contact. This time is spent in a nondirective, reflective stance by the teacher (see Banking Time in chapter 7).

At the classroom level, teachers can build Banking Time interventions with students into small-group activities that are chosen by the students from a menu of alternatives. For as little as 10 minutes, the teacher spends time with the group, taking a reflective stance, while at the same time calling attention to relationship components and qualities as is appropriate. Using this approach, a teacher can spend time with 5 to 6 children at a time, rotating groups of children so that during the course of a typical week, he or she might be involved with each child 2 to 3 times.

Implementing a Banking Time intervention for the classroom presents its biggest challenge in terms of finding time and organizing this time. Most of the same principles that govern Banking Time at the individual level apply here. Regularly scheduled time blocks that are not conditional on behavior, a nondirective stance, the use of language to label feelings and feeling–action links, predictable responsiveness, and attention to three to four relationship messages (e.g., "I am here to help you") are all possible within this small group or classroom framework. Activities available for use during these periods typically include board games, arts and crafts activities, and even projects taken from the curriculum in math, language arts, social studies, or science. To the extent that the Banking Time stance is infused into curricular activities with regular, predictable scheduling of activities, the teacher can optimize the classroom environment in terms of its support of child–teacher relationships.

Several Banking Time principles apply at the classroom level. First is the use of messages to draw attention to or to define certain roles or experiences in the relationship that can be helpful to all children. These have been elaborated earlier but include messages or themes such as "you are important or valued," "I am available," "I am safe," "I am consistent," "I important or valued," "I am available," "I am safe," "I am consistent," "I can be helpful to you when asked," "you have competencies," and "your signals to me can be read and will be responded to." These are core relational themes that play out as an undercurrent to a host of interactions and classroom situations. Even outside of the actual Banking Time sessions, teachers can be alert to situations in which these messages are salient and can verbalize these messages along with taking the appropriate action. In this way, just as in the Banking Time sessions, the teacher pairs an interactive behavior (which usually is accompanied by an emotional valence or quality) with a verbal message. Over time, and with consistent implementation, such messages will come to embody what the child and the adult believe and experience about their relationship with one another, to the extent that they will override situational stressors or perturbations in the relationship, and hence allow for greater flexibility in interactions and responses. Of course, these themes might be individualized for different children or may, in fact, be consistently applied across all children, clearly conveying the role of the teacher in relationship to students.

Language and Emotion Regulation

Consistent with the developmental perspective offered in chapter 3, the child comes to use internal representations (thoughts) and their manipulation–communication (language) to tolerate arousal states and events and to respond with behaviors appropriate to the situation and its demands. Relationships play a key role in this progression and can, in fact, be enhanced by teachers' efforts to facilitate emotional regulation.

Teachers spend a great deal of time and effort in the management and instruction of emotion regulation skills, especially links among emotion, language, and action. There are at least three ways teachers facilitate emotion regulation: (a) they teach self-control, (b) the child experiences a regulated child–teacher relationship and thereby acquires a sense of regulated experience, and (c) teachers model emotion regulation. The vast majority of these efforts are informal and oftentimes unintentional, and they are completely intertwined with teachers' relationships with students. Although the child–teacher relationship context provides input to emotional regulation, the way in which a teacher handles the management of emotion and emotional expression (such as in behavior management systems) has an impact on the quality of the relationships he or she has with students.

This discussion of emotional regulation processes, and the ways in which language and communication are involved in these processes, provides a window or a lens through which teacher–child interactions can be viewed. In a consultant-based model of intervention in a classroom (or with a particular teacher), behaviors and behavioral patterns that exemplify these processes can be identified, brought to awareness, and subjected to the problem-solving orientation of the consultant. In the case of model of intervention would typically involve a consultant's examining teachers' interaction patterns or tendencies across the classroom as a whole and working with these emotional regulation processes at that level.

The primary means of communication between children and teachers is spoken or written language. Language in these forms is one way that children receive feedback about their behavior and are given cues for the demands of tasks and assistance for behavioral or academic needs. This contrasts with the use of gestures and caregiving, which are less abstract. As was discussed in chapter 3, children differ in the extent to which they can use language to "operate" on their experience. Thus, the use of information in abstracted, less experiential forms, such as symbols, words, and representations, to mediate one's experience of the world is a fairly advanced phase of social–emotional development in which words are connected to feelings and behaviors in a functional association.

There are two ways in which emotional regulation language and its use in the classroom are important with respect to child–teacher relationships. First, language labels emotions, pairing words or symbols with experience. The accurate use of language to label emotional states, emotion–action links, and emotion–cognition links provides children with a set of self-regulatory skills. Language becomes a fundamental way in which child and teacher share meaning or develop a sense of shared meaning. It is a signal between adult and child that is used to understand one another, and it is used for the teacher to help provide an experience of emotional regulation for the child. By sharing meaning, the child–teacher relationship is strengthened.

Language helps establish a system of shared meaning between teacher and child (or even teacher and classroom), linking behavior and emotion. A core process involved in the development of child–adult relationships is this use of shared meaning or experience (e.g., "attunement"). Critical to this process is the capacity of the adult to label the child's experience accurately and in a timely manner. This aspect of adult behavior is linked to the closeness of the child–adult relationship and other outcomes relevant to school-like settings (Howes & Hamilton, 1992b). For this reason, interventions specifically directed at teaching teachers how to label and reflect emotional states in children, as part of the natural flow of classroom interactions, are valuable for enhancing relationship quality and outcomes.

Teacher–child interactions often target specific emotions and influence their intensity or expression. Teachers help children keep the intensity of emotion within acceptable limits by providing comfort, support, and help, and they assist with output and expression by facilitating discussion of the child's emotional state, providing labels for emotional experience and tolerating a wide range of emotions and expressions. Being available to help the child with respect to emotions is a critical aspect of the child–teacher relationship that has consequences for the child's classroom adjustment and coping. For example, attachment-related behavior (seeking comfort when threatened) is one means of regulating the intensity of anxiety that is expressed fairly directly (clinging or hugging) in early childhood (Cassidy, 1994; Crittenden, 1992) and less directly (wanting to talk) in middle childhood and early adolescence. How teachers respond to these bids (communicating an openness to the child, labeling emotions, commenting on the child's perspective) establishes an emotional tone for relating to the teacher that pervades the classroom.

In Greenberg's (Greenberg et al., 1991, 1993) affect–behavior–cognition model, the adult-as-emotion-regulator provides comfort for arousing experiences, then provides labels for the child's affective states. These labels form the basis for emerging links among cognition, language, and emotion and allow the adult access to the emotional world of the child. These access points involve the adult in the child's emotional regulation system and provide the basis for the communication and closeness–warmth that are hallmarks of adaptive relationships. As discussed before, these access points to the child's emotional world must be cultivated—they often do not happen systematically enough or with sufficient regularity or intensity to allow the child–teacher relationship to function to reduce the negative consequences of any number of challenges or risk factors. Thus, simple instruction in and implementation of affective labeling skills, reflective statements about emotions, and neutral responses to emotion expression are necessary to provide teachers with the relational tools they need, as exemplified in the following:

> In working with a new third-grade teacher who had a tendency to recognize only positive emotions in children (similar to the third case described in chapter 6), the consultant noticed, predictably, that the children tended to seek comfort from one another rather than from this teacher. The teacher had made a number of referrals to the special educator because of apparent learning problems in the children. The special educator suspected a problem in perceiving the children's needs and requested the consultant observe in the classroom. On noticing the pattern of uniformly positive interpretations of behavior and emotion, the consultant offered to meet with the teacher. In this meeting, the consultant wondered out loud about whether the teacher might be feeling a bit distant from this group of children and whether she would like to review some videotapes of classroom interaction. The teacher, surprised by this interpretation, was somewhat defensive and taken aback. Reluctantly, she agreed. In the session in which the tape was reviewed, the consultant adopted the role of narrator, labeling the positive and negative emotions evident on the tape. The teacher soon began predicting the consultant's statements, and soon they were jointly naming emotions. The teacher noted, "I'm not sure I noticed all this going on before . . . I see where they don't seem to come to me much . . . what do I do about all this?" The consultant noted that these emotion expressions were simply signals the children were sending her and that by labeling them, she could come closer to the children, and perhaps they would feel understood by her and come to her for help. The consultant offered to run some activities in the class in which these labeling skills could be modeled for the teacher. The teacher learned quickly.

Summary

Classroom-level practices related to stabilizing interactions between children and a particular adult, minimizing the relational tax levied by entries and exits, appropriately using rewards and punishments as feedback in the child–teacher relationship, and providing teachers with the knowledge base for infusing classroom practices and interactions with language that supports emotion regulation are all within the purview of the psychologist as classroom consultant. These are practices that support the development of relationships between teachers and children that, in turn, give rise to these relationships functioning as protective factors in the face of risk. More specifically, these practices assist children (and teachers) in communicating personal goals and information, experiencing emotional closeness and warmth, providing motivation to teacher and child to face the frustration of engaging in challenging instructional and learning tasks, and facilitating dyadic interactions that support the child's acquisition of new skills and knowledge.

These interventions complement those described for individual dyads in chapter 7 and build directly on the model of child–teacher relationships presented in earlier chapters. These classroom-level interventions can be applied on their own, as described in the examples, or can be combined with individual dyadic-level interventions for a package of efforts aimed at strengthening relationships. However, the discussion of classroom-level processes has raised issues regarding policies and practices at the school or the district level that affect classroom practices. The discussion now turns to issues related to school-wide efforts to enhance child–teacher relationships.

9

How School Policy Affects the Child–Teacher Relationship

A meeting of the program staff that serves high-risk 4-year-olds in a suburban school system is involved in a director-led discussion of an article on building resilience in children. The staff, sometimes emotionally, even painfully, expresses the hope that their program builds resilience in the often broken lives of the children it serves. Relationships with the children are a focus of the discussion for some time. There is a genuine sense that this program really supports these children.

Then, one aide raises the issue of this district-wide program not being located in the school or schools in which the children will attend kindergarten. She sees this as a really negative aspect of the way the program is structured. She recalls when the program was smaller, and the few classes were housed in the catchment elementary schools: "It was so important to the kids that they could come back and see us. They'd come for hugs, they'd come to work with the kids in the class [for 4-year-olds]. They really felt important when they came back to see us; and we could help when they got in trouble or needed us. It's really hard not to be there for them and not be able to see them." She noted that this connection often continued after kindergarten for the elementary school years. She teared up. She was upset by the notion that the children in the program, as currently configured, would miss this opportunity for continuity and support and that it hurts them. "They have no relationship continuity from year to year transitioning from the 4-year-old program into kindergarten."

This anecdote is common for teachers who connect with children within a relationship that seems to buffer the children from the stresses of their lives. Every teacher can relate to the feelings of loss and worry when a child, with whom they have worked for 9 months, leaves for the next grade. The example above is saturated with attachment-related feelings of the teacher and is framed by the staff member in terms of attachment. The child is seen as seeking contact with an attachment figure and as using that attachment figure when under stress; the presence of the attachment figure affords support for higher levels of the child's coping and competence. The adult experiences feelings of loss and abandonment, even guilt, for not being there when needed. This is an example of a transition imposed on relationships between teachers and children by the arrangements of a particular program. In this case, the location of the program or programs constrains the relationships.

> In a different staff meeting with a group of elementary school teachers from a small city school serving a heterogeneous population, there was a sense that one of the ways in which this school was a resource for the children was in making them feel at home. The staff pointed out the fact that the children really had a sense of pride and ownership in the school: "This is a place they belong." The children feel effective, and they have some control and input over their lives. Right after this, someone says "and they take care of one another," elaborating with an example of how the students generally encourage the special education students (severely handicapped program) and other students needing help. It is clear that there is a helping ethic in this school. Then, in turn, nearly every one of the staff attending this meeting (nearly 40 staff) mentions a feeling of responsibility for each child who attends the school. They offer examples of how one or another of them helped in the hallway, bathroom, or lunchroom, always mentioning the child's name and speaking personally of the child. There is very little sense of "that kid belongs to so and so" but, instead, that any teacher noticing a need would respond.

This is such a clear example of the adults' shaping a responsive community in this school (Knoff & Batsche, 1994). One can imagine the sense of safety and protection (attachment again!) that this affords the children in this school, a sense that any adult would respond to you when in need or would step in to set a limit or to use corrective feedback. As in the previous example, the scenarios invoked by teachers, the examples they use, and the language used to describe these examples typify teacher–child relationship processes (e.g., attachment).

Three things are important about these examples for the present school-level discussion of relationships between teachers and children. First, these are the experiences lived by teachers—they live in a world of attachment- and relationship-related feelings, experiences, and beliefs. No amount of focus on academics, no matter how strong or exclusive, will substantially change the fact that the substrate of classroom life is social and emotional. Second, teacher–child relationships are constrained and facilitated by school-level policies that affect staffing levels, configurations, and locations of programs and transitions between programs and classrooms, among other things. Finally, and perhaps most important, these two groups of school staff, in quite different settings and locations, worked in environments that made it possible to have open discussions among themselves about their experiences with children as well as their hopes and fears for the children and themselves in the school environment. Are these programs unique? Can what they do be emulated elsewhere? Why would it be important to have these discussions? What district- and school-level policies and practices affect relationships between children and teachers? These are the questions that frame the present chapter in a discussion of school-level policies and practices that influence the development and maintenance of robust child–teacher relationships.

This chapter addresses at least four ways, derived from the developmental perspective discussed in earlier chapters, in which school-level policies and practices (school and district levels are discussed interchangeably here) affect relationships between teachers and children. These include policies and practices related to (a) adult–child ratios; (b) length of contact between children and adults; (c) transitions and stability of contact; and (d) school organization, climate, and culture.

Adult–Child Ratios

There is literally no occasion during which school staff discuss the problems of children in schools when they do not discuss the matter of child–adult (or student–teacher) ratios. This is particularly true at the elementary school level but also occurs at the middle and junior high school level as well. Ratios are one very salient manner in which schools constrain relationships between teachers and children, and one can examine them with the perspective developed in this book. (See chapter 8 for a more thorough discussion of ratios and relationships; I briefly mention ratios in this chapter because of the extent to which school-level decisions affect them.)

For example, in the early 1990s, the city of Minneapolis went so far as to hold a special referendum on the matter of raising property taxes with the stated purpose of lowering teacher–student ratios in elementary school classrooms. Each vote for the proposal was a vote for spending additional money to lower these ratios. The referendum passed. It is interesting that a parallel initiative across the Mississippi in St. Paul failed. A child attending kindergarten in a Minneapolis school in the fall of 1993 could expect to be in a classroom with a teacher and 16 other children. In St. Paul, this child might attend with 21 other children. At the state level, Tennessee conducted a similar intervention with its kindergarten classrooms statewide (Mosteller, 1995) and California is also intiating a similar effort.

It is a fundamental belief in most school systems and communities that lowering child–teacher ratios is good. When a teacher is responsible for a fewer number of children, it is believed that the children are exposed to better instruction, the class is easier to manage, and more work gets accomplished. As was noted in chapter 8, the results of evaluations of interventions to lower ratios supported these beliefs (Bourke, 1986; McGiverin et al., 1989; Thurlow et al., 1993). The Tennessee initiative to lower ratios has demonstrated that children in the lower ratio classrooms have by and large achieved at higher levels than when ratios were higher. The child–teacher relationship processes affected by ratios were discussed in chapter 8, and decisions regarding in-class grouping to achieve better functional ratios that maximized contact between a teacher and a child were presented. In this chapter on school-wide policies, ratios continue to be relevant, in part because although within a classroom teachers can manipulate the functional ratio by grouping, school policies affect the number of teachers and children in that classroom.

In many kindergarten classrooms (and some first grades), there is a full-time teacher and a full-time aide—two adults. At the other end of the spectrum is the single adult in the classroom. In between, there exists nearly every permutation and fraction of the continuum between one and two adults. Many classroom situations also include a number of other adults who come in to help from time to time—parents, volunteers, student teachers, college students, and more. In reality, most elementary school classrooms have a fairly large number of adults in and out of the door on any given day.

Any discussion of the effect of ratios must start with the assumption that every classroom in the United States has, at the minimum, one full-time teacher. Thus, one reason that lower ratios may be associated with child success is that lower ratios more or less directly (depending on how they are computed) reflect the increased likelihood that a specific full-time teacher is responsible for fewer children in her classroom. Class size, in short, goes down. In this context, full-time adults are distributed across fewer children.

What happens to social processes in a classroom in which adult resources are distributed across fewer children? First, each child can be expected, on average, to interact more frequently with an adult with specialized training in the education of children. Interactions between child and teacher in a lower ratio classroom allows for more teacher–child interactions within individual child–teacher dyads. Thus, the opportunities for instruction and relationship (formation and maintenance) increase. If child–teacher relationships can be harnessed as buffers to risk, the opportunities for developing these relationships and for allowing them to regulate development are optimized when the child is afforded the chance to have a primary adult figure with whom to interact.

It is fundamental that educators and parents should scrutinize child–teacher ratios, and efforts to change them, in relation to the actual experience of a child in a classroom, trying to answer whether whatever ratio or change maximizes the contact between a child and a particular teacher. Thus, although a relationship focus can be used to argue for lower child–teacher ratios, it can also be used to frame analysis of existing policy. In this analysis, the psychologist has an important role as one who can provide the scientific and theoretical underpinnings of a discussion of policy related to ratios and can translate theory into the experiences of teachers and children.

Increasing Length of Contact

If one asks teachers, at the end of the school year, about the connection between their teaching and their relationships with students, they often say (in one form or another), "I was just beginning to reach him" or "I felt like we had gotten past all the 'testing to see who's tougher' stuff and now we were able to work with one another" or "she and I had just started to really communicate—she was really opening up to me." Just as often, they add a sense of disappointment that the process will have to start over with a new teacher the next year: "It's too bad we can't keep 'em for another year."

One method of improving the quality of teacher–child relationships is to lengthen the amount of time teachers and children spend together (not lengthen the school day!). Just as child–teacher ratios can be used as a strategy to increase contact between a teacher and a student within a given time period, relationships can be enhanced through school-level strategies that extend this period of time for contact between teachers and children. The most common method of accomplishing this relationship objective is to experiment with policies that allow students to stay with a particular teacher for 2 to 3 years. There are at least two kinds of contexts in which this kind of intervention has been attempted. The first is known as "looping" and is a practice increasing in frequency (Graue, in press). The second approach is functionally equivalent to looping in one sense but has its roots in the notion of "academies" for ethnic minorities, in which African American boys (typically) are taught for several years by an African American male teacher–father figure.

In the looping framework, a teacher is capable of teaching, for example, the K–2 curriculum, a cohort of children enters with the teacher as kindergartners and travels with him or her until the second grade. He or she would then start the next year with another cohort in kindergarten. Incoming and exiting students would be included as the class flows through the 3-year period, just as they are under more traditional structures. Looping is not to be confused with cross-grading, in which grades are mixed in a given classroom (e.g., K–1 or 1–2) but the children travel to another teacher each year. There is a widespread belief (although not empirically grounded because of a lack of data) that looping is effective in some broad sense (Graue, in press).

In addition, the popular press has reported on interventions that are specifically designed to build relationships between teachers and children who are considered to be at high risk for school failure: ethnic minority (primarily African American) boys. Used as an alternative program, these schools or programs within schools have been described informally by the news media as "academies." The fundamental premise on which these programs were based was the relationship formed between a child and a teacher. Educators and community members recognized that many minority boys were being raised in female-headed households and had little to no access to same-gender role models or to the experience of forming an attachment with a same-gender parent. Thus, these programs typically enrolled young (primary grade) boys in a looping arrangement with a teacher who was an African American man. These opportunities frequently do not present themselves within the public school primary grades, in which the modal teacher is a White woman. These programs were often subject to a variety of challenges, including legal challenges that they discriminated among student groups on the basis of race and gender, and systematic evaluations of these "academy-type" programs have been rare.

Common to both the looping intervention and the academy-type program is an emphasis on building, and building on, relationships between teachers and children. When a child's contact with the same teacher is extended for more than an academic year, the intervention deepens and enriches the child–teacher relationship, increasing the possibility that this relationship will produce benefits in terms of student success. Insofar as this discussion pertains to interventions, a looping-type arrangement is a way of intensifying the effectiveness of the child–teacher relationship as a buffering intervention for risk conditions. One would expect that combining low ratios with looping would provide a near-optimal context for the formation of effective child–teacher relationships. Recalling earlier discussions of relationships as buffers or protective factors against risk, one can frame policy analysis and program development around how these relationship resources can be best delivered to high-risk students, through either primary prevention or early intervention delivery systems.

Again, it is important to ask why practices that provide for extended child–teacher contact would be effective. With regard to literature on other adult–child relationships, it has been demonstrated that length of time in contact can enhance the quality of child–parent interactions and relationships and that transitions and other disruptions of continuity in the relationship can have negative effects (see Pianta & Walsh, 1996, for a summary). The mechanisms of developmental change involve complex systems in which time invariably plays an important role. Child–teacher relationships, as contexts for development, take time to form and to have an effect on development, and they always operate in a broader relational context—involving parents, peers, and others. Thus for a relationship between a child and a specific teacher to produce developmental change, time is a key ingredient of the equation.

No matter how positive in nature, a short-lived contact will not allow a relationship to act as a buffer to risk. One can consider, for example, the child who is maltreated or chronically exposed to harsh, punitive, hostile interactions with dangerous adults. The widespread and long-lasting negative effects of this kind of treatment have been documented in numerous studies, with some studies having a particular emphasis on describing the ways in which this developmental history seriously undermines school success. One mechanism thought to be responsible for the school problems of these children is their difficulty in relying on adults to explore and master the object and social worlds (Aber & Allen, 1987; Erickson et al., 1989).

To expect that a teacher's relationship with such a child will overcome a history of long-lasting inadequacies in relationships with adults is simply unrealistic. The intervention literature is filled with documentation of the difficulty of changing well-established relationship patterns. However, entrenched patterns of interactions with adults can be changed so that children can use adults effectively. Under what conditions? Typically, the rule is "the earlier the better" and "the less severe the case, the more likely the positive outcome." Thus, hopes for success need to be tempered with reality.

Because most children who have some difficulty in school—those typically labeled high risk—are not maltreated, their risk coefficient with respect to relationships is not as high as that for children fitting the example above. Thus, development is somewhat more open to the influence of child–teacher relationships for most high-risk children. A key issue to bring into any analysis of the role of child–teacher relationships in relation to risk is that building educational systems to combat risk is a process requiring a long view of the child's development over many years and involving many contexts, not just what occurs between a child and a given teacher (Pianta & Walsh, 1996).

Finally, several other issues are germane to discussing relationship continuity as a buffer to risk and to examining school policies with this lens in mind. First is an age-related issue. Most people believe that the primary grades are those in which relationships between children and adults should be attended to and possibly used in interventions of the sort being discussed here (e.g., looping, using academies). However, limiting the use of interventions to the primary grades to provide continuity to child–teacher relationships neglects the influence of child–adult relationships on children in early adolescence and beyond (Lynch & Cicchetti, 1992; Wentzel, 1996). Although the nature of the child–adult relationship changes with adolescence, moving from a caregiving focus to a mentoring, monitoring, problem-solving focus (Lynch & Cicchetti, 1992; Wentzel, 1996), relationships with adults still play a key role in development particularly in school performance. For children with compromised relationship histories, relationships with adults are likely to take on even greater importance in the middle and junior high school years, as children can be more active in seeking resources that promote their social and mental health (Lynch & Cicchetti, 1997).

Yet, most school policies related to children's contact with teachers in middle and junior high school (and beyond) fraction or distribute contact between teachers and children into increasingly smaller units. It is interesting that most attempts to address the needs of high-risk students in these years involve lowering or constraining child–teacher contacts through the use of "schools within a school" or "academic houses" that have the effect of redistributing adult resources. Analysis of the relationship needs and capacities of many high-risk youth in middle and junior high school suggests that drawing adult–child interactions into a tighter, more focused unit is a step in almost every form of intervention. For example, as special education interventions increase in "restrictiveness," at the same time, they reduce the number of teachers with whom a youngster deals. Yet interventions such as these are limited, when viewed from a relationship or a prevention perspective. They are "too little, too late" for many of the children they serve, when analyzed with respect to their relationship needs (Aber & Allen, 1987).

Furthermore, this analysis can be extended to school policies that affect children's transition into school (Rimm-Kaufman & Pianta, 1997). Teachers have almost no contact with children and families before they enter school; however, it is widely believed (although again not grounded in empirical support) that teacher–child contact before school can ease a child's transition, in part because it begins the processes of establishing a relationship between child and teacher earlier and can be more individualized than the kind of group open house that is the typical practice. Viewed in the context of preventive interventions (Weissberg et al., 1991), policies that extend child–teacher contacts throughout the day, across transitions, and across academic years and settings can increase resources available to all children and to particular children whose needs for relationship stability and contact are high.

Decreasing Transitions

Related to the discussion of extending child–teacher contacts across years or grades is the broader principle of formulating school-level policies and practices that decrease relationship transitions in any form (switching teachers from grade to grade is just one form of relationship transition). This topic has been addressed in previous discussions of classroom-level interventions, in which school policies are examined for how they tend to maximize "exit and entry" events in the classrooms.

From a school-wide perspective, many of the points made earlier in the discussion of classroom-level interventions still apply (see chapter 8). Exits and entries that fraction a given child's experience with an adult (or adults) pose risks to the establishment of an effective relationship between a child and a teacher. These issues, however, can be framed in terms of school-level policies as well.

The most common, nearly ubiquitous, manner in which schools seek to solve the problem of individual differences in children is to increase contact with specialists and to fraction the contact between the child and the classroom teacher (Gartner & Lipsky, 1987; Pianta & Walsh, 1996). Unfortunately, as almost double jeopardy, it is often the most "at-risk" youngsters who are enrolled in these services and are required to make most of the changes. Each occasion in which pull-out services are offered requires some form of transition (which can be disruptive). In attachment terms, the time away from the home teacher negatively affects the degree to which a sense of stability and security (secure base) can be provided by that teacher. In extreme form (such as the child making two to three such transitions each day), this arrangement of services is itself a form of risk. How to best integrate services needed by children into the flow of the classroom is a significant management problem that has consequences for building, and building on, relationships between teachers and children. This problem can be addressed, at least in part, when services are delivered in consultation form by the specialist to the teacher, not to the child (Goldstein, 1993; Gutkin, 1997; Hughes, 1992; Meyers et al., 1979; Shriner et al., 1989).

In a consultation, or an indirect services model, the specialized training of the special services personnel is put to use by the classroom teacher in his or her interactions with the child (Gutkin & Conoley, 1990; Hughes, 1992). The specialized personnel conduct an assessment of the child's needs in their area of expertise; develop treatment programs to be integrated into the classroom schedule and flow; train teachers to deliver such programs; and monitor, troubleshoot, and evaluate these programs as implemented. Evidence has indicated that specialized services provided on a consultation basis are at least as effective (or more so) for the vast majority of cases that are presented to specialized personnel (see Zins, Kratochwill, & Elliott, 1993). The training that takes place with teachers with whom consultation has been successful has the added benefit of increasing teachers' competence to address similar needs down the road, which has a preventive effect, and lowers the incidence of more serious problems.

Given the pros and cons of consultation, a shift to delivering routine, specialized services through consultation is an ideal way of shifting resources to more effectively support child–teacher relationships. In this context, even for children with needs for specialized support services, contact with a primary teacher is preserved at the same time specialized support is delivered. Fractioning of the teacher–child relationship is reduced, as are entry and exit occasions—threats to stability of contact and sources of noncompliance. Contact with multiple adults, with their own idiosyncratic interaction styles, tolerances, and sensitivities, is also reduced so that the child has the opportunity to learn one relationship, learn it well, and glean the developmental benefits of learning it. These are just some of the direct and indirect benefits of a shift to consultation, which, from the perspective of Pianta and Walsh (1996), fights the tendency of special services and programs to fraction resources for children. Thus, school-level policies on the delivery of services to children can be scrutinized with respect to their effects on another resource—child–teacher relationships—in terms of the extent to which they increase or decrease the "tax" on relationships caused by transitions.

School-Level Organization, Climate, and Culture

It should be clear from the discussion of lowering child–teacher ratios, ensuring more continuity in child–teacher contacts, decreasing transitions as threats to continuous contacts, and moving to consultation-based services that the interventions suggested by the preceding discussion most optimally form an intervention package that results in schools looking quite different organizationally than they now do (e.g., Adelman, 1996; Holtzmann, 1992; Knoff & Batsche, 1994; Wang & Kovach, 1995).

Organization

To the extent that school organization is a major focus of school reform (Wang & Kovach, 1995), organizational structures and procedures that affect relationships between teachers and children need to be part of the analysis. The relationship–systems perspective described in earlier chapters identifies the developmental benefits of contexts that, in social terms, are fairly small and stable. These are schools in which social networks are manageable and children are clearly linked to a specific adult or a small number of adults, these adults know they have primary responsibility for a specific child, and, most important, each child knows they can seek and find resources from a specific adult. In other words, teachers are engaged with children (Louis, 1995). Optimally, these contexts address decisions about ratios, grade-based class assignments, service delivery, and transitions in such a way that adults can invest heavily in interactions with children (e.g., banking time is possible) and that the quality of these interactions can be characterized as sensitive and responsive. This may involve any of a variety of organizational patterns, and a flexible approach to optimizing adult resources when the organizational pattern is in place is challenged by external demands and stressors (Wang & Kovach, 1995). Frequent, direct contact with a small number of adults who are invested in optimizing developmental outcomes in the context of a manageable and knowable social network are just some of the qualities of a context that can reduce risk. Contexts that mirror these properties are associated with competence across a range of child outcomes (Holtzmann, 1992; Louis, 1995; Pianta & Walsh, 1996; Wang & Kovach, 1995).

Although some elementary schools are organized in this way, pressures on school systems and misguided understanding of "development" and "maturity" cause middle and high schools not to look like this at all. Increasingly, elementary schools are adopting the fractioned structure of middle schools. Multiple classes organized by content area, increasing numbers of specialists, and large, distributed networks of adult responsibility for children can contribute to risk in part because these factors undermine relationships between children and an adult or adults who can serve as a source of security and stability (see Graue, in press). A "team" or "family" or "inclusive" approach to restructuring schools, in which children are exposed to fewer teachers, has counteracted this tendency toward fractioning adults and children (e.g., Louis, 1995; Wang & Kovach, 1995).

Risk for school failure in the United States is largely the result of social processes that have undermined the child's capacity to adapt and to respond to the challenges of learning and performance in school. Homes that are less homelike produce risk for school failure (Pianta, Egeland, & Sroufe, 1997). Countering the risk and vulnerability mechanisms set in place by these social processes requires compensatory action on these processes themselves—social networks (especially with adults) in schools need to be made small, manageable, and sensitive–responsive and to be invested in particular children if there is the possibility of overcoming the risk that travels with these children (Pianta & Walsh, 1996).

School Culture: Giving Voice to Teachers' Experiences of Relationships

In the programs that were described in the vignettes at the beginning of the chapter, one early childhood program had just been moved from being distributed in several elementary schools to one central location. The teachers, without exception, felt this was a more homelike atmosphere in part because of the way they could now arrange for children's needs on a more individualized, flexible, as-needed basis. They developed a stronger, more coherent vision of themselves in relation to the children and an identity in which investment in each child was supported and encouraged by all the staff. The staff of the program in the second vignette described the way that the children felt at home in the school and that all the staff, not just the teacher, were invested in each child.

The investment and homelike atmosphere in these programs created closer relationships between teachers and children than would have occurred in other organizational structures. The emotions generated by these close relationships and investment by teachers were actually a challenge to maintaining these values in this school. Teachers could burn out easily, become discouraged by the forces operating against them, and feel saddened and discouraged by seeing children move on each year to school contexts that were different and were perceived to be less homelike.

How these teachers managed their feelings about children was a central aspect of these organizations. One of the clear similarities in these two contexts was the freedom, and encouragement, to talk about their relationships with children and their feelings in these relationships. Often, these conversations took place just between teachers, or between teachers and administrators, but more often, the conversations were encouraged and were catalyzed in conversations at staff meetings in which a consultant was present. The purpose of these conversations was to help staff understand their experiences and their roles with children in relationship terms. On a staff- or a school-wide level, these conversations were like the individualized consultations with teachers that work with teachers' representational models of relationships with children.

By formalizing these conversations in regular meetings, and by permitting openness about staff's feelings and beliefs about these children, the staff's representations were not consigned to second-tier status, hallway, or staff-lounge talk or considered a by-product of teaching. They were placed at the forefront of how the school defined itself (Louis, 1995). In short, they were a major part of the culture of these schools. These conversations were the school's way of extending to teachers the benefits of valuing relationships that the teachers were trying to extend to children. Consistent with this valuing of relationships, these schools and programs all had classes in which a variety of practices related to enhancing child–teacher relationships were being implemented, the practices included Banking Time, individual consultation with teachers concerning children or concerning their own perceptions of relationships, and school-wide programs for informing staff about relationships with more didactic methods.

Furthermore, relationships between children and teachers figure prominently in more generic efforts for school reform such as the School Development Program or programs that make consultants more available to teachers, lower class size, or encourage teacher collaboration (e.g., Comer, 1988; Knoff & Batsche, 1994). These efforts are complex and are outside of the purview of this chapter; however, two points are worth mentioning. First, successful school reform efforts often place a value on relationships and social networks, collaboration and teams at the staff level, and shared responsibility for children (Comer, 1988; Knoff & Batsche, 1994). These emphases are the accrued wisdom of local decision making and local efforts that, in turn, validate a systems theory view of schooling, with interpersonal relationships among staff and children playing a prominent role. Second, many school reform efforts strategically target relationships between children and teachers as outcomes. Thus, signs of successful school reform efforts are a sense of teachers knowing children better and children having feelings of belonging.

What factors allow teachers or schools to place representations and relationships as central to the mission of the organization or as important to a goal of reform? At the school level, how does one alter the school culture to make it permissible to share relationship experiences as a central part of teaching, not just something that has to be dealt with after the fact as a burnout issue? Clearly, leadership is critical; both the schools described in this chapter had leaders that saw the value of relationships between teachers and children and, at the same time, encouraged teachers to discuss their experiences.

What about situations when leadership or knowledge is limited? Psychologists have a role to play in framing discussions and changing attitudes of staff so that these kinds of discussions can take place. The idea that school psychologists engage in interpersonal persuasion (e.g., Gutkin & Conoley, 1990; Hughes, 1992; O'Keefe & Medway, 1997) is consistent with working toward the goal of creating school cultures in which relationship-focused conversations can take place. As information about the importance of adult–child relationships penetrates the popular media and teacher-education programs, and is reflected in educational leadership training in the context of school reform, openings will be created for psychologists to advance information on child–teacher relationships to a place of prominence in school culture.

Summary

In this chapter, school-wide perspectives on child–teacher relationships have been addressed, consistent with the goal of presenting information that enables schools to build, and build on, these relationships as resources for child development. School-level policies or practices were discussed in relation to four factors affecting the formation and maintenance of child–teacher relationships: (a) adult–child ratios; (b) length of contact between children and adults; (c) transitions and stability of contact; and (d) school organization, climate, and culture.

One important theme presented in this discussion is the fact that the relationship perspective offers a lens for the analysis of policy and practice that has not been yet articulated or applied in educational contexts. This lens is wedded to theories of social development, the role of relationships with adults in the development of child outcomes, and the ways in which these relationships are affected by the social context in which they develop and are maintained. Attention to these issues in schools, with a focus on relationships between children and teachers, is novel yet not without precedent in many educational contexts. As schools contend with the challenges of educating more and more children who are at high risk for educational failure because of eroded social development, this relationship lens will become increasingly valuable as a tool for supporting the construction of school and classroom contexts that make use of the resources of adults.

10 _____

Strong Relationships Mean More Resources: An Agenda for Practice and Research

As an applied child and adolescent psychologist, your professional practice involves many children for whom school is not a place of personal success and reward, either interpersonally or academically. Their relationships with adults in the school context reflect these broader problems in adjustment. Some are alienated from adults in one form or another, perhaps disengaged and uninvolved, or involved only to the extent that they have to participate in a relationship that allows certain forms of expression, such as was the case for Deborah in chapter 6. Other children are embroiled in conflict with their teachers. Many are angry, uncertain as to whether this adult will behave like other adults and reject them, or are unable to confidently trust this person with whom they spend most of the day.

You also see many examples of good relationships, relationships that enrich the child's life, build confidence and self-esteem, support the child's learning and performance, and motivate the child to explore new ideas and new roles. Many children in your practice also experience relationships of this type.

Your practice affords you some opportunities to engage individual teachers concerning their interactions with particular children as well as opportunities to influence groups of teachers and to be called upon for advice on school and community policy related to children and adolescents. What ideas from this book are relevant to your work?

This chapter summarizes key points presented throughout the book, links these ideas to professional practice, and describes an agenda for research that will advance the study of child–teacher relationships. The present ideas can be applied in many different ways but, to some extent, can be reduced to applications that are attempted in the context of a preventive orientation to service delivery and to those that are in a more remedial context.

Practice for Prevention

Applied child and adolescent psychologists are usually consulted after a problem has developed to a fairly serious level. Rarely are psychologists involved early enough to prevent the kind of problems that they see most often. Yet, much of the information I presented in the early chapters, and the classroom- and school-level applications I described in chapters 8 and 9, can be used in the context of preventive interventions. In short, they can be used to provide information to educators that, in turn, can be used to support and enhance the quality of child–teacher relationships for all children as well as those at most risk.

The need for a focus on preventive mental health services, with schools as contexts in which to deliver such services, has been articulated by many professionals (e.g., CSBPSC, 1994; Henggeler, 1994; Roberts, 1996; Weissberg et al., 1991). This requires that the professional understand the mechanisms for delivering services that have a preventive effect (e.g., Hughes, 1992; Weissberg et al., 1991). In the present context, this involves one's viewing schools as a context for development and relationships between children and teachers as one mechanism by which school contexts influence development. Once professionals understand these terms, they can use resources present in the child–teacher relationship more systematically.

Some authors have argued that the survival of applied child and adolescent psychology depends in large part on the degree to which psychologists become involved in the design and delivery of prevention services (CSBPSC, 1994; Henggeler, 1994; Roberts, 1996). The changing landscape of third-party payment, the increasing use of paraprofessionals in direct service to children and families, as well as the emerging knowledge on best practices in intervention come together to create opportunities to reexamine and redesign how services are delivered to children (Henggeler, 1994; Roberts, 1996). Child–teacher relationships are an ideal resource for preventive intervention—they are available to all children, options exist for strengthening and intensifying their benefits to children, and systems are already in place for teacher training (inservice and preservice) that can reflect this knowledge about relationships. The following sections address key themes from the previous chapters that need to be infused into the design of preventive services and used to identify areas for future work.

Systems Theory

General systems theory provides a set of principles that can help educators wade through, and make sense of, the complex nature of developmental pathways through the school years and the role of schools in influencing those pathways. Because one of the problems facing educators is the sheer complexity of the task of understanding the links among risk, outcome, and education, systems theory can be helpful in ordering analysis. It is important to note that systems theory cannot provide all the answers to the many dilemmas facing educators. In fact, many educators are made uncomfortable with systems theory's emphasis on uncertainties in predictions, holistic perspectives, and highly dynamic interactions among multiple forces or influences on behavior. Nonetheless, achieving some level of familiarity and comfort with systems theory, and its applications to the specific topic of child–teacher relationships, can be helpful in advancing preventive interventions (Pianta & Walsh, 1996).

The importance of adopting a systems theory perspective cannot be overemphasized. To the extent that a range of school-related problems for children are understood in terms of the invidious triangle of "child," "home," or "school" causes, a preventive intervention orientation will be impossible. Those who design current models of training teachers, psychologists, and other helping professionals too frequently oversimplify models of development, relying on a dated perspective emphasizing stages or specific domains of development (e.g., Goodlad, 1991). Furthermore, the dominant explanation for child behavior (problems) in present-day American culture appears to be the biological processes that appear correlated with children's performance. Such perspectives are narrow and likely to truncate alternatives available to children. Systems theory counters these oversimplified views of development and, although complex and uncertain to some degree, offers a view of development that opens up possibilities for preventive intervention.

The Role of Context

Perhaps the single most important contribution of systems theory to preventive intervention in education is the emphasis on the role of context in developmental processes—even those for which there are biological correlates (Gottlieb, 1991; Reid et al., 1993; Sameroff, 1989). In addition, systems theory provides a way of thinking about how contexts interact with child characteristics to produce developmental change. From this perspective, preventive service delivery that uses the child–teacher relationship as a resource capitalizes on the distributed nature of development during childhood. Competence, with respect to the key themes of development in childhood, is a function of many contexts' support with respect to that theme. In the same vein, risk can be conceptualized as the inability of social contexts to adequately support development. Relationships with adults are a cornerstone of development—they are responsible for a large proportion of school success. Too often, the role of the adult–child relationship is underestimated either because it is not well understood or because the role of the context itself is not understood or emphasized in the prevailing models for understanding development.

To use the resources inherent in child–teacher relationships preventively, psychologists must become active in advancing educators' understanding of the role of contexts in development. A focus on the role of social processes in learning, instruction, and socialization that is integrated into dominant theories of and approaches to instruction and classroom management would be a considerable leap from current conceptualizations and approaches to professional training and practice. Psychologists have a central role to play in facilitating this leap—who among professionals involved in education is better suited to provide knowledge about the role of context and social processes in education and development?

Information on Child–Adult Relationships

A more specific focus on relationships emphasizes the need for psychologists to communicate information about child–adult relationships, particularly child–teacher relationships, and their importance in development. This information helps teachers and other education professionals understand children's behavior and their own experiences and also lays the groundwork for the kind of interventions presently discussed. Because preventive intervention systems by and large capitalize on naturally occurring contacts between children and resources (Henggeler, 1994; Roberts, 1996), the successful design and implementation of such systems are dependent on the people implementing interventions to thoroughly understand the rationale behind their actions.

As has been described in earlier chapters, child–adult relationships serve a regulatory function with respect to emotional and academic skills development. In so doing, these relationships enormously influence a child's competence in childhood. There is evidence that child–parent relationships provide infrastructure for these processes and that child–teacher relationships, in turn, operate on this infrastructure. Thus, any discussion of child–adult relationships must rely, in part, on summaries of the literature on child–parent relationships. (The references provided in the discussion of these issues in chapters 3 and 4 can provide the interested reader with necessary information.)

There is also a need to focus on child–teacher relationships apart from child–parent relationships. Child–teacher relationships influence development through processes characteristic of dyadic systems. These processes, involving representational models, feedback or exchange processes (tolerance, timing, and contingency of interactions), and other relationship systems in which the child and teacher are embedded (e.g., relationships with parents, with spouses, with other staff), need to be considered in any analysis of child–teacher relationships.

Furthermore, providing teachers with information on practices is easily within the purview of a consultant. Classroom-level practices were discussed that related to stabilizing interactions between children and a particular adult, minimizing the relational tax levied by entries and exits, insulating child–teacher relationships from negotiating rewards and punishments, and infusing classroom practices and interactions with language that supports emotion regulation.

Finally, school-level policies and practices can be influenced by information provided by psychologist consultants. Four factors affecting the formation and maintenance of child–teacher relationships can be considered in school policy. These include (a) adult–child ratios, (b) length of contact between children and adults, (c) transitions, and (d) school organization, climate, and culture. For each of these factors, a set of considerations for policy analysis has been presented, and suggestions for policy decisions intended to enhance child–teacher relationships have been discussed. Comprehensive efforts to harness teacher–child relationships as a preventive resource for child development will include a focus on school-level policy, in which psychologists can be expected to take an active role.

Assessment for Prevention

As described in chapter 5, the available measurement systems for child–teacher relationships are somewhat underdeveloped. In a preventive intervention context, early and quick detection of relationship problems in the population is highly valued. Thus, most observational systems, such as adaptations of the Attachment Q-Set, are not practical. Teacher or child report methods are more feasible, but there are limits on child-report validity. Lynch and Cicchetti's (1997) report on a school-wide administration of a brief, child-report measure of the quality of relationships between teachers and children in upper elementary and middle school grades is encouraging. Pianta (1992) reported on a district-wide administration of the 30-item STRS, of which a 15-item short-form version has been recently developed. These, and other child-report and teacher-report instruments, show adequate psychometric properties and could be integrated into screening batteries for preventive interventions (Weissberg et al., 1991).

Advances in using child–teacher relationships preventively are predicated in part on a second generation of research on assessment. This next generation of research must extend the current generation of research that is basically descriptive and based on convenience samples to focus on developing instrumentation reflecting normative features of the population. Several issues will be important in advancing this research agenda for it to be supportive of prevention services.

First, prevention assessments must be brief and efficient, yet valid and reliable. This is a challenge to test developers, and in the area of relationship assessment, the challenge is even greater because of the need to include multiple perceptions of the relationship from all participants. There is some evidence that certain items in teacher-report instruments such as the STRS can be used as broad screens for relationship problems (Pianta, 1994). To date, there is not any empirical support for such items from child-report measures or observations.

Second, advancing the assessment of child–teacher relationships for the purposes of prevention will require attention to developmental issues. Child–adult relationships transform and reorganize with development— the nature of a sixth-grader's relationship with his or her teacher is different than that of a first grader. These developmental issues will need extensive consideration in the next generation of research—both descriptively and from an assessment perspective. Thus, there is a need for much more information that describes these transformations in normative samples, as well as the best ways to assess relationships at different developmental phases. It can be expected, for example, that child interviews and other means of self-report could play a more prominent role in assessment for prevention as children age.

Third, the assessment of relationships for the purposes of prevention requires careful attention to sampling, especially with respect to different populations of children. To date, not enough is known about how child ethnicity, for example, is a factor in child or teacher reports of relationship quality. Although some data suggest that child ethnicity is not a factor (Saft, 1994), these data are preliminary and need to be extended before developing instruments that can be used for large-scale screening.

In sum, successfully using child–teacher relationships as a resource for children requires careful attention to the need of educators for information on relationships. Currently, this type of information is basically absent in their training and practice. This information needs to adequately reflect the use of systems theory and the role of contexts and relationships in development. Furthermore, to use the ideas regarding intervention that I have described in a prevention context, considerable research is necessary to develop appropriate instrumentation for screening and assessment batteries.

Remediation and Practice with High-Risk Groups

Applied child and adolescent psychologists spend most of their time working with children who have already been identified as having learning, behavioral, or emotional difficulties and as being at some unacceptably high level of risk. These children frequently experience conflict in relationships with teachers or are disengaged from the resources of the child–teacher relationship (Pianta et al., 1995). In these instances, the teacher's or the child's interactions with one another, and their representational models of experiences with one another, can be related to the problems they are having. More important, for children already identified as having school-related problems, it is through their relationships with their teachers that social behavior, self-control, and motivation to achieve can be improved. Most other interventions (e.g., a behavior modification plan) must be delivered in this relational context.

Thus, regardless of a child's needs, and the intervention applied to meet those needs, relationships between teachers and children play a role in identification and treatment. Efforts to improve the relationship between a teacher and a child will almost always have the added benefit of improving the response to any other interventions and, as I have argued throughout, is an intervention worthy of consideration on its own merit.

Assessment

Once engaged in a consultation with a teacher, a psychologist can use a mix of observation, questionnaire, or teacher interview techniques to provide in-depth information reflecting the richness of the relationship experiences of the teacher and information for subsequent planning and be-havior change. Furthermore, the more standardized of these techniques (such as the STRS or standardized observations) can be used as outcome measures for consultation and intervention. The TRI, described in chapter 5 and profiled in chapter 6, appears promising in terms of its capacity to elicit teachers' representational models of relationships with children. Teachers appear comfortable in responding to the questions, and their re-sponses are consistent with conceptualizations of adults' responses to other relationship-oriented interviews. It is important that the TRI pro-vides the consultant with a structured way to start working in an area (relationships with children) that can be hard to define.

Information

As in preventive service delivery, there is a role for informing teachers of the developmental perspective on children and relationships that has been outlined in earlier chapters. This information can be passed along through a series of didactic workshops, through in- or preservice training, or through ongoing group consultation meetings. Topics to cover include (a) the presence of key themes of socioemotional development, (b) the role of relationships in socialization, (c) the definition of relationships and their components, and (d) the recognition of relationships in trouble.

Child–Teacher Relationship Interventions

The Banking Time intervention discussed in chapter 7 presents a method for intervening in both remedial and preventive approaches but is more likely to be used with children and teachers for whom relationship, or other, problems have been identified. This intervention—defining the teacher's role relationally and tying experience and emotion to words de-scribing the relationship—is a way to deliberately shape the classroom context in ways that provide a structure to social interactions that take place in that context. This structure is of importance to many children who enter classrooms having experienced relationships with adults that are confusing, unpredictable, or negative in some form. For many children, the idea that an adult can be unconditionally accepting, safe, trusted, con-sistent, and available violates their expectations of relationships with adults. If carried through consistently across the many adult–child inter-actions in which the child engages, these messages can form a powerful intervention for high-risk children.

Furthermore, the design of behavior management systems can be in-formed, and perhaps improved, when considered from a relationship-enhancing perspective. Behavior management systems directly affect the feedback and exchange processes involved in child–teacher interaction and can indirectly affect teachers' and children's representations of rela-tionships. Current conceptualizations and implementation of behavior management practices do not reflect this linkage with a relationship perspective. As developmental theory becomes a dominant paradigm for understanding risk and problem outcomes (e.g., Sameroff, 1989), there will be increasing opportunities to identify the connections between behavior change with operant techniques and behavior change as a function of developmental processes. Understanding and exploiting these connections (as when behavior management systems are used to enhance child–teacher relationships) are likely to result in more efficient and powerful interventions for children in need.

An Agenda for Research

The conceptual and theoretical perspectives I have described have strong empirical validation, yet, as previously mentioned, many of the practices described have not been subject to strong tests of their validity. Furthermore, despite the strong empirical support for the perspectives on relationships between children and teachers that have been described, there is much more research needed on these relationships to advance both theory and practice. With these points in mind, the following recommendations for future research are forwarded.

Research on Basic Processes

Several directions for research are recommended. The first is research related to describing the dimensions and organization of child–teacher relationships as they transform over time. Such research might involve describing the different relationship roles that teachers play during different developmental periods and the manner in which relationship patterns are carried over from one relationship to another both over time and within a given grade for multiple teachers. Related to this program of research is information needed on the ways in which practices such as looping affect the quality and the nature of child–teacher relationships.

A second area of research on basic relationship processes involves the correlates, determinants, and consequences of relationships between children and teachers. This area of research would do well to rely on the hundreds of studies that have examined similar issues concerning the effects of social context, maternal characteristics, neighborhood settings, and demography on child–parent relationships. Adopting that framework would lead to research on the determinants of child–teacher relationships that examined teacher characteristics and developmental history, child characteristics and developmental history, school climate and organization, curriculum, and wider community-level variables such as funding. In this way, the study of the determinants of child–teacher relationships would proceed within a developmental frame. Relatedly, research on the consequences of child–teacher relationships would examine how children and teachers are affected by relationships of varying quality—areas related to risk and protective processes for both child and teacher and relevant here.

In basic research on child–teacher relationships, it will be important to undertake studies with a longitudinal, prospective design. Thus, samples of children and teachers will need to be enrolled in studies prior to the emergence of certain relationship phenomena and studied over time through windows in which the phenomena of interest develop. Studies are needed that focus on the child, the teacher, and the child–teacher relationship as the units of analysis, and it may be necessary to conduct such studies on separate populations to satisfy the need for longitudinal research. Furthermore, one needs to conduct such studies from a systems theory point of view and to include instrumentation of a wide array of contexts and constructs, not focusing just on classroom interactions, for example.

Applied Research

This book has clear implications for research on applications of information on child–teacher relationships, particularly with regard to interventions. In the present professional practice context that strongly emphasizes the use of empirically validated interventions, it will be important to buttress local practice decisions with empirically based rationales.

However, the press for professionals to practice using only empirically validated interventions should not proceed without caution and without careful consideration of the weaknesses of most intervention study designs. For example, even in the best designed and implemented studies in which treatment groups' performance on desired outcomes exceeds that of control groups, it has to be noted that by and large, empirical validation of the success of these treatments is in the form of a difference between group means. Statistical significance tests of this form, however significant, mask the fact that treatment groups nearly always contain some individuals who do not change and that the level of change is often variable within the group. Furthermore, as was mentioned earlier, it is possible to generate empirical support for interventions that neither make theoretical sense nor are generalizable.

Thus, even when there is strong empirical support for a given practice, there will always be a need for local decision making. One could argue that this is more often the case than not in education, given the ubiquitous arguments about whether one or another practice is effective. In this context, empirically validated theories of the process or problem under consideration are of paramount importance because very often, educators' understanding of an issue guides practice with respect to that issue.

This perspective suggests that research on basic child–teacher relationship processes that builds an empirically validated theory of these relationships has considerable implications for practice. Notwithstanding this argument, research on child–teacher relationship practices is sorely needed. A research agenda in this area could include studies of banking time interventions or variants in behavior management approaches that affect child–teacher relationships. It is important that research of this nature focus on these interventions in the context of the kind of child-, teacher-, classroom-, and school-level variables that are likely to affect these interventions. Thus, even intervention research needs to be conducted in the longitudinal, developmentally informed designs that characterize research on basic relationship processes. Research on classroom-, school-, and policy-level interventions require the same kind of considerations in design.

Conclusion

Applied child and adolescent psychologists are well situated and well suited to apply developmental theory in an educational context. Because the role of the psychologist involves program development, consultation, and policy analysis as well as assessment and intervention, there are a wide range of opportunities to shape how relationships with teachers can be enhanced and supported for many children.

As has been noted earlier, the relationship perspective presented here offers a lens for the analysis of policy and practice that has not been articulated or applied in most educational contexts. This perspective integrates theories of social development, particularly the developmental importance of relationships with adults, with methods of professional practice in child and adolescent psychology. This perspective is especially suited to professional practice that has a prevention orientation, one that recognizes the enormous potential of teacher–child relationships as resources for all children. And, as schools contend with the challenges of educating more and more children who are at high risk for educational failure because of eroded social development, this relationship perspective can become increasingly valuable as a tool for supporting the construction of school and classroom contexts that use these resources.

References

Aber, J. L., & Allen, J. P. (1987). The effects of maltreatment on young children's socio-emotional development: An attachment perspective. *Developmental Psychology, 23,* 406–414.

Adelman, H. S. (1996). Restructuring education support services and integrating community resources: Beyond the full service school model. *School Psychology Review, 25,* 431–445.

Ainsworth, M. D., Blehar, M. C., Waters, E., & Wall, D. (1978). *Patterns of attachment: A psychological study of the Strange Situation.* Hillsdale, NJ: Erlbaum.

Alexander, K. L., & Entwisle, D. R. (1988). Achievement in the first two years of school: Patterns and processes. *Monographs of the Society for Research in Child Development, 53*(2, Serial No. 218).

Alexander, K. L., Entwisle, D. R., & Dauber, S. L. (1995). *On the success of failure.* New York: Cambridge University Press.

Alexander, K. L., Entwisle, D. R., & Thompson, M. S. (1987). School performance, status relations, and the structure of sentiment: Bring the teacher back in. *American Sociological Review, 52,* 665–682.

American Psychiatric Association. (1994). *Diagnostic and statistical manual of mental disorders* (4th ed.). Washington, DC: Author.

Barkley, R. (1987). *Defiant children: A clinician's manual for parent training.* New York: Guilford Press.

Belsky, J., & MacKinnon, C. (1994). Transition to school: Developmental trajectories and school experiences. *Early Education and Development, 5,* 106–119.

Bergmann, S., Egeland, B., & Sroufe, L.A. (1986). *Peer competence and anxiety in middle childhood: Prediction from infant–caregiver attachment.* Unpublished manuscript.

Berlin, L., Cassidy, J., & Belsky, J. (in press). Loneliness in young children and infant mother attachment. *Merrill-Palmer Quarterly.*

Birch, S., & Ladd, G. (1996). Interpersonal relationships in the school environment and children's early school adjustment. In K. Wentzel & J. Juvonen (Eds.), *Social motivation: Understanding children's school adjustment* (pp. 199–225). New York: Cambridge University Press.

Birch, S., & Ladd, G. (1997). The teacher–child relationship and children's early school adjustment. *Journal of School Psychology, 35,* 61–79.

Blatt, S. J. (1995). Representational structures in psychopathology. In D. Cicchetti & S. Toth (Eds.), *Rochester Symposium on Developmental Psychopathology: Vol. 6. Emotion, cognition, and representation* (pp. 1–34). Rochester, NY: University of Rochester Press.

Bornstein, M. H. (1989). Sensitive periods in development: Structural characteristics and causal interpretations. *Psychological Bulletin, 105,* 179–197.

Boulding, K. E. (1985). *The world as a total system.* Beverly Hills, CA: Sage.

Bourke, S. (1986). How smaller is better: Some relationships between class size, teaching practices, and student achievement. *American Education Research Journal, 23,* 558–571.

Bowlby, J. (1969). *Attachment and loss: Vol. 1. Attachment.* New York: Basic Books.

Bradley, R. H., Caldwell, B. M., & Rock, S. L. (1988). Home environment and school performance: A ten year follow up and examination of three models of environmental action. *Child Development, 59,* 852–867.

Brantley, D. C., & Webster, R. E. (1993). Use of an independent group contingency management system in a regular classroom setting. *Psychology in the Schools, 30,* 60–66.

Bredekamp, S. (1987). *Developmentally appropriate practice in early childhood programs serving children from birth through age 8.* Washington, DC: National Association for the Education of Young Children.

Breger, L. (1974). *From instinct to identity.* Englewood Cliffs, NJ: Prentice-Hall.

Bronfenbrenner, U. (1979). *The ecology of human development: Experiments by nature and design.* Cambridge, MA: Harvard University Press.

Brophy, J., & Good, T. (1986). Teacher behavior and student achievement. In M. Wittrock (Ed.), *Handbook of research on teaching* (pp. 328–375). New York: Macmillan.

Bus, A. G., & van IJzendoorn, M. H. (1988). Mother–child interactions, attachment, and emergent literacy: A cross-sectional study. *Child Development, 59,* 1262–1273.

Campbell, S. B. (1990). *Behavior problems in preschool children.* New York: Guilford Press.

Campbell, S. B. (1994). Hard-to-manage preschool boys: Externalizing behavior, social competence, and family context at two-year follow-up. *Journal of Abnormal Child Psychology, 22,* 147–166.

Campbell, S. B., March, C. L., Pierce, E., Ewing, L. J., & Szumowski, E. K. (1991). Hard-to-manage preschool boys: Family context and stability of externalizing behavior. *Journal of Abnormal Child Psychology, 19,* 301–318.

Carlson, V., Cicchetti, D., Barnett, D., & Braunwald, K. (1989). Disorganized/disoriented attachment relationships in maltreated infants. *Developmental Psychology, 25,* 525–531.

Cassidy, J. (1994). Emotion regulation: Influences of attachment relationships. In N. A. Fox (Ed.), The development of emotion regulation: Biological and behavioral considerations. *Monographs of the Society for Research in Child Development, 59*(2–3, Serial No. 240), 228–249.

Christenson, S. L., & Ysseldyke, J. E. (1989). Assessing student performance: An important change is needed. *Journal of School Psychology, 27,* 409–425.

Cicchetti, D. (1994). Advances and challenges in the study of the sequelae of child maltreatment. *Development and Psychopathology, 6,* 1–4.

Cicchetti, D., Ackerman, B. P., & Izard, C. (1995). Emotions and emotion regulation in developmental psychopathology. *Development and Psychopathology, 7,* 1–10.

Cohn, D. A. (1990). Child–mother attachment of six-year-olds and social competence at school. *Child Development, 61,* 152–162.

Cohn, J., Campbell, S., Matias, R., & Hopkins, J. (1990). Face-to-face interactions of postpartum depressed and nondepressed mother–infant pairs at 2 months. *Developmental Psychology, 26,* 15–23.

Comer, J. P. (1988). Educating poor minority children. *Scientific American, 259,* 42–48.

Consortium on the School-Based Promotion of Social Competence. (1994). The school-based promotion of social competence: Theory, research, practice, and policy. In R. J. Haggerty, L. Sherrod, N. Garmezy, & M. Rutter (Eds.), *Stress, risk, and resilience in children and adolescents: Processes, mechanisms, and interventions* (pp. 268–316). New York: Cambridge University Press.

Cost, Quality and Child Outcomes Study Team. (1995). *Cost, quality and child outcomes in child care centers: Public report.* Denver: University of Colorado at Denver, Economics Department.

Crittenden, P. M. (1992). Quality of attachment in the preschool years. *Development and Psychopathology, 4,* 209–242.

Cummings, E. M., Hennessy, K., Rabideau, G., & Cicchetti, D. (1994). Responses of physically abused boys to interadult anger involving their mothers. *Development and Psychopathology, 6,* 31–42.

Denham, S., & Burton, R. (1996). A social-emotional intervention for at-risk four-year olds. *Journal of School Psychology, 34,* 225–246.

de Ruiter, C. & van IJzendoorn, M. (1993). Attachment and cognition: A review of the literature. *International Journal of Educational Research, 19,* 5–20.

Diaz, R.M., & Berk, L. E. (1995). A Vygotskian critique of self-instructional training. *Development and Psychopathology, 7,* 369–392.

Dodge, K. (1991). Emotion and social information processing. In J. Garber & K. Dodge (Eds.), *The development of emotion regulation and dysregulation* (pp. 159–181). New York: Cambridge University Press.

Dodge, K., Pettit, G., & Bates, J. (1994). Effects of maltreatment on the development of peer relations. *Development and Psychopathology, 6,* 43–57.

Doll, B. (1996). Children without friends: Implications for practice and policy. *School Psychology Review, 25,* 165–183.

Duncan, G., & Brooks-Gunn, J. (1997). *Consequences of growing up poor.* New York: Russell Sage Foundation.

Dwyer, K. P., & Gorin, S. (1996). A national perspective of school psychology in the context of school reform. *School Psychology Review, 25,* 507–511.

Eaton, W. (1981). Demographic and social-ecologic risk factors for mental disorders. In D. Regier & A. Gordon (Eds.), *Risk factor research in the major mental disorders*. Washington, DC: Department of Health and Human Services.

Egeland, B., Pianta, R. C., & O'Brien, M. (1993). Maternal intrusiveness in infancy and child maladaptation in early school years. *Development and Psychopathology, 5,* 359–370.

Elicker, J., Englund, M., & Sroufe, L. A. (1992). Predicting peer competence and peer relationships in childhood from early parent–child relationships. In R. Parke & G. W. Ladd (Eds.), *Family–peers relationships: Modes of linkage* (pp. 77–106). Hillsdale, NJ: Erlbaum.

Entwistle, D. R., & Alexander, K. L. (1993). Entry into school: The beginning school transition and educational stratification in the United States. *Annual Review of Sociology, 19,* 401–423.

Epanchin, B. C., Townsend, B., & Stoddard, K. (1994). *Constructive classroom management: Strategies for creating positive learning environments*. Pacific Grove, CA: Brooks/Cole.

Erickson, M. F., Egeland, B., & Pianta, R. C. (1989). The effects of maltreatment on the development of young children. In D. Cicchetti & V. Carlson (Eds.), *Child maltreatment: Theory and research on the causes and consequences of child abuse and neglect* (pp. 647–684). New York: Cambridge University Press.

Erickson, M. F., & Pianta, R. C. (1989). New lunchbox, old feelings: What kids bring to school. *Early Education and Development, 1,* 15–23.

Erickson, M. F., Sroufe, L. A., & Egeland, B. (1985). The relationship between quality of attachment and behavior problems in preschool in a high-risk sample. In I. Bretherton & E. Waters (Eds.), Growing points of attachment: Theory and research. *Monographs of the Society for Research in Child Development, 50*(1–2, Serial No. 209), 147–166.

Fonagy, P., Steele, H., & Steele, M. (1991). Maternal representations of attachment during pregnancy predict the organization of mother–infant attachment at one year of age. *Child Development, 62,* 891–905.

Ford, D. H, & Ford, M. E. (1987). *Humans as self-constructing living systems*. Hillsdale, NJ: Erlbaum.

Ford, D. H., & Lerner, R. M. (1992). *Developmental systems theory: An integrative approach*. Newbury Park, CA: Sage.

Garbarino, J. (1982). *Children and families in the social environment*. New York: Aldine.

Garbarino, J., Dubrow, N., Kostelny, K., & Pardo, C. (1992). *Children in danger: Coping with the consequences of community violence*. San Francisco: Jossey-Bass.

Garmezy, N. (1994). Reflections and commentary on risk, resilience, and development. In R. J. Haggerty, L. Sherrod, N. Garmezy, & M. Rutter (Eds.), *Stress, risk, and resilience in children and adolescents: Processes, mechanisms, and interventions* (pp. 1–19). New York: Cambridge University Press.

Gartner, A., & Lipsky, K. K. (1987). Beyond special education: Toward a quality system for all students. *Harvard Educational Review, 57,* 368–395.

George, C., & Solomon, J. (1991). *Children's representations of the practicing family using a doll play technique*. Paper presented at the biennial meeting of the Society for Research in Child Development, Seattle, WA.

Goldstein, S. (1993). *Understanding and managing children's classroom behavior*. New York: Wiley.

Goldstein, S. (1995). *Clinical Interview Form*. Salt Lake City, UT: Neurology, Learning and Behavior Center.

Goodlad, J. I. (1991). *Teachers for our nations's schools*. San Francisco: Jossey-Bass.

Gottlieb, G. (1991). Experimental canalization of behavioral development: Theory. *Developmental Psychology, 27,* 4–13.

Graue, E. (in press). Kindergarten classroom contexts and the transition to school. In R. C. Pianta & M. Cox (Eds.), *Transition to kindergarten: An ecological/developmental perspective*. Baltimore: Paul Brookes.

Greenberg, M. T., Kusche, C. A., & Speltz, M. (1991). Emotional regulation, self-control, and psychopathology: The role of relationships in early childhood. In D. Cicchetti & S. Toth (Eds.), *Rochester Symposium on Developmental Psychopathology: Vol. 2. Internalizing and externalizing expressions of dysfunction* (pp. 21–55). Hillsdale, NJ: Erlbaum.

Greenberg, M. T., Speltz, M. L., & DeKlyen, M. (1993). The role of attachment in the early development of disruptive behavior disorders. *Development and Psychopathology, 5*, 191–213.

Greene, R., Abidin, R. R., & Kmetz, K. (in press). The Index of Teaching Stress: A measure of student–teacher compatibility. *Journal of School Psychology.*

Greenough, W. T., & Black, J. E. (1991). Induction of brain structure by experience: Substrates for cognitive development. In M. Gunnar & C. A. Nelson (Eds.), *Minnesota Symposia on Child Psychology: Vol. 24. Behavioral developmental neuroscience* (pp. 155–200). Hillsdale, NJ: Erlbaum.

Greenspan, S. I. (1989). *Development of the ego.* Madison, CT: International Universities Press.

Greenspan, S. I., & Greenspan, N. (1991). *Clinical interview of the child* (2nd ed.). Madison, CT: International Universities Press.

Gutkin, T. B. (1997). An introduction to the Mini-Series: The Social Psychology of Interpersonal Influence with Adults. *Journal of School Psychology, 35*, 105–106.

Gutkin, T. B., & Conoley, J. C. (1990). Reconceptualizing school psychology from a service delivery perspective: Implications for training, practice, and research. *Journal of School Psychology, 28*, 203–223.

Hamilton, C. E., & Howes, C. (1992). A comparison of young children's relationships with mothers and teachers. In R. C. Pianta (Ed.), *New Directions in Child Development: Vol. 57. Relationships between children and non-parental adults* (pp. 41–60). San Francisco: Jossey-Bass.

Hennessy, K. D., Rabideau, G. J., Cicchetti, D., & Cummings, E. M. (1994). Responses of physically abused and nonabused children to different forms of interadult anger. *Child Development, 65*, 815–828.

Henggeler, S. W. (1994). A consensus: Conclusions of the APA Task Force Report on Innovative Models of Mental Health Services for Children, Adolescents and Their Families. *Journal of Clinical Child Psychology, 23*, 3–6.

Hinde, R. (1987). *Individuals, relationships, and culture.* New York: Cambridge University Press.

Hirsch, E. D. (1997, April). *Address to the California State Board of Education.* Paper presented at a meeting of the California State Board of Education, Sacramento.

Hofer, M. A. (1994). Hidden regulators in attachment, separation, and loss. In N. A. Fox (Ed.), The development of emotion regulation: Biological and behavioral considerations. *Monographs of the Society for Research in Child Development, 59*(2–3, Serial No. 240), 192–207.

Holtzman, W. H. (1992). *School of the future.* Washington, DC: American Psychological Association.

Howes, C., & Hamilton, C. E., (1992a). Children's relationships with caregivers: Mothers and child-care teachers. *Child Development, 63,* 859–866.

Howes, C., & Hamilton, C. E. (1992b). Children's relationships with child-care teachers: Stability and concordance with parental attachments. *Child Development, 63*, 867–878.

Howes, C., Hamilton, C. E., & Matheson, C. C. (1994). Children's relationships with peers: Differential associations with aspects of the teacher-child relationship. *Child Development, 65*, 253–263.

Howes, C., & Matheson, C. C. (1992). Contextual constraints on the concordance of mother–child and teacher–child relationships. In R. C. Pianta (Ed.), *New Directions in Child Development: Vol. 57. Relationships between children and non-parental adults* (pp. 25–90). San Francisco: Jossey-Bass.

Howes, C., Matheson, C. C., & Hamilton, C. E. (1994). Maternal, teacher, and child-care history correlates of children's relationships with peers. *Child Development, 65*, 264–273.

Hughes, J. N. (1992). Social psychology foundations of consultation. In F. J. Medway & T. P. Cafferty (Eds.), *School psychology: A social psychological perspective* (pp. 269–304). Hillsdale, NJ: Erlbaum.

Jacobvitz, D., & Sroufe, L. A. (1987). The early caregiver–child relationship and attention deficit disorder with hyperactivity in kindergarten. *Child Development, 58*, 1488–1495.

Johnson, D. W., Johnson, R. T., Buckman, L. A., & Richards, P. S. (1985). The effect of prolonged implementation of cooperative learning on social support within the classroom. *Journal of Psychology, 119*, 405–411.

Johnson, D. B., Malone, P. J., & Hightower, A. D. (1997). Barriers to primary prevention efforts in the schools: Are we the biggest obstacle to the transfer of knowledge? *Applied and Preventive Psychology, 6*, 81–90.

Katz, G. S., Cohn, J. F., & Moore, C. (1996). A combination of vocal, dynamic and summary features discriminates between three pragmatic categories of infant-directed speech. *Child Development, 67*, 205–217.

Kazdin, A. E. (1992). Child and adolescent dysfunction and paths toward maladjustment: Targets for intervention. *Clinical Psychology Review, 12*, 795–817.

Knoff, H. (1996). The interface of school, community, and health care reform: Organizational directions toward effective services for children and youth. *School Psychology Review, 25*, 446–464.

Knoff, H. M., & Batsche, G. M. (1994, October). *Project ACHIEVE: A collaborative, school-based school reform process improving the academic and social progress of at-risk and underachieving students.* Paper presented at the conference "Safe Schools, Safe Students: A Collaborative Approach to Safe, Disciplined and Drug-Free Schools Conducive to Learning," Washington, DC.

Knoff, H. M., & Curtis, M. J. (1996). Introduction to the mini-series: Organizational change and school reform: School psychology at a professional crossroad. *School Psychology Review, 25*, 406–408.

Kopp, C., & Wyer, N. (1994). Self-regulation in normal and atypical development. In D. Cicchetti & S. Toth (Eds.), *Rochester Symposium on Developmental Psychopathology: Vol. 5. Disorders and dysfunctions of the self* (pp. 31–56). Rochester, NY: University of Rochester Press.

Kozol, J. (1991). *Savage inequalities: Children in American schools.* New York: Crown Books.

Ladd, G. W., & Price, J. M. (1987). Predicting children's social and school adjustment following the transition from preschool to kindergarten. *Child Development, 58*, 1168–1189.

Ladd, G. W., Price, J. M., & Hart, C. H. (1988). Predicting preschoolers' peer status from their playground behaviors. *Child Development, 59*, 986–992.

LaFreniere, P. J., & Sroufe, L. A. (1985). Profiles of peer competence in the preschool: Interrelations among measures, influence of social ecology, and relation to attachment history. *Developmental Psychology, 21*, 56–69.

Laparo, K., & Pianta, R. C. (1996). *System for observing kindergarten classrooms.* Unpublished manuscript, University of Virginia, Charlottesville.

Lieberman, A. F. (1992). Infant–parent psychotherapy with toddlers. *Development and Psychopathology, 4*, 559–574.

Loeber, R. (1990). Development and risk factors of juvenile antisocial behavior and delinquency. *Clinical Psychology Review, 10*, 1–41.

Louis, K. S. (1995). Teacher engagement and real reform in schools. *Closing the achievement gap: A vision to guide change in beliefs and practice* (pp. 81–102). Washington, DC: U.S. Department of Education Regional Educational Laboratory Network.

Lynch, M., & Cicchetti, D. (1992). Maltreated children's reports of relatedness to their teachers. In R. C. Pianta (Ed.), *New Directions in Child Development: Vol. 57. Relationships between children and non-parental adults* (pp. 81–108). San Francisco: Jossey-Bass.

Lynch, M., & Cicchetti, D. (1997). Children's relationships with adults and peers: An examination of elementary and junior high school students. *Journal of School Psychology, 35*, 81–100.

Main, M. (1996). Introduction to the special section on attachment and psychopathology: 2. Overview of the field of attachment. *Journal of Consulting and Clinical Psychology, 64*, 237–243.

Main, M., & Goldwyn, R. (1994). *Adult Attachment Interview Scoring Manual.* Berkeley: University of California at Berkeley, Department of Psychology.

Main, M., & Hesse, E. (1990). Is fear the link between infant disorganized attachment status and maternal unresolved loss? In M. Greenberg, D. Cicchetti, & M. Cummings (Eds.), *Attachment in the preschool years* (pp. 161–182). Chicago: University of Chicago Press.

McBurnett, K., Lahey, B., & Pfiffner, L. (1993). Diagnosis of attention deficit disorders in DSM-IV: Scientific basis and implications for education. *Exceptional Children, 60,* 108–117.

McGiverin, J., Gilman, D., & Tillitski, C. (1989). A meta-analysis of the relation between class size and achievement. *Elementary School Journal, 90,* 47–56.

Meyers, J., Parsons, R. D., & Martin, R. (1979). *Mental health consultation in the schools.* San Francisco: Jossey-Bass.

Molnar, A., & Lindquist, B. (1990). *Changing problem behavior in schools.* San Francisco: Jossey-Bass.

Mosteller, F. (1995). The Tennessee study of class size in the early school grades. *The Future of Children, 5,* 113–127.

Motti, F. (1986). *Relationships of preschool teachers with children of varying developmental histories.* Unpublished doctoral dissertation, University of Minnesota, Minneapolis.

National Center for Children in Poverty. (1993). *Five million children: 1993 update.* New York: Author.

National Center for Health Statistics. (1993). *Children's health index.* Hyattsville, MD: Public Health Service.

O'Keefe, D. J., & Medway, F. J. (1997). The application of persuasion research to consultation in school psychology. *Journal of School Psychology, 35,* 173–194.

Pancake, V. R. (1985, April). *Continuity between mother–infant attachment and ongoing dyadic peer relationships in preschool.* Paper presented at the biennial meeting of the Society for Research in Child Development, Toronto, Ontario, Canada.

Pederson, E., Faucher, T. A., & Eaton, W. W. (1978). A new perspective on the effects of first grade teachers on children's subsequent adult status. *Harvard Educational Review, 48,* 1–31.

Pennington, B. F., & Ozonoff, S. (1991). A neurological perspective on continuity and discontinuity in developmental psychopathology. In D. Cicchetti & S. L. Toth (Eds.), *Rochester Symposium on Developmental Psychopathology: Vol. 3. Models and integrations.* Rochester, NY: University of Rochester.

Pianta, R. C. (1990). Widening the debate on educational reform: Prevention as a viable alternative. *Exceptional Children, 56,* 306–313.

Pianta, R. C. (1992). *New Directions in Child Development: Vol. 57. Beyond the parent: The role of other adults in children's lives.* San Franciso: Jossey-Bass.

Pianta, R. C. (1994). Patterns of relationships between children and kindergarten teachers. *Journal of School Psychology, 32,* 15–32.

Pianta, R. C. (1997a). Adult–child relationship processes and early schooling. *Early Education and Development, 8,* 11–26.

Pianta, R. C. (1997b). *Banking Time: Manual and procedures.* (Available from the author, Curry School of Education, University of Virginia, P.O. Box 9051, Charlottesville, VA 22906-9051).

Pianta, R. C. (1997c). *Teacher Relationship Interview.* (Available from the author, Curry School of Education, University of Virginia, P.O. Box 9051, Charlottesville, VA 22906-9051).

Pianta, R. C., & Button, S. (1997). *Mothers' representations of relationships with their children: A psychometric analysis.* Unpublished manuscript, University of Virginia, Charlottesville.

Pianta, R. C., Egeland, B., & Sroufe, L. A. (1990). Maternal stress and children's development: Prediction of school outcomes and identification of protective factors. In J. Rolf, A. Masten, D. Cicchetti, K. Nuechterlein, & S. Weintraub (Eds.), *Risk and protective factors in the development of psychopathology* (pp. 215–235). New York: Cambridge University Press.

Pianta, R. C., Egeland, B., & Sroufe, L. A. (1997). *Poverty, pathways, and pathology.* Unpublished manuscript, University of Virginia, Charlottesville.

Pianta, R. C., Erickson, M. F., Wagner, N., Kreutzer, T., & Egeland, B. (1990). Early predictors of referrals for special services: Child-based measures vs. mother–child interaction. *School Psychology Review, 19,* 240–250.

Pianta, R. C., & Ferguson, J. (1997). *Prediction of behavior problems in children from mother–child interaction.* Unpublished manuscript, University of Virginia, Charlottesville.

Pianta, R. C., & Harbers, K. (1996). Observing mother and child behavior in a problem-solving situation at school entry: Relations with academic achievement. *Journal of School Psychology, 34,* 307–322.

Pianta, R. C., & McCoy, S. (1997). The first day of school: The predictive utility of an early school screening program. *Journal of Applied Developmental Psychology, 18,* 1–22.

Pianta, R. C., & Nimetz, S. L. (1989). Educators' beliefs about risk and prevention: The context for changing beliefs. *Early Education and Development, 1,* 115–126.

Pianta, R. C., & Nimetz, S. L. (1991). Relationships between teachers and children: Associations with behavior at home and in the classroom. *Journal of Applied Developmental Psychology, 12,* 379–393.

Pianta, R. C., Nimetz, S. L., & Bennett, E. (1997). Mother–child relationships, teacher–child relationships and adjustment in preschool and kindergarten. *Early Childhood Research Quarterly, 12,* 263–280.

Pianta, R. C., O'Connor, T. G., Morog, M. C., Button, S., Dimmock, J., & Marvin, R. S. (1993). *Scoring guide for the Parent Development Interview.* Unpublished manuscript, University of Virginia, Charlottesville.

Pianta, R. C., Smith, N., & Reeve, R. (1991). Observing mother and child behavior in a problem-solving situation at school entry: Relations with classroom adjustment. *School Psychology Quarterly, 6,* 1–16.

Pianta, R. C., & Steinberg, M. (1992). Relationships between children and kindergarten teachers from the teachers' perspective. In R. C. Pianta (Ed.), *Beyond the parent: The role of other adults in children's lives* (pp. 61–80). San Francisco: Jossey-Bass.

Pianta, R. C., Steinberg, M., & Rollins, K. (1995). The first two years of school: Teacher–child relationships and deflections in children's classroom adjustment. *Development and Psychopathology, 7,* 297–312.

Pianta, R. C., & Walsh, D. (1996). *High-risk children in the schools: Creating sustaining relationships.* New York: Routledge.

Reed, S., & Sautter, R. C. (1990, June). Children of poverty: The status of 12 million young Americans. *Phi Delta Kappan,* 1–12.

Reid, R., Maag, J. W., & Vasa, S. F. (1993). Attention deficit hyperactivity disorder as a disability category: A critique. *Exceptional Children, 60,* 198–214.

Resnick, L. B. (1994). Situated rationalism: Biological and social preparation for learning. In L. Hirschfield & S. Gelman (Eds.), *Mapping the mind: Domain specificity in cognition and culture* (pp. 474–493). Cambridge, England: Cambridge University Press.

Resnick, M. D., Bearman, P. S., Blum, R. W., Bauman, K., Harris, K. M., Jones, J., Tabor, J., Beuhring, T., Sieving, R. E., Shew, M., Ireland, M., Behringer, L. H., & Udry, J. R. (1997). Protecting adolescents from harm: Findings from the National Longitudinal Study of Adolescent Health. *Journal of the American Medical Association, 278,* 823–832.

Riccio, C. A., Hynd, G. W., Cohen, M. J., & Gonzalez, J. J. (1993). Neurological basis of attention deficit hyperactivity disorder. *Exceptional Children, 60,* 118–124.

Richman, N., Stevenson, J., & Graham, P. J. (1982). *Preschool to school: A behavioral study.* London: Academic Press.

Rimm-Kaufman, S., & Pianta, R. C. (1997). *An ecological model of the transition to kindergarten.* Unpublished manuscript, University of Virginia, Charlottesville.

Roberts, M. C. (1996). *Model programs in child and family mental health.* Hillsdale, NJ: Erlbaum.

Rogoff, B. (1990). *Apprenticeship in thinking: Cognitive development in social context.* New York: Oxford University Press.

Rubin, K., Coplan, R. J., Fox, N. A., & Calkins, S. D. (1995). Emotionality, emotion regulation, and preschoolers' social adaptation. *Development and Psychopathology, 7,* 49–62.

Rutter, M. (1987). Psychosocial resilience and protective mechanisms. *American Journal of Orthopsychiatry, 57,* 316–331.

Saft, E. W. (1994). *A descriptive study of the psychometric properties of the Student–Teacher Relationship Scale.* Unpublished doctoral dissertation, University of Virginia, Charlottesville.

Sameroff, A. J. (1983). Developmental systems: Context and evolution. In P. H. Mussen (Series Ed.) & W. Kessen (Vol. Ed.), *Handbook of child psychology: Vol. 1. History, theory and methods* (pp. 237–294). New York: Wiley.

Sameroff, A. J. (1989). Principles of development and psychopathology. In A. Sameroff & R. Emde (Eds.), *Relationship disturbances in early childhood* (pp. 17–32). New York: Basic Books.

Sameroff, A. J., & Emde, R. N. (1989). *Relationship disturbances in early childhood: A developmental approach.* New York: Basic Books.

Sameroff, A. J., & Haith, M. (1996). *The 5 to 7 shift.* Chicago: University of Chicago Press.

Sander, L. (1975). Infant and caretaking environment: Investigation and conceptualization of adaptive behavior in a system of increasing complexity. In E. J. Anthony (Ed.), *Explorations in child psychiatry* (pp. 129–166). New York: Plenum.

Sattler, J. (1997). *Clinical and forensic interviewing of children and families.* San Diego, CA: Sattler.

Shepard, L. A., & Smith, M. L. (1986). Synthesis of research on school readiness and kindergarten retention. *Educational Leadership, 44,* 78–86.

Shriner, J. G., Ysseldyke, J. E., & Christenson, S. (1989). Assessment procedures for use in heterogeneous classrooms. In S. Stainback & W. Stainback (Eds.), *Educating all students in the mainstream of regular education.* Baltimore: Paul Brookes.

Sroufe, L. A. (1983). Infant–caregiver attachment and patterns of adaptation in preschool: The roots of maladaptation and competence. In M. Perlmutter (Ed.), *Minnesota Symposium on Child Psychology: Vol. 16. Development of cognition, affect, and social relations* (pp. 41–81). Hillsdale, NJ: Erlbaum.

Sroufe, L. A. (1989a). Pathways to adaptation and maladaptation: Psychopathology as developmental deviation. In D. Cicchetti (Ed.), *Rochester Symposium on Developmental Psychopathology: Vol. 1. Emergence of a discipline* (pp. 13–40). Hillsdale, NJ: Erlbaum.

Sroufe, L. A. (1989b). Relationships and relationship disturbances. In A. Sameroff & R. Emde (Eds.), *Relationship disturbances in early childhood* (pp. 97–124). New York: Basic Books.

Sroufe, L. A. (1996). *Emotional development: The organization of emotional life in the early years.* New York: Cambridge University Press.

Sroufe, L. A., & Fleeson, J. (1988). Attachment and the construction of relationships. In W. Hartup & Z. Rubin (Eds.), *Relationships and development* (pp. 27–47). Hillsdale, NJ: Erlbaum.

Sroufe, L. A., & Rutter, M. (1984). The domain of developmental psychopathology. *Child Development, 55,* 17–29.

Stern, D. (1989). The representation of relationship patterns: Developmental considerations. In A. J. Sameroff & R. Emde (Eds.), *Relationship disturbances in early childhood* (pp. 52–69). New York: Basic Books.

Stewart, S., & Rubin, K. (1995). The social problem-solving skills of anxious-withdrawn children. *Development and Psychopathology, 7,* 323–336.

Stigler, J. W., & Fernandez, C. (1995). Learning mathematics from classroom instruction: Cross-cultural and experimental perspectives. *Minnesota Symposium on Child Psychology: Vol. 28. Basic and applied perspectives on learning, cognition, and development* (pp. 103–130). Mahwah, NJ: Erlbaum.

Super, C., & Harkness, S. (1986). The developmental niche: A conceptualization at the interface of child and culture. *International Journal of Behavioral Development, 9,* 545–569.

Swanson, J. M., McBurnett, K., Wigal, T., Pfiffner, L. J., Lerner, M. A., Williams, L., Christian, D. L., Tamm, L., Willcutt, E., Crowley, K., Clevenger, W., Khouzam, N., Woo, C., Crinella, F. M., & Fisher, T. D. (1993). Effect of stimulant medication on children with attention deficit disorder: A "review of reviews." *Exceptional Children, 60,* 154–162.

Taylor, A., & Machida, S. (1996, April). *Student–teacher relationships of Head Start children.* Paper presented at the annual meeting of the American Educational Research Association, New York.

Thompson, R. A. (1991). Emotional regulation and emotional development. *Educational Psychology Review, 3*, 269–307.

Thompson, R. A. (1994). Emotion regulation: A theme in search of definition. In N. A. Fox (Ed.), The development of emotion regulation: Biological and behavioral considerations. *Monographs of the Society for Research in Child Development, 59*(Serial No. 240), 25–52.

Thurlow, M. L., Ysseldyke, J. E., Wotruba, J. W., & Algozzine, B. (1993). Instruction in special education classrooms under varying student–teacher ratios. *Elementary School Journal, 93*, 305–320.

Toth, S., & Cicchetti, D. (1996). The impact of relatedness with mother on school functioning. *Journal of School Psychology, 34*, 247–266.

Troy, M., & Sroufe, L. A. (1987). Victimization among preschoolers: The role of attachment relationship history. *Journal of the American Academy of Child Psychiatry, 26*, 166–172.

U.S. Department of Education. (1996). *Implementation of the Individuals with Disabilities Education Act: 18th annual report to Congress.* Washington, DC: U.S. Government Printing Office.

van IJzendoorn, M. H., Sagi, A., & Lambermon, M. W. E. (1992). The multiple caretaker paradox: Some data from Holland and Israel. In R. C. Pianta (Ed.), *New Directions in Child Development: Vol. 57. Relationships between children and non-parental adults* (pp. 5–24). San Francisco: Jossey-Bass.

Walker, H. M. (1994). *The acting out child: Coping with classroom disruption.* Longwood, CO: Sopris West.

Walsh, D. J. (1991). Reconstructing the discourse on developmental appropriateness: A developmental perspective. *Early Education and Development, 2*, 109–119.

Walsh, D. J., Baturka, N. L., & Smith, M. E. (1992). The two-year route to first grade: Administrative decisions and children's lives. *Educational Foundations, 6*, 67–84.

Walsh, D. J., Baturka, N. L., Smith, M. E., & Colter, N. (1991). Changing one's mind— maintaining one's identity: A first grade teacher's story. *Teachers College Record, 93*, 73–86.

Wang, M., & Kovach, J. (1995). Bridging the achievement gap in urban schools: Reducing educational segregation and advancing resilience-promoting strategies. *Closing the achievement gap: A vision to guide change in beliefs and practice* (pp. 9–24). Washington, DC: U.S. Department of Education Regional Educational Laboratory Network.

Waters, E. (1987). *Attachment Behavior Q-Set, Revision, 3.0.* Stony Brook: State University of New York at Stony Brook.

Waters, E., & Deane, K. E. (1985). Defining and assessing individual differences in attachment relationships: Q-methodology and the organization of behavior in infancy and early childhood. In I. Bretherton & E. Waters (Eds.), Growing points of attachment theory and research. *Monographs of the Society for Research in Child Development, 50*(1, Serial No. 209), 41–65.

Weissberg, R. P., Caplan, M., & Harwood, R. L. (1991). Promoting competent young people in competence-enhancing environments: A systems-based perspective on primary prevention. *Journal of Consulting and Clinical Psychology, 59*, 830–841.

Wellborn, J. G., & Connell, J. P. (1987). *Rochester Assessment Package for Children.* Rochester, NY: University of Rochester.

Wentzel, K. (1996). *Effective teachers are like good parents: Understanding motivation and classroom behavior.* Paper presented at the annual meeting of the American Educational Research Association, New York.

Werner, E., & Smith, R. (1980). *Vulnerable but invincible.* New York: Wiley.

Young, K. T. (1994). *Starting points: Meeting the needs of our youngest children, The report of the Carnegie Task Force on Meeting the Needs of Young Children.* New York: Carnegie Foundation.

Ysseldyke J. E., & Christenson, S. (1987). *The Instructional Environment Scale.* Austin, TX: PRO-ED.

Zeanah, C. H., Benoit, D., Barton, M., Regan, C., Hirschberg, L., & Lipsitt, L. (1993). Representations of attachment in mothers and their one-year old infants. *Journal of the American Academy of Child and Adolescent Psychiatry, 32*, 278–286.

Zeichner, K. (1995). Educating teachers to close the achievement gap: Issues of pedagogy, knowledge and teacher preparation. *Closing the achievement gap: A vision to guide change in beliefs and practice* (pp. 39–52). Washington, DC: U.S. Department of Education Regional Educational Laboratory Network.

Zins, J., Kratochwill, T., & Elliott, S. (1993). *Handbook of consultation services for children.* San Francisco: Jossey-Bass.

Index

About the Author

Robert C. Pianta, PhD, is a professor in the Curry School of Education's Programs in Clinical and School Psychology at the University of Virginia. A former special education teacher, he is a developmental, school, and clinical child psychologist who enjoys integrating these multiple perspectives on children in his work. In addition to his work on relationships between teachers and children, Pianta studies parent–child relationships. He is interested in the role of a range of social contexts in the development of children and particularly the role that social contexts play in the production and reduction of risk for poor development outcomes. Dr. Pianta is a principal investigator on the National Institute of Child Health and Human Development Study of Early Child Care, a senior investigator with the National Center for Early Development and Learning, and editor of the *Journal of School Psychology*. He teaches courses on intervention with children and the role of social and emotional processes in development. Dr. Pianta is also the father of three children, is a soccer coach, and is learning to play the piano.